G000166398

Thousands of Roads

Thousands of Roads

*A Memoir of a Young Woman's Life
in the Ukrainian Underground
During and After World War II*

by
MARIA SAVCHYN PYSKIR

Translated by ANIA SAVAGE
Foreword by JOHN A. ARMSTRONG

McFarland & Company, Inc., Publishers
Jefferson, North Carolina, and London

Frontispiece: Maria Savchyn in 1955

Library of Congress Cataloguing-in-Publication Data

Pyskir, Maria Savchyn.
    [Tysiacha dorih. English]
    Thousands of roads : a memoir of a young woman's life in the
Ukrainian underground during and after World War II / by
Maria Savchyn Pyskir ; translated by Ania Savage ; foreword by
John A. Armstrong.
       p.   cm.
    Includes index.
    ISBN 0-7864-0764-6 (softcover : 50# alkaline paper) ∞
    1. World War, 1939–1945—Underground movements—
Ukraine, Western.   2. Pyskir, Maria Savchyn.   3. Ukraèns§'a
povstans§'a armiëi—Biography.   4. World War, 1939–1945—
Personal narratives, Ukrainian.   5. World War, 1939–1945—
Women—Ukraine, Western.   6. Ukraine, Western—History—
Autonomy and independence movements.   I. Title.
    D802.U4P9413   2001
    940.53'477—dc21   00-46459

British Library cataloguing data are available

Cover background image: ©2000 Index Stock. *Foreground image:* Maria as
a student in Lviv in 1940.

Manufactured in the United States of America

McFarland & Company, Inc., Publishers
  Box 611, Jefferson, North Carolina 28640
    www.mcfarlandpub.com

This book is dedicated
to the men and women
who fought and died heroically
in the struggle for a free Ukraine.
It is also dedicated to
my family and my two oldest sons
who were as much casualties of this struggle
as those who bore arms.

Contents

Foreword

by JOHN A. ARMSTRONG

To say that this book reads like a novel is a compliment to the vivid writing of the author and her translator. To recognize that this poignant memoir is fully credible is to acknowledge the prevalence of terrifying episodes in the history of the twentieth century. If, in the new century we have just entered, we are to avoid repeating such episodes, we must carefully study accounts by their survivors like Maria Pyskir.

The author began life as the daughter of a peaceful peasant family in the village of Zadviria, twenty miles east of Lviv (variously known as Lemberg, Lwów, and Lvov). Because Lviv is the principal city of Western Ukraine, this area of the otherwise typical Western Ukrainian countryside is exceptionally open to urban contacts. As a result, Maria's childhood was shadowed by the hostility between Ukrainians and Poles arising from the latter's determination to create a unified Polish culture by stifling minority activities.

In adolescence Maria was determined to attain freedom for her ethnic group. A classmate urged that the best patriotic course was to join the youth auxiliary of the Organization of Ukrainian Nationalists (OUN). Its "Decalogue" adopted the integral nationalist stance that, for patriots, violence, including sabotage and assassination, was obligatory in resisting forceful Polish suppression of Ukrainian culture. To Maria, then fourteen years old, the implications of joining were probably not fully apparent, but she accepted.

In contrast to the experience of older members of the youth organization, and especially of the adult members of OUN itself, Maria's concern with Polish oppression was quickly overshadowed by Soviet conquest of her native province, Galicia, following the 1939 Nazi-Soviet

1

pact for partitioning Poland. For the next twenty months, her classmates and her family endured numerous impositions and restrictions by the Soviet occupation authorities, but their life was not yet totally disrupted, as were the lives of many neighbors deported to Siberia.

Maria's initial reaction to the German invasion of June 1941 was relief. But it soon became apparent to her that Nazi totalitarianism would be as intolerant as the Communist type. Jaroslaw Stecko, the leader of the "Bandera" branch of the OUN, was arrested by the Gestapo when he tried to set up a Ukrainian independence regime in Lviv. Clearly Maria, still a teenager, did not understand all the ramifications of the split in the OUN. However, in 1940, she agreed to become assistant to the director of the clandestine security service (Sluzhba Bezpeky) of the Bandera OUN in Galicia.

In 1942, forcibly taking over guerrilla activities begun in nearby Volhynia by other Ukrainian resistance elements, the Bandera OUN developed a "Ukrainian Insurgent Army" (UPA) designed to undermine German occupation and to resist the return of the Soviet forces. When German troops withdrew from Galicia in late 1944, the UPA became for nearly a decade the principal force resisting complete totalitarianism in East Central Europe. It was in that decade that Maria's services to the resistance became prominent.

Why was Maria, and why were tens of thousands of Ukrainians like her, willing to undertake such a desperate resistance to two ruthless totalitarian regimes? In addition to her adolescent romantic outlook, Maria had a strong religious background. Her family was Catholic of the Ukrainian rite (sometimes termed "Uniate"); this religious outlook permeated her curtailed gymnasium schooling as well. She emphasizes that she grew up believing in humanitarianism and individual rights as well as national self-determination, which an American should remember was also part of Woodrow Wilson's legacy in East Central Europe.

Maria occasionally exhibited a remarkable degree of tolerance for ethnic groups that many extreme Ukrainian nationalists did not. It seems that revenge as such was foreign to her nature. Although she oversimplified the origins of Polish-Ukrainian antipathy (fortunately largely overcome in recent decades), Maria recognized good qualities in many Poles she encountered in the months she stayed in western Galicia. Later, after innumerable injuries inflicted by Russian-speaking officials, she still praised the achievements of Russian literature. In a general way she acknowledged Slavic deficiencies: The fierce determination of the strictly organized UPA was necessary "to overcome the fatalism of the Ukrainian Slav." Passing references to Jewish neighbors suggest that she rejected attempts to demonize Jews.

During her underground resistance career, Maria Pyskir maintained her religious connections. When she eventually married the prominent UPA leader Vasyl Halasha ("Orlan"), two Ukrainian Catholic priests officiated. Other Ukrainian clergyman sheltered her—evidently at great risk—when she was hiding from the Polish security forces dominated by Communists. Her own family and some of Halasha's relatives loyally supported her and her second son while she carried on later resistance work. Her family values are also demonstrated by her long faithfulness to her marriage and her fortitude when confronted by poignant loss—separation from the two sons whom she courageously bore while in hiding (the first was permanently lost to adoption by a high Polish Communist official).

Apparently Maria was not involved in OUN internal violence that preceded resistance to Soviet forces, nor, in practice, in violent resistance to the latter. She did, however, subscribe to the basic resistance creed that suicide was preferable to capture that might endanger one's comrades. Ordinarily she firmly rejected the "cult of death" sometimes prevalent in resistance forces. At one point, however, when she was suffering extreme pain from bomb fragments, Maria begged her husband to shoot her, even seeming to doubt God's providence. But who could cast the first stone at a Christian driven to such extremities by years of utter hardship, fear, and apparent hopelessness?

In addition to her humanitarian outlook, Maria was also motivated by the hope that Soviet occupation would soon be curbed by some kind of Western pressure. In the meantime, resistance networks, especially the more or less "above-ground" camps in Volhynia during the German occupation and in the Carpathian Mountains until the late 1940s, would serve the practical purpose of preserving young Ukrainian men from forced labor in Germany or as Soviet "cannon fodder" during the renewed occupation (1944). In addition, resistance might delay collectivization accompanied by (as in the 1930s Eastern Ukraine) mass starvation. Thus, for a brief transition period, resistance would serve both to preserve the nation's demographic strength and to demonstrate its fervent opposition to the outside world.

By the late 1940s, it had become evident that such optimism was ill founded. Resistance could be maintained only by literally going underground, i.e., by building bunkers (dugouts) in which astounding perseverance enabled small partisan groups to hide throughout the winter when every move was revealed by the snow cover. There it was that Maria, often separated from her husband, spent most of her partisan career. An earlier lengthy stay in the part of Western Ukraine assigned by Moscow to Poland was almost as discouraging. Material circumstances were relatively good, but the environment was alien (Maria had learned fluent Polish, but realized that prewar friction had made the Poles of Cracow and Przemysl [Ukrainian *Peremyshl*] hostile). After forced evacuation of Ukrainian villages, the countryside was also unsupportive. One lesson she fully absorbed is that, as Mao Tse-Tung wrote, partisans could not operate effectively unless surrounded by friendly civilians. For example, some small UPA groups continued to exist, barely, in the forest and swamps of Polissia but had little scope for action. By the late 1940s the Soviets more or less achieved the same results in Volhynia and Galicia by ruthlessly expelling Ukrainian peasants, thereby replicating the unsupportive environment for resistance achieved in Eastern Ukraine fifteen years earlier by Stalin's extreme collectivization.

Under these circumstances, the last years Maria and Orlan remained in hiding were devoted almost exclusively to propaganda rather than to attacking Soviet agents. The propaganda objective was threefold: (1) to gather information about Soviet oppression; (2) to get it to the West via OUN agents, or at least to preserve the evidence for the future; and (3) to spread it by practical methods such as attaching leaflets to school doors. For this reason Orlan and his counterparts spent long winter months dispatching and receiving couriers like Maria, writing and duplicating propaganda reports. Here some friction arose between the leaders, nearly all men, and the assistants including many women, who were usually excluded from decision-making.

There was one additional resistance possibility; infiltration of UPA members into the work force of Eastern Ukraine, where they would bring the OUN message (considerably modified by the UHVR, the new civilian counterpart of the UPA command, to stress social and economic goals) to the huge population that had had little or no contact with organized nationalism. In fact, planned infiltration of the eastern provinces began in the mid–1940s, as soon as Soviet military and police pressure made the large UPA enrollment (in the tens of thousands) a vulnerability rather than an asset. Demobilized partisans were equipped with false identity papers and directed to take jobs in war-torn eastern areas such as the Donbas. As Maria notes, however, Soviet security forces soon detected the forgeries. When exposed, the ex-partisans were helpless amidst a population that was highly skeptical of men with Western Ukrainian customs and speech patterns claiming to be able to resist Soviet might. Unfortunately, events since 1991 have provided little evidence of such direct impact of Western Ukrainian propaganda in the industrial centers.

Yet Maria remained convinced that the UPA epic was crucial for the future of the Ukrainian nation: "As I look back over the years I will argue that Ukraine would not have become independent in 1991 had it not possessed the memory of the bloody and bitter UPA war." In the short run, this assertion appears unfounded. Without reviewing the peculiar combination of circumstances that led to independence for all Soviet Union republics, one may point out that the Western Ukrainians played a significant role in demonstrations during the late 1980s centering on demands for religious freedom, but the critical decisions at that time were still being made in Moscow and Kyiv (Kiev).

The longer-range implications of the memory of UPA are more significant. It has served to counteract the myth of Soviet partisan heroism and to reinforce recent exposure in Afghanistan and Chechnya of official Russian incapacity in dealing with popular guerrilla oppositions. More concretely, the lesson of Western Ukrainian resistance has produced a current generation determined to emulate their ancestors by fierce resistance to a return of Moscow rule. Surely this lesson has also stiffened the readiness of the current Ukrainian elite (still predominantly composed of ex–Communist *apparatchiki*) to hang on to their new freedom from centralized control based in Moscow. Moreover, the ability of the Ukrainian state to form and indoctrinate a new army depends on the loyalty of former Soviet officers like General Kostiantyn P. Morozov, of half–Russian parentage from Eastern Ukraine, who opted for Ukrainian citizenship as soon as independence was attained. In his recent post as Ukrainian Minister of Defense he can scarcely fail to be impressed by the valor and fortitude of the kind of Western Ukrainians whom Maria Pyskir depicts. He must be aware that, in a crisis, Ukraine can count on devoted, self-sacrificing defenders.

Apart from physical hardships and bitter anguish caused by loss of loved ones (children and, for years, siblings and parents exiled to Siberia), the author lived for a decade under the threat of arrest. "Only someone who has been arrested by Soviet security authorities can comprehend the terrible terminality of a gate—or a door—closing behind them." As one who has had this experience, brief and relatively banal as it was in Minsk 1956, I can begin to grasp her psychological trauma.

Actually Maria was arrested three times—once in Cracow, where she lost her first born; one in Lviv, where the police tried to use her as bait to seize her husband; and a third time in Eastern Ukraine, where she and Orlan were making a desperate move in the spring of 1953 to arouse local support for the UPA. By fortunate coincidence, the third arrest came shortly after Stalin's death, which led to insecurity and dissension among the security authorities themselves. Maria recounts that she and her husband were interrogated by T. A. Strokach, Ukrainian State Security chief, and M. V. Slon, minister of Ukrainian Internal Affairs. Ultimately these officials took the chance (inconceivable under Stalin and probably under Khrushchev or Brezhnev as well) of letting her leave the Soviet bloc to contact UHVR headquarters in emigration. This time she lost her husband, who was eventually released but gave in to pressure and recanted his involvement with the UPA—a factor, apparently, in Maria's obtaining an American divorce.

In spite of such distressing circumstances, reinforcing the horror of arrest, Maria had the fortitude to retain a clear head while negotiating her departure and reporting her remarkable experiences to the UHVR émigré headquarters and to the American authorities who gave her asylum. I had the privilege of becoming acquainted with her about that time. Her account impressed me; although then, as now, I of course cannot confirm all details, the written version is even more plausible.

The Ukrainian-reading public in North America has had access to Maria Pyskir's published memoir for several years, and her three visits since 1991 to independent Ukraine have enabled her to convey some of these experiences to Ukrainians at home. Her observations in independent Ukraine doubtless confirmed partisan concerns (echoing those of French and Belgian resistance elements in 1944) that it would take a long time to overcome the alienation to all authority that resistance had necessarily entailed. In closing, Maria cogently remarks, "The years of servitude have been hard to shed and I think it will be the mission of the next generation to create a really independent Ukraine."

Now, with the publication of her book, the English-speaking world should be grateful to be able to weigh this extraordinary experience while considering how, in the future, to avert the terrible, prolonged traumas imposed on civilization as well as individual nations by twentieth-century totalitarianism.

1. Early Years

As I grow older and my thoughts return to my youth, I ask myself several questions: Why did I choose this kind of life and not another kind? What made me select a way that from the very beginning augured many difficult days and dangers? Even today, I do not know the answers. Perhaps it was typical girlhood romanticism, or perhaps I was influenced by the example of my parents who believed that in order to achieve something you had to fight for it. Or perhaps I was influenced by the stories my parents and their contemporaries told about the heroism in the earlier war, and I wanted to be heroic.

The first world I knew was the village Zadviria, near Lviv, the capital of Western Ukraine. That distant memory glistens under the dust of accumulated years. Barefoot, with tiny steps, I run to the crossroads not far from our house. I cross the road, jump over a ditch, and climb a hill to the Cross of Freedom. The cross was erected long, long ago to commemorate the ending of serfdom in this land. Every spring, village girls whitewash it and hang garlands from the crossbeams. Standing under the cross, I squint into the distance at the three roads that radiate from the crossroads like the spokes of a wheel. Two of the roads disappear into a stand of trees. The third one runs straight through fields until it is swallowed by the horizon. Where does this road end? The question vexes me. As soon as I learn the alphabet, I run to the crossroads and decipher the three-armed sign. This is how I learn that one road goes to Kamianka Strumylova, that the second road leads to Hlyniany, and that the third road terminates in the great city of Lviv.

Even when I was little, the names of these places evoked a secret world, a world that was different from the one in which I lived.

I lived a quiet, ordinary life with my mother and father, a grandfather, and four younger siblings. I was the eldest. Olia was two years younger, Stefa, four, and Lesia, five. Ivanko was nine years my junior. We cared about each other and our parents. Our childhood flowed placidly one day into the next, one season into the next one. During summer, my parents worked in the fields and we were left with our paternal grandfather. When our chores were finished and we became bored, grandfather would tell us stories of long ago. In his gentle voice, he would sing the songs of his youth, describe the feasts and great holidays of the past, and evoke a history that held us spellbound.

My mother and her God reigned over our childhood. Mother's God was not a good-natured God. He sat high in the heavens and was sometimes demanding. Thankfully, there was also the Mother of God who interceded for all sinners, namely for children like me. I prayed to her fervently. My mother believed in the power of prayer, and as soon as we could put sentences together, she taught us the Our Father, the Hail Mary, and eventually the Apostles' Creed.

My father was home in the evenings and during holidays. Whatever the weather, he worked on our farm from morning to night. He was a tall, thin, and quiet man. He worked very hard. Perhaps the hard work made him silent and a little sad. He had a nice tenor voice, and sang in the church choir, and sometimes in the evenings he hummed to himself.

Because of my status as the eldest daughter, I was expected to help with the housekeeping and with tending the youngest children. Yet, my mother was not strict, and her good nature permeated my childhood. Her voice floats back through the years like water trickling over a stream bed. She knew how to tell a story, select the right word, relate the telling anecdote, proffer the pithy example. I remember how I would sit with her at the table making dumplings. The ball of dough was huge and, as I studied it, I knew that my morning would be wasted making dumplings while the other children played outside. She would see the expression on my face, and she would begin one of her stories. Her words would draw me in, and I would forget everything: "I was not much older than you, when they took your grandfather—my father—away into the army," she would say as she rolled out the dough. "It was wartime and your grandfather—my father—had been called up. My mother—your grandmother—was left alone with five small children. Then the authorities came and took away the horses. Your grandmother was able to hide some of the grain before it was requisitioned also. Otherwise we would have had nothing to eat. I remember how she would wake me up before dawn, and I would go with her to the barn where we would thresh the grain. We had to do this in secret because we were afraid that the thresher would also be requisitioned."

My mother didn't know that when I went to bed at night, I would repeat her stories over and over again, and my heart would ache for her and for my grandmother and for all those blameless people who were shot, who were hanged in that terrible war. World War I. How much I heard about it in my childhood.

Our village Zadviria lay about thirty kilometers east of Lviv. It stretched along three roads, which I mentioned before. The village was large and well-to-do. It had many city conveniences, including a railroad station. In the center of the village stood a beautiful wooden church of the Ukrainian Catholic

Maria's father Petro Savchyn, in a photograph taken in exile in Siberia in the 1950s.

rite, and not too far from it, a Roman Catholic church. There was also a police station, a post office, several grocery stores, and a government building. A factory that made railroad ties had been built a short distance outside the village, and its red smokestacks dominated the sky. The factory whistles in the morning and in the evening signified the beginning and end of the workday.

Most of the villagers worked in the fields, and on Thursdays they would take their produce to the market in Hlyniany. As I was growing up, the complexion of the village began to change. More workers moved in when the factory was hiring, and a layer of the intelligentsia developed. Because of our proximity to Lviv, many of the villagers worked in the city, and many young people studied at schools there. The nearness of a big city had other, more subtle influences. Folk traditions still observed and costumes still

Maria's mother Anastasia Savchyn, in a photograph taken in exile in Siberia in the 1950s.

worn in far-flung villages had disappeared from Zadviria shortly after the turn of the century.

Most of the villagers were Ukrainians, although there were about a dozen Polish families as well as a number of Jewish families. Before World War I, most everyone spoke Ukrainian. After the annexation of Western Ukraine to Poland in the 1920s, the Warsaw regime insisted on the use of the Polish language, and this created a widening chasm between the Ukrainian population and the Poles and the Jews. I do not recall when I realized my national heritage. I know I knew this very early. I remember that I had a friend whose mother spoke to her in a language that was different from the one we used at home. This is how I knew that we were different from our neighbor.

Because I did well in school, our parish priest counseled my parents to send me to Lviv to a classical gymnasium (secondary school). I took the entrance exam in the spring of 1939. I did very well on the test, placing not at the entry level but in the second level. We had barely started school that autumn when we heard the news over the public address system: Poland was at war with Germany. In two short weeks, Poland was no more. Then, Western Ukraine was annexed to the Soviet Union.

I was home when the Red Army marched in. Our village received the Bolsheviks with reserve and uncertainty. People did not leave their homes to welcome the columns of soldiers and tanks, but stood in their front yards and looked on silently. There must have been prior contact between the Red Army and our village elders, because we were told that a general meeting would be called when the Red Army passed through. This happened soon. The soldiers and the tanks came to a halt at the crossroads and, slowly, the villagers gathered. A Red Army political officer clambered to the top of the hill where the Cross of Freedom stood and began to shout that the Red Army had come to rescue us from Polish capitalistic oppression. People listened in silence. After finishing his diatribe, which he delivered in Russian which not everyone understood, the officer scrambled down from the hill, got into a tank, and the columns of tanks and soldiers rolled on west. People went home in silence, their faces worried; hopes of freedom and independence, sparked by the new war, were extinguished.

Although I was only fourteen, I took these changes very seriously, like an adult. Perhaps my contemporaries and I matured more quickly because the times were so dramatic. I realized that my country, like my village, stood at a crossroads and that hopes for an independent Ukraine might very well be a pipe dream. True, Poland no longer existed and we did not rue its disappearance, but instead of Poland, we now belonged to the Soviet Union, and that was a greater calamity than Polish rule. We all knew that in 1932–33 Stalin had brought about the Great Famine in Eastern Ukraine that caused the death of nearly seven million people. People hoped that the Soviet occupation was temporary and that the war would push the Red Army back east. The local wisdom was that we only had to wait for the right moment to rid ourselves once and for all of the foreign yoke.

The author as a student at the gymnasium in Lviv in 1940.

I knew my job was to continue studying, and I soon returned to the gymnasium. The atmosphere in the city was electrifying. People were waiting for change, but they were also afraid of it and envisioned it in different ways. Poles, for example, believed that the Polish Army would rescue them. It did not, and many thousands of Poles were deported from Lviv and other parts of Western Ukraine to Siberia. At school, the curriculum changed. Each school was given a number, and our academy earned the distinction of being number one. In the next few months, Soviet teachers replaced many of our professors. New subjects and textbooks appeared, while other classes and textbooks were dropped.

I remember, in particular, an evening in November. The leaves had already fallen and crunched under my feet as I made my way back to the dormitory from the library. A friend, Olia Zeleniuk, one of the best pupils at school, was walking with me. I had been reading a book about a young heroine who defends her country, and I turned to Olia to ask, "Tell me what can I do to help my country?"

She thought about my question for a moment, and then said, "Learn all you can about it."

"How can I do this?" I asked her.

"Join a group where you can learn the true history of your country, not what the Soviets teach."

I did join Olia's group and once a week we traveled across Lviv to a meeting. I discovered that Olia led many of the meetings. One day

in early spring, she said to me: "You are now in Yunatsvo OUN [Orga-
nization of Ukrainian Nationalists–Youth]. Remember, you cannot tell
anyone about this."

She handed me a piece of paper on which she had copied OUN's
Decalogue, the rules of the organization.

The OUN has been vilified by Moscow for nearly half a century
and is largely misunderstood in the West, where, ironically, it was
formed. Following the disastrously unsuccessful attempts during and
after World War I to unify Western and Eastern Ukraine and create a
sovereign Ukrainian state, Ukrainian political activists who fled into
exile and Ukrainian students studying abroad met in the late 1920s in
Berlin and Prague and established the OUN. If defined in its strictest
sense, the OUN was a Ukrainian political movement dedicated to the
establishment of an independent Ukrainian state. But it became much
more than that and, in fact, shaped the thinking of and instilled Ukrainian patriotism in a whole generation of Ukrainian youth, including me,
who matured prior to and during World War II. Most OUN activities
in the interwar years were directed against the Polish regime that
acquired Western Ukraine after World War I and instituted anti–
Ukrainian policies, including restrictions on the use of the Ukrainian
language and political assembly. The OUN staged and took responsibility for hundreds of acts of sabotage and a number of assassinations,
including those of two high-ranking Polish officials. Many OUN
activists were arrested and tried, and many were in Polish prisons when
World War II broke out.

I equated OUN with patriotism and was enormously proud of being
accepted into the youth section. At fourteen, I found it extremely difficult to harbor a deep secret. I wanted to tell my mother about the OUN
but remembered Olia's words: "Don't tell anyone," and I didn't. My
weekly studies changed now. They were still wholly devoted to Ukrainian subject matter but, in addition to history, we studied geography and
ethnography. At each meeting we were questioned on what we had been
given for homework, then discussed it in terms of what was happening
around us. Olia became my first ideological instructor and, although I
would have older and more experienced teachers, her place as one of
the people who forged my thinking has not diminished.

My contemporaries and I searched for an answer to the baffling
and painful question: "Why was Ukraine not an independent sovereign
nation?" It was difficult to understand why, after so many revolutions
and uprisings, Ukrainians had been unable to establish a sovereign state.

Where did the fault lie? What was missing? We discussed these questions over and over again at our weekly meetings. This self-evaluation coupled with our patriotism made us painfully aware of our second-class status, which we had inherited from our fathers, our grandfathers, and our great-grandfathers. We talked about the unsuccessful attempts to create an independent Ukraine during World War I, and we could not forgive our parents for letting that opportunity slip through their hands. We learned in the OUN's Youth Section that it was our duty to fight for our land, our customs, and our proud heritage.

Eventually I was transferred to another group where I learned about the goals and organization of the OUN. I knew that the purpose of these meetings and of all the study was to prepare us to fight for our country's independence. But as we talked about resistance, I grew afraid, since I knew I had a fearful nature, did not like conflict, and wondered whether I could stand side by side with the others.

The winter of 1939–40 was severe. Food shortages forced people to stand in long lines and often go home empty handed. The countryside was overwhelmed by requisitions of animals and materials and could not produce enough food for the city. There was also a lack of fuel. This is when schools were closed and those of us who were from the outlying villages were sent home. I finished that school year in Zadviria. In the fall of 1940, I returned to Lviv and spent the school year living in a dormitory and continued my clandestine membership in the OUN.

♦ ♦ ♦ ♦ ♦

One of the most riveting moments of my life came in June of 1941. Exams were over, and we were going home, leaving behind Lviv and the empty, quiet dormitory. I was always eager to see my family, although I felt a twinge of regret that I was leaving friends behind. I guess I was not the only one who felt this way. Several in our group organized a return trip to Lviv the following week and an excursion up Devil's Bluff, a steep hill that towered over the city.

Four of us met at the train station in Zadviria. The day was gorgeous, great for a hike. I noticed that the train station was unusually empty, but this did not worry my companions or me since it was Sunday morning. The train was late. At first, this fact did not worry us either since trains became notoriously unpredictable after the arrival of the Bolsheviks in 1939. Yet, the train was very late. Finally, we saw the stationmaster hurrying toward us. From the expression on his face, we could tell that something was very wrong.

"Don't you know a war has broken out?" he asked us. "With Germany."

"What?" we chorused in disbelief.

Secretly, I was glad, and I think so were my companions and other passengers on the platform. I was saying to myself, "Thank the Lord. This means that the Russians will soon be gone. This means the end of arrests, deportations to Siberia, collective farms." Looking back, I realize that neither my friends nor I comprehended the consequences of this great war that was just beginning. We did not, and could not, imagine what the war would do to us and to our families, to our land. Even if someone had told us, we would not have believed—I would not have— that the life we knew was at an end, and a much more difficult life lay before us.

But, being young and foolish, we still wanted to return to Lviv and climb Devil's Bluff. We saw a freight train rumbling toward us. It had several empty wagons, and we climbed in. Before we reached the city, several more friends joined us.

Just after our arrival, sirens began to howl an air raid warning. Militiamen appeared on the streets and shepherded pedestrians, including us, into courtyards of nearby apartment buildings. Soon, we heard bombs exploding in the center of the city. The bombers disappeared as suddenly as they had appeared. The air raid was over, people poured out on the sidewalks, and we continued on our way. When we reached Devil's Bluff, we found the way blocked. Red Army soldiers had dragged anti-aircraft artillery up the hill, and its summit was now off limits.

The late train, the air raid, the futile hike—none of these events dampened our spirits. Since trains were no longer running, we had to walk back home. We were not alone on the road. Many Lviv residents were leaving the city for the relative safety of the countryside. I arrived home long after midnight. My mother was waiting for me, and she was not happy.

"Some people have children who stay put, but I have a daughter who wanders no matter how dangerous the times are. Do you know how worried we were? Especially after we heard that the city was bombed? Can you imagine my state of mind?"

To tell the truth, I had not given my parents a thought that day. I could not understand my mother's worry. For I was sure, I was positive, that nothing, nothing, could happen to me.

In a few days, the Germans marched in. Their tanks rolled through our village the same way Soviet tanks had rolled through two years earlier. The only difference was the direction in which the tanks were going. The Soviet tanks had gone west, while the German tanks were rolling east.

Everyone was impressed by German weaponry. It was so superior to the broken down Red Army tanks littering the ditches along major roads. Also, German soldiers were friendly, and we responded in kind. We secretly were hoping for a better, more stable life, a life without arrests, funerals, and deportations to Siberia.

When the Soviets arrived in 1939, many members of the OUN went into exile. They returned with the German Army but fractured into two bitter factions. Andrii Melnyk led one faction, while the other one recognized Stepan Bandera. Bandera, who had been imprisoned by the Polish government, had served as the national leader of OUN prior to the war. I did not know which faction to side with. As happens in such circumstances, there were several reasons for the breach in the OUN. Perhaps the bitterest arguments centered on how the OUN should respond to the Nazi invaders. Older OUN members had matured in exile and were pro–German. The younger generation had been active at home. Both sides were convinced they knew better. Both factions espoused independence, but the younger generation urged a radical revolutionary tactic, while the older generation urged a moderate position toward Nazi Germany. The results of this split were sad and sometimes tragic. The Bandera faction was popular among young idealists like myself who began organizing an anti–German resistance. This increased frictions. Occasionally, differences over tactics led to fistfights, sometimes even death. This internal OUN tension continued through the entire German occupation. When the Red Army returned, those who had started the split went into exile again, while the young Turks stayed behind to fight Stalin.

Events were coming in swift succession. In the first days of July, a poster appeared in the village that announced the formation in Lviv of a government headed by Stepan Bandera's OUN faction. The poster said that Bandera had promulgated an act of Ukrainian independence on June 30, 1941. A crowd gathered in front of the poster to read and comment. Joy shone in people's eyes. It was hard to believe that suddenly Ukraine was a sovereign nation. How quickly and easily it had happened. When I read the poster, I thought my heart would burst with pride and joy. I was proud of my clandestine membership in the OUN. The decree of independence was promulgated as the Red Army retreated in chaos under the pressure of a new, mightier invader. As these two giants fought for control of Europe, the vassal country decided to become independent. As we rejoiced, we also wondered about tomorrow.

I decided to go to Lviv to renew my OUN contacts. I was convinced that there was great work to be done, the work of building a new nation. Besides, I had to learn more about the two factions and choose sides. My mother was wondering out loud at this time: "Don't be so glad about the arrival of Germans. Do you think Hitler sent his armies because he wanted us to be rid of the Bolshevik yoke? Think again. He will be as bad as the Bolsheviks. He wants to rob and enslave us."

"No, mother," I argued back. "Germany wants to get rid of its worst enemy in Europe. Let them fight, but why should we do nothing in the meantime? Anyway, you always suspect other people's intentions and color things black."

"I don't color things black, young lady, but I've lived longer in this world than you have and know how things are. The Germans came not to free us but to take what we have. In this they are no different from all other conquerors who came this way."

Although I suspected that my mother might be right, I did not want to believe her. A fifteen-year-old girl is not motivated by logic.

When the new war broke out, passenger trains stopped running. What service there was was sporadic and could not be relied on. Thus, when I heard that a neighbor was going to Lviv to sell produce on the black market, I got into his wagon and went with him.

The city had changed. I found out that all my friends had joined the Bandera faction. I headed to where the Ukrainian government had opened offices, but the street was clogged with people, many of them young, who had come to obtain instructions on how to build an independent country in their towns and villages. I met a friend in the crowd who told me that Myron Litynsky was working for the new government. My heart skipped a beat. I was half in love with Myron, and he had taken me to the movies several times. So I pushed my way to the guard at the gate and asked him to deliver a note to Myron. I did not have to wait long. Myron came out himself and invited me into his office. We talked for a long time. I remember how impressed I was with him. He was good-looking, always well turned out, but now, sitting behind a desk covered with documents, he also seemed very serious and important. He wanted to give me something for a memento of our conversation and began rummaging on his desk. He found a pile of maps and gave me the two lying on top. They were topographical maps of Pidliasha and Kholmshchyna, a rather odd present. As I left, I wondered what use these maps would be to me, a girl who lived in a village on the outskirts of Lviv in Halychyna, a hundred and fifty kilometers or so east of the lands shown in the maps. If only I could have imagined, but I would not have believed my future.

Two weeks later, the Gestapo arrested the Ukrainian Premier Yaroslav Stecko and other members of the new government. Stepan Bandera was also arrested as were other OUN leaders. Ukraine was declared a colony of Germany. From this time on, OUN engaged in anti–German activity and continued its opposition until the end of the war. The Soviet retreat brought to light the atrocities the Bolsheviks had committed. They had murdered thousands of political prisoners and prisons in Lviv, and other cities were filled with decaying corpses. The OUN declared a period of national mourning. The murdered were buried in communal graves on the outskirts of the cities and villages. These were Cossack-style burial mounds that were topped with birch crosses and reminded all of us of the need to fight for national independence.

The advancing German armies kept pushing the front further east. The roar of cannons and the detonation of bombs were replaced by the thunder of bombers that darkened the sky as they flew east. As soon as the front passed, life in Zadviria began to return to a semblance of normality. Schools reopened. The village administration and police were taken over by local people. Young people began to organize self-help militia units.

One hot July afternoon, a month or so after Hitler declared war on Stalin, a group of girls and boys were congregating in the street, and a friend and I joined them. I saw a stranger in the group. I looked at him and he at me, and it was as if we both were thunderstruck. We were introduced and began to talk as if we had known each other all our lives. I listened to him and was amazed how he could read my thoughts and knew my dreams. And besides, he was so handsome. I had just turned sixteen. He was twenty. His name was Sofron Bezubko, and he was visiting relatives in the village. Before he left, we exchanged addresses and began to correspond. When he visited our village again, we went to a performance at the local Prosvita library and afterwards walked home together. At the gate to our yard, he kissed me.

Sofron was my first love. We met infrequently after that, but each meeting was like a celebration of our dreams and hopes. Even the intervening years cannot erase the quiver of joy I feel when I remember him. We met too infrequently to disappoint each other and too many times to forget. He gave me his photograph, which I carried with me. Each of his letters brought great joy. Perhaps that is what first love should be—sunny and untroubled by any doubts.

Early that fall, Germany took administrative control of Ukraine. The new German governor declared that only two classical gymnasiums would reopen in Lviv, and only a few girls would be admitted. Although I applied, I was not chosen, and I enrolled in a trade school.

During this time, secondary schools became fertile ground for organizing anti–German resistance. At our school, I was told to recruit students to the OUN. My superior was Iryna Savycka, whose nom de guerre was Bystra, which translates as "the swift one." The name was apt. She was an energetic young woman whose forthright behavior sometimes grated. She trained me and gave me several OUN cells that she had already organized at the school to manage. She also told me to organize new cells. I did, but with less success than was expected of me. The problem was that my requirements for the recruits were so lofty that I recruited very few students, although at this time many young people were joining the OUN. My generation opposed Germany because we felt we were being reduced to serfs, as the Gestapo implemented restrictions on the freedom of movement and assembly and began to arrest activists. This is not to say that we had a developed ideology vis-à-vis Nazism. Most of my contemporaries grew up in deeply religious homes and learned the Christian ethic in schools. We believed in humanitarianism, in the rights of the individual, and the rights of self-determination by nations. If I were to delineate our ideology, these beliefs would be its foundation.

In 1942, I was one of four girls to pass an examination for entry into the regular OUN. During the ceremony, we pledged our allegiance to the organization. I spent that school year living with a relative in an apartment in Lviv and doing courier work for the OUN when the need arose.

The OUN was growing quickly, its popularity no longer restricted to students. Many young people in the countryside were caught up in the fervor of national independence and flocked to the organization. Although I did not tell anyone at home about my membership in the OUN, my family soon realized my involvement, since I received letters that were not delivered by normal mail but by couriers. Soon I was doing double work for the OUN. I did courier work in Lviv and, when I was home in Zadviria, I trained new local cadres.

In the fall of 1942, I graduated from the technical school and obtained work as a typist in the Psychological Testing Institute. This institute was a German invention, an example of Germany's low opinion of the Slavs. Students from secondary schools in the Lviv area were brought to the institute for psychological and aptitude assessments. My job was to type the completed evaluations. I soon noticed that every student was evaluated as having an aptitude for manual labor. Not one in the hundreds tested was deemed suitable for an "intellectual" job. My position at the institute carried a great benefit. It earned me a document that said I was gainfully employed. This document protected me from deportation for work in Germany.

Because of my status, Hryhory Pryshliak, whose nom de guerre was Mikushka, drafted me into his entourage. He was chief of the SB (Sluzhba Bespeky), the security service of the OUN in Western Ukraine. I became his personal courier and liaison agent in the Lviv district. Unlike many OUN leaders who were careless about their security, Mikushka led a very circumspect life. He lived in Lviv but maintained several apartments and changed his location often. I was occasionally asked to pretend that I was his fiancée, and he would hug me as we made our way to one of these apartments. I did not like pretending I was in love with him and objected, but he would only laugh at my skittishness. However, our conversations invariably dealt with OUN matters, although I was never consulted how to carry out a task. Our relationship was that of an adult (him) instructing a child (me). I did not like this, either.

My duties as a courier consumed all my free time. I delivered Mikushka's mail to his associates in the city and in the outlying districts and brought mail back from them. The job was not complicated, but neither was it boring because I always met new people. Occasionally, these contacts were closer in age to me than Mikushka, who was in his early thirties. These people treated me as an equal, and

Hryhory Pryshliak, whose nom de guerre was "Mikushka," was chief of the SB (*Sluzhba Bespeky*), the security service of the OUN in Western Ukraine. Maria served as one of his couriers.

I enjoyed their company. Being a courier made me learn the city well, knowledge that would prove very useful in the future. When I was sent into the countryside, I performed additional duties. Often, I would be given a typewriter, which I would use to copy manuals that would be used to train new OUN cadres. I was treated well on such excursions and looked forward to them.

At this time, overt and clandestine political activity was at a fever pitch. In the neighboring region of Volyn, groups of partisans were being organized into what would soon become the Ukrainian Insurgent Army (UPA). This fledgling armed resistance was engaging the Germans in battles. Gestapo pressure and terrorism of the population was becoming increasingly brutal. Jews had been rounded up and taken away to concentration camps. Political activists faced sudden arrest, while young, able-bodied men and women were seized and forced onto trains that took them to labor camps in Germany. Every day the population was subjected to senseless brutalities. On one of my delivery runs, I also became a victim. This happened at the train station where the Gestapo intimidated passengers by patrolling train platforms with vicious German shepherds. Train stations, train platforms, and trains themselves were usually packed, since this was the principal means of mass transportation. Only two trains a day would accept civilians, and when the trains arrived they were already stuffed with people. As soon as a train came to a halt, people would rush at it and try to squeeze inside or at least get a foothold on one of the tiny platforms at either end of a train car. I made one of these mad dashes for the train and was climbing up the steps of a train car, when suddenly a Gestapo guard released his dog and it jumped at me. The dog grabbed me by the leg and pulled me off the train as it began to move. Eventually, I was released and I was unhurt, but this incident would have driven me to join the OUN resistance if I had not already been part of it.

There were many other indignities that the civilian population had to endure. Food was extremely scarce in Lviv, and people tried to smuggle foodstuffs from the countryside. The Gestapo tried to stop the smuggling by initiating frequent searches. Not only would a woman's purse be searched, but she was also subjected to a body search with the Gestapo guard fondling her breasts to see if she had anything "hidden" there.

I always looked forward to my weekend trips to Zadviria and especially to seeing my mother. I usually managed to get away on Sunday morning, and my mother got into the habit of coming out to the crossroads to meet me. I would see her standing there, and I would run up to her and kiss her callused hand, while she would hug me and kiss my forehead. Many years later, after my parents returned from ten years of exile in Siberia where they were deported because of me, my mother would remember our Sunday meetings; whenever she would hear the rumble of an approaching train, she would go to the window and look out to see if I was coming home. Her wish would never come true.

One such Sunday in 1943, Mikushka met me in Zadviria at my home. My father was outside in the yard getting the horses and the wagon ready to take Mikushka to a neighboring village. Mikushka and I were alone in the room.

"Marusia," Mikushka suddenly said and in a low voice laden with emotion. When I turned toward him, his eyes burned with a strange fire. In the next instant, he grabbed me and kissed me. I had never before experienced such a kiss. At that moment, the outside door opened and someone stepped into the vestibule. Mikushka let go of me and began to talk about something. I ran past him and out the door and walked briskly down the road to Sunday mass. During the service I prayed for forgiveness for committing such a grave sin. After that incident, there was a marked change in our relationship, although neither he nor I referred to that kiss. Mikushka was kinder and less gruff, but he continued to treat me more as a child than an equal. Nonetheless, I decided that it would be better to end this relationship, and when an opportunity presented itself, I grabbed it.

At this time, a course was being organized in Peremyshl for young people like me whose education in the gymnasium had been interrupted by the war. This course prepared one for a test that would then grant a gymnasium diploma. I convinced my parents to let me apply and went to the institute to quit my job. However, I was denied permission to leave. I ran out of the director's office in tears—and left my job anyway. A few weeks later, a notice appeared in a local paper that listed me as well as many others who had left their jobs and were being sought by the authorities. My parents were very upset, because this meant that if I were arrested I would be deported for labor in Germany. They contacted Mikushka and asked him to intervene on my behalf with the institute's director, which he did.

In the fall of 1943, it became obvious that Germany was losing the war. The retreating troops overwhelmed the cities and the countryside. They bivouacked in large buildings, especially schools. This was not a good time to study. Nonetheless, young people from throughout

Halychyna flocked to Peremyshl for the gymnasium course. (Peremyshl was a historically significant Ukrainian political, cultural, and religious center, although by the 1930s only 15 percent of its inhabitants were Ukrainians.) In 1943, the city swelled with refugees fleeing from Eastern Ukraine and the advancing Red Army.

I came to Peremyshl with a letter of introduction from Mikushka to the local OUN network, but I did not get involved immediately. I lived in a dormitory with other girls, and the lectures and study for the test consumed all my time. I met Natalka Kozakevych, a friend from Lviv, who had joined the local underground. She was, at this time, the regional head of the Ukrainian Red Cross, which organized women medics to treat wounded UPA partisans. She mostly worked in the countryside, although she had an apartment in Peremyshl.

Vasyl Halasa, Maria's first husband, in 1942. He adopted the nom de guerre "Orlan."

Sometime during the early months of 1944, at Natalka's apartment, I met Vasyl Halasa, who was an OUN leader in the area. Natalka was in love with him and had told me much about him, so I was curious to make his acquaintance. At that time he was using the nom de guerre of Zenon, which he later changed to Orlan. He was of medium height and had a very high forehead and thick, dark blond hair that he wore brushed back. He was friendly, yet his keen blue eyes seemed to see right through me. He was about twenty-five years old then, but he greeted me like an equal and his smile lit up his whole face. Our conversation was interesting, and he showed a keen sense of humor. We saw each other several more times at Natalka's apartment, and our friendship developed. Then he stopped coming to Peremyshl, and I began to miss him. His ability to make lasting friends was one of his greatest talents.

In the meantime, I continued attending lectures and studying. The course moved from building to building, the lectures were interrupted many times by bombardments and the war, but finally in the spring of 1944 we took the test. I passed and received a gymnasium diploma, which would enable me to enroll for university studies.

The OUN had been active among the students attending the lectures, and many joined the underground at this time. I, too, decided to stay in Peremyshl and work for the OUN. I was assigned to Solovii (Mykola Dudko), who contacted Mikushka and completed my transfer. I was given the nom de guerre of Zirka and became Solovii's secretary.

In May 1944, a two-week training camp for OUN women was organized in a forester's house in the woods outside the village of Kniazhychi in the Carpathian foothills. My friend Zoya (Zena Khymka) and I were among the twenty-two young women who participated in the course. Zenon was our principal ideological instructor, although we also received training in nursing, battle strategy, and how to handle weapons. We were protected by a group of armed partisans, while local police units cooperated with the OUN and would have given us warning in the event of a Gestapo raid. I enjoyed the training, and it did not pose any difficulties. Although much of the material was familiar, Zenon delivered the lectures in such a fresh and interesting manner that he had my full attention as well as that of the other girls.

The course was almost at an end when, in the middle of the night, a guard burst into the house and woke us up. He said that a Gestapo unit was approaching the house. His words created a panic, and everyone forgot what we had just learned about an organized retreat. Some of the girls were crying, others were praying out loud. Everyone was crying, packing her things, and then unpacking because not everything would fit in the backpacks. My conduct, however, was exemplary. I did not panic but followed orders and packed my things. Then I shouldered my backpack and waited, ready for further instructions. As I watched the other girls running around trying to decide what to do, I was hard pressed not to laugh. I suspected that this alarm was being staged to test us. I could see that our instructors were very calm and perhaps a little too poised. This turned out to be the case.

Finally, our instructors quieted us down, and led us out the back door into the forest. Some of the girls had simply rolled their things into a bundle and now began to lose items. Once we were in the forest, we were told the alarm had been a test. Our instructors told us what we had done wrong and pointed out that if the raid had actually happened, the Gestapo would have found us simply by following the trail of our lost garments.

At the end of the course, I was to report to commander Taras (Petro Kavula) who was stationed in the village of Viis'ko. Zenon told me he was also going in that direction, and we set out together before dawn the next morning. I followed Zenon along a trail, some distance from the main road. Now and again we would meet people who were working in nearby fields. They would wish us good morning, and we would exchange a few words. After a while, Zenon stopped and took my backpack. He said that I must be tired. Then he took me by the hand and we, like children on a pleasant hike, kept on walking, carefree and happy, convinced of the righteousness of the life path we had chosen. Now and again, Zenon would squeeze my hand, and an inkling of what could happen between us overcame me; I wondered whether I wanted this to happen.

We did not find Taras as we had expected and had to wait. In order not to waste time, Zenon began to dictate a letter and I began to transcribe it on the typewriter we found in Taras' room. The tension that had developed between us during our trip intensified as we waited for Taras. However hard I tried to control my emotions, I could not. I found it difficult to concentrate and made many mistakes as I typed. Although Zenon noticed my clumsiness he did not say anything; I realized he understood my agitation, and this made me even more nervous. Then suddenly he came over to me, lifted my face to his and kissed me. A moment later, Taras entered the room, but by then, Zenon, who had seen Taras approaching through the window, was again pacing the room and dictating. I blushed crimson. Taras, who was a tall handsome man, a year or so older than Zenon, looked at me and smiled. His eyes betrayed his understanding of what had been going on.

A day later, Taras gave me new orders, and I left for the village of Kormanychi. This village stretched along a stream, while behind it lay a thick forest. It was reasonably easy to monitor any new arrivals, and Solovii, to whom I was to report, had brought his family here and established his headquarters.

At this time, the Germans were retreating west, and the front was passing through the Carpathian mountains. Couriers would bring mail to Solovii. One day there was a letter for me from Zenon, who had now assumed the name Orlan. He apologized for his earlier conduct and wished me the best. Yet between the lines of the letter I sensed sadness and a yearning for something he thought could not ever happen. Our relationship could have ended with that letter, and my life would have taken a different course. However, I decided to answer his letter. In my note, I asked why he was so sad, since he was not going away and neither was I; we could be friends. I received a second letter very quickly. He asked me to visit him in the next village, and he would send one of his men to accompany me.

Thus, we began to meet every Sunday, alone. Sometimes he came to my quarters. At other times we would meet in a meadow or by the stream. I was eighteen and in love. He opened his heart to me and told me his most secret hopes and dreams. He told me about his life and the people he had met, and I marveled how he was always able to find goodness in those he knew. Sometimes I envied him this gift, since most people that I met I perceived as ordinary and unremarkable. I felt that, after every one of our meetings, I came away a better and more understanding person. He was for me what a spring of cool water is to a thirsty pilgrim. I wanted to stay by that spring and drink my fill.

But my conscience troubled me. Wasn't I already in love with Sofron? Was I deceiving Orlan? When Orlan kissed me and I closed my eyes, I saw Sofron's face. I loved them both.

The war came nearer. In August 1944, the front ground to a halt at Brody. I asked Solovii for permission to visit my parents. Although in the previous two years I had been home only occasionally, nonetheless Zadviria was the center of my existence, the place where I gained strength. Everyone knew that Germany would retreat further west and that Lviv and Zadviria would once again fall under Soviet rule. I did not know when I would be able to visit my parents again.

I took the train to Lviv, and once there I went to visit friends. As soon as I greeted my friends, they told me that Sofron had come to them several times to ask about me and had left several messages where I could find him. I immediately went to see him.

After a year apart, we were together again, but this meeting was different from those earlier ones. Our emotions were like a spring flood, tempestuous and raging. We again confessed our love, but this time without any doubts in our voices. We were afraid that we would not have enough time to explain to each other the entire year of yearnings and dreams. But what about Orlan? I relegated him to a corner of my mind and concentrated my attention on my first love.

We did not have much time together. Sofron's UPA unit had been devastated in the fighting, his parental home lay in ruins. He was shattered by what was happening and told me that the future was bleaker than anything we had ever imagined. I did not share his fears. I was more optimistic and, as I tried to convince him that all was not lost, I remembered Orlan and his confidence and enthusiasm. Suddenly I was ashamed of myself. I asked Sofron if he knew Orlan and told him a little about our relationship, but not everything, of course. Sofron had met Orlan earlier at one of the OUN training courses. He looked at me and said, "If something should happen to me, marry him. He is a good person."

He was about to say something else but changed his mind. That evening, we took the train to Zadviria to see my parents, and the next morning we returned to Lviv as the Red Army began its bombardment of the city. Sofron took me to the train station and waited with me for the train to Peremyshl. He kissed me good-bye.

A week later, the Red Army occupied Lviv. A year later, I learned that Sofron had fled West. I also learned that he had already made plans to leave when we met and that was the thing he had hesitated to tell me. I think I know why he did not tell me his plans. He suspected, rightly, that I would look down on him for abandoning the struggle and fleeing West to safety.

As soon as I returned to my post, Orlan came to see me. He said he had worried about my safety. He tried to hug and kiss me. I turned my face away.

"What's the matter?" he asked and his smile disappeared.

I did not tell him the truth. I found an excuse. I told him I knew that Natalka Kozakevych was in love with him and I could not betray a friend.

He looked at me with a puzzled expression. "You certainly are big hearted," he said. "I wonder why you didn't think before that our relationship would hurt her."

Eventually, Orlan learned the truth—from Natalka herself. "What? She said she did it for me? She saw this guy in Lviv, a guy she used to go with before she met you." And so Natalka had her revenge.

The German army was retreating west, and the OUN was feverishly working to prepare itself to face the Soviet invader. Confrontations with either army were avoided at all costs. The OUN and the UPA were conserving their manpower and their weapons for the partisan war that lay ahead.

Right behind the Red Army came the special security troops of the NKVD, the Soviet security agency. These detachments immediately encircled villages and towns and searched for partisans. At greatest risk were women partisans who lived among the population. In order to safeguard them, the UPA leadership ordered these women to join partisan detachments in the forests. There the women were trained as nurses and couriers.

At this time, some OUN members, especially those that had families, were deciding to immigrate West. Orlan gave them safe passage through the territories under his control. One day I received a letter from him suggesting that I join one of the groups heading West. He said he would arrange the details. To underscore the seriousness of his proposal, he warned that circumstances would soon become very difficult and that I was not strong enough to lead a harsh life in an armed guerrilla army. His comment hurt me, although I suspected he was paying me back for turning him down. I wrote back declining his offer, saying that I planned to join the UPA since I did not think it could be restricted to people with robust physiques.

2. Recruitment
into the Resistance

In August 1944, I joined the UPA. According to Ukrainian military historians, at least twenty-five thousand and at most forty thousand men fought in the UPA between 1942 and its near annihilation in 1949, although Nazi and Soviet military documents would set the figure at around two hundred thousand.

Organized in 1942 as self-defense units during Nazi control of Western Ukraine, UPA evolved into an effective guerrilla army by 1944 under the ideological control of the Bandera faction of the OUN. German attempts to destroy the UPA failed. Soviet attempts in 1944 and 1945 also were unsuccessful until the "Great Blockade" in the Carpathian mountains from January to April 1946. At this time, special contingents of NKVD troops were stationed in all towns and villages, while mobile combat units scoured the forests. Forty percent of UPA troops died or were captured during this blockade. The UPA was demobilized, and the struggle against Stalin continued as an underground resistance.

The 1946 demobilization did not apply, however, to companies of the Sixth Military District of the UPA, also known as the Sian Division of UPA West. This force operated in the Ukrainian ethnic territories in Poland. This area was called the *Zakerzon krai*, which translates as "the region beyond the Curzon Line." The evolution of this name dates to December 8, 1919, when the Allied Supreme Council drew Poland's eastern frontier, as Europe sorted itself out at the conclusion of World War I. In July 1920, during the Soviet advance on Warsaw, British Foreign Secretary Curzon proposed the same line as the border between Poland and Soviet Russia to halt the fighting. The Treaty of

28

Riga in 1921 between Poland and the newly formed Soviet Union moved Poland's eastern border further east to encompass Western Ukraine (using the old Austro-Hungarian border), and the Curzon line became a nonissue. The Curzon Line was resurrected in February 1945 at the Yalta Conference, as Stalin, Churchill, and Roosevelt drew a map of post–World War II Europe. Implementation of the Curzon Line gave Stalin Western Ukraine, a territory on which he insisted, but ceded to Poland ethnic Ukrainian territories, primarily along the Sian River and in the foothills of the Polish Carpathian mountains. Viis'ko, the village where I had worked under Taras, became part of Western Ukraine, while Peremyshl, where I had studied to obtain my gymnasium diploma, became the Polish city Przemysl. Its location on the Sian River and the frontier would make it a volatile border town. The Curzon Line remains Poland's eastern frontier to this day (minor adjustments that were made in 1951), and Peremyshl remains a Polish city.

Throughout 1944, I served as a nurse and intelligence courier for the Druzhynnyky UPA company in the *Zakerzon krai*. I occasionally crossed into Western Ukraine to deliver mail and other documents to UPA groups there. This was the time when the German Army was retreating, while the Red Army was pressing across Europe.

As mentioned earlier, the arrival of the Red Army brought back the NKVD special troops whose task was to destroy resistance and pacify the countryside. Those of us who were couriers were assigned to the *sotnya* (a company numbering one hundred men) of Commander Chernyk (Mykhailo Marushchak). We set out to rendezvous with Chernyk's company in a carefree mood, as if we were going for a recreational hike and not to join partisans who would very likely involve us in battles. Not that we did not comprehend the seriousness of the political situation or realize that the return of the Soviets had to be resisted with force—we knew that we, as well as those we loved, would probably die in the guerrilla war we were being trained for. We understood all this, yet our fears were lulled by the thought, "This will not happen to me. It will happen to someone else." Our youth made us feel invincible; what we thought about was our heroism. I remember thinking, "Now I will be fighting in the UPA. I will be involved in what really matters. I will no longer have to spend my time typing orders or delivering mail. This is the place where I will show my bravery, my heroism, and my dedication." If only the battle were joined!

Chernyk, on the other hand, had no intentions of pitting his company against superior NKVD forces. He did everything possible to evade direct confrontations with the well-equipped and motorized enemy. Instead of fighting, he took his men and us deep into the forests where we continued our studies. We learned map reading, some military science, and how to handle weaponry won in battles. We were also detailed to the kitchen.

We soon realized that the NKVD forces usually did not stay in the countryside or in the villages at night. They would search the villages and raid the forests during the day, but depart to more secure camps along major roads at night. Thus, Commander Chernyk and other UPA leaders worked out this strategy: We spent the days in the forests, but, as night approached, we would march toward the nearest village where we would find food.

One evening, as we left the forest in a single file and were approaching a village for a meal being readied by friendly village women, bullets from hidden machine guns began to rain on us. Several of the men cried out in pain as bullets found their mark. We women panicked. A pleasant evening changed into war in an instant, and we were not prepared.

"Back into the forest," Chernyk commanded, while ordering a squad to cover our orderly retreat. I guess none of us understood the order. As the machine gun fire intensified, we turned and dashed headlong through the fields toward the forest.

"What are you doing?" Chernyk bellowed, and we stopped in our tracks. "Get behind the squad."

We did as we were told, and eventually we were able to escape the pursuing enemy without suffering any serious casualties. Once we were safe, Chernyk told us to halt. We built a fire, boiled water, and cleaned and bandaged the wounded. As tensions receded and the men settled down around the campfire, someone wondered out loud whether the women deserved medals for that evening's show of "bravery." We were silent, ashamed of ourselves. Eventually one of the women said that this was the first time—it would not happen again. This is when I and, I think, the others understood the difference between our dreams of heroism and the reality of battle. The barrage of bullets made us understand that glory costs dearly.

We did not spend all those weeks hiding in the forests. On occasion Chernyk would dispatch us in pairs to deliver or bring mail or to gather intelligence about the enemy. One spring day, I remember that Chernyk sent Zoya, who had joined the UPA at the same time I did and had participated in the same training courses, and me to a nearby village to learn about the strength and movements of the NKVD special forces. We did what we were assigned to do and set out on the return journey late in the afternoon, staying ahead of a Red Army infantry detachment in the area. The soldiers were marching on the road while we were on a path that ran parallel with the road through nearby fields. Dusk was falling; some of the soldiers were swilling vodka from hip bottles, talking and singing. They had seen us earlier and now began looking our way more often. We knew that we had been noticed, and we accelerated our strides until we were almost running.

"Hey, you girls," one of the soldiers shouted. "Come with us to Germany."

At that moment, one of the soldiers turned and tried to jump over the ditch on the side of the road, but an officer grabbed him by the shoulder. The soldier whirled around and hit the officer. The column came to a halt as the soldier and the officer exchanged blows. Then the soldier pulled out his revolver and shot the officer in the hand.

We watched in horror as the officer tried to stem the flow of blood. We began to run in earnest, afraid that we would be blamed for provoking the incident and that the soldiers would shoot us.

We did escape and late that night reached a small village. We knocked at the door of the first house, then at the door of the next house, but the village was deserted. We spent the night in a barn and toward morning were awakened by the arrival of two soldiers. We hid behind some bales of hay and held our breaths. I looked at Zoya. Her eyes were large and round with fear; I guess mine were too. If the soldiers found us, we were sure they would take us to their commander to be questioned. If the commander thought we were partisans, couriers, or sympathizers, he could summarily execute us. But the soldiers did not see us. Eventually, we made our way safely back to Chernyk.

Another time, two of us set out with mail we were to drop off at a village on the outskirts of the forest. Somehow we took a wrong turn and became lost. Every path we took ended in a ravine. Then to make things worse, clouds rolled in and it began to rain. A little later the rain became a cloudburst. We were cold and soaked, and night was falling. Somehow we found a small forester's hut. We spent the night curled into balls pressing against each other to stay warm. We awoke before daybreak and started out again. If it had not been for an old man who had driven his wagon into the forest to gather wood, we might have stayed lost for another day. He pointed out the way to us and, after thanking him profusely, we carried out our assignment.

When in the fall of 1944 the retreating German Army halted in the Carpathian mountains, most of the partisan units found themselves inside the German front. It took them until late autumn to fight across the German line. This was a critical time for our detachments, since we had not yet established contact with the UPA that had formed in Western Ukraine under the aegis of the OUN-Bandera faction. At this time, the detachments active in the *Zakerzon krai* were operating on their own, their strikes against the enemy decided at meetings of the commanders of the companies. Since I was increasingly used as a courier, I saw Orlan, who was the OUN regional representative and ideological instructor, fairly often. Zoya, who had become my best friend, was assigned to be his secretary.

The relationship between Orlan and me did not change that spring and summer. We treated each other in the same way we treated others around us. What I did notice was that he had a remarkable effect on rank-and-file partisans. Not only did they respect him, he also inspired them and quelled their unspoken fears. Somehow, he gave them confidence that what they were fighting for was not only just, but that their sacrifice would someday result in a sovereign Ukrainian state. As I watched how the partisans listened to him, my feeling toward him also began to change. I began to regret my earlier rejection of his affection. Sofron's image began to slip from my thoughts and dreams.

When autumn arrived and deepened, my mood became as gloomy as the changing season. The forests were darker and quieter, the songbirds disappeared, and cobwebs ensnared the underbrush as if to protect it from the gusting cold winds.

The first meeting between UPA units in the *Zakerzon krai* and those in Western Ukraine was about to take place and I, as liaison coordinator of the Peremyshl UPA Military Region, would deliver documents and be debriefed. This was early October, and the meeting place agreed upon was behind the war front that now stood west of Peremyshl. This meant that I had to cross the Polish frontier. I would be passed from contact to contact until I was across the frontier and in Western Ukraine; after that I would be on my own, since no one knew if the old OUN routes established during the German occupation still existed or were safe. I sewed the documents I was given into my clothing and learned my oral report by heart. Just before I was to depart, I went together with an escort to Orlan to get his instructions and collect his mail.

By coincidence, that day was also my nineteenth birthday. No one around me knew this, and those that might have known had forgotten. My spirits were at a low point. I wished that at least one person would remember and wish me a happy birthday.

Orlan acknowledged my arrival, rolled his letter into a thin long tube, and handed the tube to me. He shook my hand in farewell and escorted me to the door, then followed me outside. The night was as bright as day. Moonlight shone on the hills around us, and the horizon glowed with a silver luminescence. I stopped to wait for the arrival of my escort who had gone to a nearby house on an errand. Again, Orlan bade me farewell and picked up my hand, held it in his and said, "Happy birthday and good luck."

Suddenly I was in his arms and he was whispering, "I can't get you out of my mind."

"I think about you, too," I whispered back just in time, since my escort appeared from the shadows. I stepped away from Orlan and turned to follow my escort. But my steps were light and my thoughts as resplendent as the moonlight.

I was passed from village to village along normal OUN channels and was escorted across the frontier by a UPA platoon without incident. In the first village in Western Ukraine I sensed the change. People were so frightened they trembled. In the *Zakerzon krai*, I was used to UPA operating cautiously but only semi-covertly, but in Western Ukraine the resistance had already been driven deep underground. I discovered that I would be traveling without the new documents that had been issued to the resident population a few months earlier when the Soviets re-established control. No one in the OUN had yet found a method for accessing or forging the new credentials. However, my further transportation was arranged, and I continued on toward Lviv in the back of a truck. In Lviv, I stopped to visit friends and get news about my family. To my relief I learned that the NKVD's "Red broom" had swept past my home. No one had been arrested, and everyone was well. From Lviv, I again traveled in the back of a truck, mingling with other passengers that were picked up by the driver along the way. I got off at the town of Bibrka, as I had been instructed. From there, I made my way to a remote village. This village was in a forested region and, as I learned later, was the destination of all the couriers, who were lodged in practically every house. Later that evening, I was taken by a platoon to an even more remote village. That village was protected by an UPA *sotnya* stationed just beyond the village in the forest. All night the village buzzed with partisan activity, then in the morning, the partisans moved into the forest to return back to the village again after dark. I delivered the mail I carried and waited to be debriefed. Several important OUN and UPA leaders were conducting the debriefings. I learned that three prominent men were in the forest: Dorosh (Petro Duzhiy), a member of central leadership of the OUN, Horbenko (Rostyslav Voloshyn), a member of the Ukrainian Supreme Liberation Council (UHVR), and Perebyinis (Dmytro Hrytsai), who would later become UPA chief of staff.

I waited my turn to report and in the afternoon was summoned by Dorosh, a thin, blond man with a narrow face. He had already looked through the mail and documents I had brought and asked me in detail about how our units had handled the passage of the German-Russian front, what casualties we had suffered and how we were adjusting to being and operating inside Poland. Dorosh was interested in the morale among the partisans and among the Ukrainian population and what kind of repression the Warsaw government was instituting against ethnic Ukrainians. Finally, he asked me about my journey and if I had encountered any adventures, which I had not. That evening, Perebyinis summoned me. He questioned me at length about the morale in the *Zakerzon krai* and had me recount the details of recent battles. He was worried about our preparations for the coming winter.

I woke up the next morning to learn that a detachment of NKVD troops was approaching the village. The entire village went on battle alert, but debriefings of couriers continued in the forest. That afternoon I was summoned to one more debriefing. Unlike Dorosh and Perebyinis, this man was not in uniform. He introduced himself as Osyp Diakiv (Hornovii), a name I recognized from my conversations with Orlan. Osyp and Orlan grew up in the same village, and now Osyp wanted to know about his childhood friend. Osyp also asked me to tell Orlan that Orlan's mother had died in exile in Kazakhstan. She had been deported in 1940, during the first Soviet occupation. Osyp also told me of other deaths among his and Orlan's mutual friends who had joined the resistance.

I was then given mail, instructions, some propaganda material, and then returned to the village. I went back to Bibrka, and from there a truck took several other couriers and me back to Lviv. Among the mail was a copy of a satirical magazine called *Ukrainian Pepper*. I enjoyed reading it so much that I hid it among my things, although I had been told that I did not have to take it with me. Only the mail and its delivery were important.

Emboldened by the fact that I had not encountered any document checks, I decided to take the train from Lviv to Zadviria to visit my family. As soon as the train departed the Lviv station, the door of the train car opened and a conductor began to collect tickets. I had a ticket, but what made my heart pound was the NKVD soldier who accompanied the conductor and was checking identity cards. The only document I had was a forged German identity card, which was still in use in Poland. When my turn came, I gave my ticket to the conductor and handed the NKVD soldier my identity card. He did a double take. It was obvious from his expression that he had not seen this kind of document before. He turned it this way and that, and I saw him trying to read the German script. He eventually put the card in his pocket and motioned to me to follow him. When the train stopped at the first station outside Lviv, the NKVD soldier led me to a train car filled with Soviet soldiers. He told me to take a seat and then sat down opposite me. I was in despair. This was the end, I thought, and could not forgive myself for deciding on this side trip home. I tried to talk my way out of the predicament. I told the NKVD soldier that I was from Zadviria and that once the train stopped there he could ask practically anyone to identify me. He did not contradict me but did not listen either. I heard him repeat several times under his breath, "I'll take her to Krasne where she can be interrogated."

In Zadviria he told me to follow him, and I had the feeling that I was about to be passed on to someone else. My despair deepened. Here I was so near my home and safety, yet both were beyond my reach. How many times I had taken the train from this station, and how many times I had arrived here. Today would be the last time.

Dusk had fallen, and passengers were pouring from the train and crowding the platforms and tracks. We had halted on the outside track, so in order to get to the train station, we had to cross the inside tracks where a freight train had stopped. People were squeezing between the wagons, and there was no way that two people could walk abreast. As the NKVD soldier stepped in front of me to push his way through the crowd, I saw my chance to get away. I knew the station well. As the soldier elbowed his way forward, I spun around and began to push my way in the opposite direction. In seconds I was swallowed by the crowd, which carried me past the station to the road that led into the village. Behind me, the passenger train began to move.

My unexpected appearance at home created joy that was tinged by the fear of my close brush with the NKVD. I listened more than I spoke and tried to be very circumspect about my UPA activities. I tried to calm my mother by saying that "where I had settled, the oppression was not as great and I was safer than I would be at home." I don't know whether she believed me or not.

I did not dare to take the train back to Lviv. In the morning, my father harnessed his remaining horse to a wagon and drove me to Lviv. (We used to have three horses, Arabian bred, which were his joy and which had made him famous in our area. The Germans took one horse. The second horse had been conscripted by the Soviets.) I glanced at my father as he urged the emaciated horse down the road. My father did not look well; he had aged suddenly. I think he guessed my thoughts. He said, "Two horses are gone, and soon they will take even this one. All my work has been for nothing." Then after a pause he added, "I don't know whether we will be allowed to stay here in Zadviria. We might be exiled."

In Lviv, I sewed the mail into my clothing, but did not have room for the *Ukrainian Pepper*, which I rolled into a tube and placed in a bag with some grain. This bag went at the bottom of a bigger bag, under my clothing, which I had taken from home. I had no documents, no identity card, and this worried me. Fortunately, the truck in which I was given a ride was not stopped at any roadblocks, and I reached my destination at the border without incident. Soon I would communicate with the OUN underground, and someone would lead me back across the frontier to the *Zakerzon krai* and safety.

I was nearing the village where I was to meet my contact, the first house was just ahead of me, when suddenly, as if he had risen out of the ground, a NKVD soldier barred my way. He was short, grim, and had Asiatic features, "Your documents, please," he said in Russian.

"Documents?" I cried. "I don't carry documents in the village. I'm just going down the road to exchange some clothing for food."

"Well, let's go inside and I'll check your bag," he said and led me into the house. We found a woman busy at the stove in the kitchen, but she stopped what she was doing and followed us into the main room. She sat down, and we too sat on a bench as the NKVD soldier began to examine my things. I froze. He would find the magazine buried in the grain. I will be arrested and taken to the county seat for interrogation. There, they will find the mail hidden in my clothing. Why did I take the magazine Dorosh had told me to read and leave behind? He had warned me that it was dangerous to travel with this kind of material.

Methodically, the NKVD soldier examined everything in my bag. He finally pulled out the bag of grain and fingered it. He soon felt the roll of paper hidden inside, untied the knot, reached inside and pulled it out.

"What's this?" he asked as he smoothed out the magazine. He glanced down at it, then looked up at me with reproach on his face. "You're carrying this and you haven't even taken the trouble to get decent documents?" He now examined the cover more closely and did a double take when he realized that the caricature on the cover was that of Stalin. He next flicked to the inside and began to read aloud the first feature, "A letter of kolkhoz members to Father Stalin." He had some difficulty with reading Ukrainian, but the satire drew him in, and he soon forgot about me.

I thought I was going to faint. The woman realized what the magazine was and grew pale. She got up and went back to the kitchen. I stood up, said I had to get a drink of water, and followed her. I had no plans yet, but I knew I had to get a drink of water because otherwise I was certain I was going to faint. In the kitchen I turned to the woman and whispered, "Is there any way out of here?"

"This way," she whispered back and opened the door that led into the barn. I slipped through it, then ran through the barn and out the other door. I looked around, saw that the ground behind the barn sloped down to a creek, and plunged down into its shelter. My boots filled with water, and I found it harder and harder to run. At any moment, the NKVD soldier would shoot me. I hoped that I would die and not be taken alive.

I reached the next house, climbed out of the stream, and ran into the house. I begged the startled people there to help me. The man took me out the back to his orchard where he had built a bunker in which the family had hid during the passage of the front through the area. I crawled inside the mildewed and wet bunker. I fell to my knees and began to pray, praying so fervently it seemed I was talking to a real person.

Although the NKVD soldier raised an alarm, the search patrol did not find me. News about my escape reached the right ears, and in the evening my OUN contact found me and delivered me to a second contact, who had been waiting to lead me to the frontier. He could not help me cross, however, since the villages along the border were filled with NKVD troops. I spent a few days in these villages, searching out women who had been active in the Ukrainian Red Cross. Not everyone was willing to help, since people were afraid of being found out and snitched on to the NKVD. Eventually, some women did help me, and I crossed the frontier back into Poland without any more incidents. However, I soon faced a new calamity. In one of the houses where I had stayed, I must have been exposed to dysentery. I did not know this at the time I brought my mail to the agreed-upon meeting place. I found no one waiting for me—Orlan and the UPA unit he was with had moved into the forest to escape NKVD raids. I realized that I could not stay in the village either and, as I tried to decide what to do, my friend Zoya, sent by Orlan, came to get me. I do not know why he had chosen her and not someone else, but her selection proved to be providential. Smiling, broad-faced Zoya had become my closest friend in the UPA, and I soon needed someone who loved me and would care for me. Zoya warned that we were in danger and urged that we leave immediately for a remote mountain village. The distance was not too great, and I agreed readily, but we soon discovered that I could hardly walk. Cramps stopped me every few minutes, and I would double up in pain.

With Zoya's help, we reached the village, where I collapsed. I was very ill for two weeks. I writhed in pain on the pallet, soiled my clothing and the linens with blood, and wished I were dead. There was no doctor, no medicines, and almost no food since the village was very poor and food was scarce. Despite hunger and the absence of medical help, or perhaps because I took nothing except water and let my body fight the disease alone, I recovered. I had become so thin that I was but a shadow of myself. Zoya had refused to leave me the entire time I was sick, and I owed her my life. She took care of me as if I were her own sister. On most days, after washing me for the umpteenth time that day and removing my blood-soaked clothing, remaking my pallet with clean sheets and carrying me back to it, she would sit beside me and sing softly. Perhaps her songs, to which I listened with my whole being, pulled me through.

During my absence and subsequent illness, conditions in the *Zakerzon krai* had become grim. UPA *sotnyas* had been decimated in constant battles with NKVD troops, and many of the men were ill, hungry, and cold since not everyone had winter clothing. Organizing their winter quarters and food supplies fell on Orlan. With his help, UPA units managed to create a supply network, which obtained food and medicines. New weapons and new clothing were won in battles. That winter, UPA units wore a combination of uniforms and civilian clothing.

◆ ◆ ◆ ◆ ◆

The winter of 1944-45, the first winter under Soviet domination, was harsh. The so-called "Red broom" was sweeping villages empty of people, and the NKVD troops did their utmost to discover and destroy partisan activity. Not only did the NKVD troops comb the forests, they also ransacked every village and homestead and terrorized inhabitants. The NKVD also established its own network of informers through threats, coercion, and bribes. Those who were suspected of helping or even sympathizing with the UPA were summarily deported to Siberia.

One of the problems the UPA faced was that it had few well-hidden underground bunkers since, until the return of the Soviets, UPA detachments lived in camps deep in the forests, not underground. The bunkers that did exist had been constructed with the help of the local population, and many people knew their location. The NKVD terror and its inhuman treatment of captured partisans forced the OUN-led resistance literally underground. While large military detachments still controlled and lived in the forests, individuals in the resistance hid in bunkers or in hideouts built into houses or barns. In the meantime, women partisans were placed with families living in strategic villages. They dressed and acted like local women. Their role was to keep information and food flowing to the partisans. The UPA Red Cross obtained medicines as well as candles and kerosene, necessary ingredients for life underground. Whenever and wherever possible, I trained local girls in basic first aid.

As winter deepened, four of us, including Zoya and me, asked Orlan for permission to visit our families at Christmas. He agreed, and we were escorted across the frontier, then found room in a truck that took us to Lviv. There we went our separate ways. To my surprise, I discovered that people in Zadviria wholeheartedly supported the UPA and were not, as in other places I had visited, circumspect about their contacts with the partisans. The partisans themselves were less circumspect than the groups I had been with recently, visiting the village often and staying for a day or so with their families. One of these partisans had returned home for Christmas as I had, and he came to see me. We spent the night telling each other our experiences. We celebrated Christmas by going to services at the church and also caroling in the village. My mother objected to my lack of discretion, but I insisted on going to church and caroling because I knew that this would be the last time I would do this at home. My mother proved to be right in worrying about the open way in which everyone was acting.

One morning just before the New Year, a platoon of NKVD troops, accompanied by bloodhounds, entered the village. Partisans visiting their families hid in a bunker that had been built near one of the houses located not too far from the church. The NKVD, however, did not do a house-to-house search, but headed straight for the house with the bunker.

Ten partisans were inside. The NKVD knew exactly where the bunker was, surrounded it, and began digging with shovels to find the hidden entrance. The partisans broke out, loped several grenades at the enemy, and tried to escape. They were all brought down by enemy fire. Those who were not killed outright used their last bullets to kill themselves so that they would not be taken alive.

The awful news of the discovery of the bunker and the death of every one of the partisans swept through the village. People took the deaths personally, as if the dead were family members, sons, nephews, brothers. I reacted as did the others. I was devastated and shocked. I had grown up with these men, had gone to school with them. "How will their mothers bear this tragedy? Some of the boys were only sons," my mother cried, looking at me in dismay and fear.

The NKVD troops conducted several other cursory searches, then left the village as abruptly as they had come. When dusk fell, my father and several other men took their large sleds to the bunker to remove the corpses lying on the snow that had turned a deep red. They found the mothers of the dead men wailing over the bodies. The women would not let the men remove the corpses. They held on to their dead sons, kissing their cold faces, and had to be torn away with force. Only one mother did not weep. She sat by her dead son in silence. Her eyes and face were that of a person going mad. She had had three sons. They had not been a well-to-do family, but she had given them all she could. The son lying in the red-stained snow was the last one. Her two other sons were already dead, one killed by the Nazis and the other one by the NKVD.

The corpses were wrapped in white linens and were buried that night in a communal grave. Our village did not sleep that night. My father came home pale, quiet, and heartbroken. I wept bitterly, not only for the dead men and their mothers, but also for all of us, for our nation. And as our hearts filled with grief, they also filled with hatred—it could not be otherwise.

Everyone wanted to know who had betrayed the bunker. The blame fell on a partisan from a neighboring village who had taken the opportunity of an amnesty the Soviets offered periodically, had turned himself in, and was cooperating with the NKVD. Later it turned out that he was not to blame. A group of NKVD men, dressed as partisans, had visited the village a week or so earlier and had gained the trust of one of the neighbors who had pointed out the location of the bunker to them.

I returned to my unit with a heavy heart. I spent the remainder of that winter moving from village to village, hiding during searches by the NKVD and visiting the bunkers in the forest only occasionally. A few months earlier, I had been elevated to the position of director of the Mostyska district Ukrainian Red Cross. In the spring of 1945, I became the director of the Peremyshl megadistrict Ukrainian Red Cross. My new position and area of activity necessitated that I change my nom de guerre. I had never liked Zirka. I chose Marichka, a variant of my own name. I reasoned that if I were to live the life I foresaw for myself, I might as well do it under my own name.

Despite the NKVD blockades and searches, the work of the Ukrainian Red Cross continued without interruption. We were able to equip several clinics, train many women in the underground in first aid, and also conduct first aid courses in a number of villages. We also assembled food packages that were sent to partisan units in the Lemko district.

Despite the constant pressure by the NKVD and the need for utmost conspiracy, Orlan and I found opportunities to see each other occasionally. We were in love, and the hours we spent together gave us strength and determination to survive. I no longer harbored any doubts that I loved him. However, we never discussed marriage. In fact, I shied away from considering marriage and its responsibilities. Then one day Orlan surprised me.

He had been called to mediate a lovers' quarrel in the partisan ranks. Taras, who was the commander of the OUN in the Peremyshl megadistrict, had been engaged for a while to one of the UPA secretaries, Sviatoslava. Once when visiting a village, Taras met a girl and flirted with her. She apparently welcomed his advances and bragged to her friends about her new romance. Her friends told others who, in turn, told Sviatoslava. Sviatoslava broke off the engagement and demanded to be transferred to a different district. Taras wrote to Orlan begging him to act as mediator. When Orlan met with the two lovers, he suggested that the only viable solution was for them to get married. Both agreed. As they began to plan the place and time for their wedding, Orlan said, "Why don't we have a double wedding?"

Taras, who had known about Orlan and me from the very beginning, said a double wedding was a great idea. A few days later, as several women and I were discussing the logistics of arranging Easter services and holiday food for the various partisan groups, I received a letter from Orlan in which he wrote, "I have decided that you and I should cross the threshold of the church together."

What a way to propose.

"What's the matter?" one of the women, who had noticed my expression, asked.

"Nothing much. I guess I'm getting married."

"You must be joking," the others chorused, since I had kept my relationship with Orlan secret from everyone, including my dear friend Zoya.

I did not relish the idea of marriage, but I knew I would do as Orlan asked.

I had an opportunity to write home to tell my parents about my plans. My letter was answered immediately by my mother who wrote, "Dear child, It is difficult for me to give you advice, but if you think you will be happy, your father and I give you our blessing. Perhaps it is better that you marry. There will be someone to take care of you."

I could not find a place for myself. My head was bursting with all kinds of fears. I knew that in the midst of war, my personal happiness was like the mythical firebird, impossible to snare. Will I have the strength and the will to match his, I wondered? He had told me that I differed from all the other girls. Although that had been pleasant to hear, I now wanted to turn to him and say, "Vasyl, you are mistaken. I'm like all the other girls. I dream of a life with you, not about a heroic death. And if death comes, I want to find the strength to face it with honor, but that will not be easy. No. I am also dazzled by your popularity and by your rank, as are the other girls. The only difference between them and me is that I know the price I will have to pay for marrying you, because I want to be the woman you say I am."

No one knew of my fears, and I did not share them with anyone, not even Zoya. I was told not to interfere in the wedding preparations, and I was happy to stay out of the way. One day Orlan told me he wanted a simple wedding with no fuss. He then left to confer with other commanders. His men and the women attached to his staff had different ideas. Although I noticed that some of the women would glance at me sideways in speculation and I could read in their eyes the question, "Why did he pick her?," nonetheless, they joined in the preparations with gusto. Orlan by then had become the OUN deputy leader of the *Zakerzon krai*. I understood their thinking. Their leader was getting married and they would arrange a proper wedding for him, even if he objected to the fuss.

I watched the preparations and could find no joy in them; this was not the wedding I had dreamt about. I wanted to be married in my village, in my church, in my home. I wanted my mother and my father to be there. I wanted to wear a white wedding dress and a veil. I wanted to have my procession to the altar serenaded by the choir in which my father sang and whose songs I knew and loved. But what I dreamt was not to be.

We were married on Sunday, May 27, 1945. Two priests, Father Hoza and Father Hrab, officiated at the double wedding. The wedding was in a chapel on the edge of the forest. Orlan and I, and Taras and Sviatoslava, led the procession to the chapel. Behind us came several unit commanders who had come to pay their respects to Orlan, and behind them ranks of UPA fighters.

As we approached the chapel, my heart began to pound. "Farewell youth," I thought. "Farewell, my first love. I am stepping over the threshold into a new life and new responsibilities, and I am scared to death that I will not know how to handle this new gift."

An honor guard came to attention as we entered the chapel. Inside, the pews and all available space were filled to overflowing with partisans. I looked for the other women. They were there too, dressed for the occasion with flowers in their hair. Every candle in the candelabras was lit and glowing, and for a moment I was blinded.

Later I heard myself repeating after the priest, "I, Marichka, take you, Orlan," I said using his and my noms de guerre as the priest had done, but silently I substituted Vasyl for Orlan.

"I, Sviatoslava, take you, Taras," I heard Sviatoslava repeat after the priest, and soon the ceremony was over.

Not only had the women decorated the chapel for the wedding and had gone out of their way to obtain the array of candles, they had also prepared a wedding feast at a school in the nearby village. I marveled at their efforts when they produced not only a wedding cake but also several bottles of wine for the toasts.

We celebrated far into the night and were guarded by two UPA *sotnyas*. Before dawn the merrymaking ended and partisan units disappeared into the forested hills.

◆ ◆ ◆ ◆ ◆

During 1945, Orlan and other UPA leaders had to face and deal with the growing enmity between Poles and Ukrainians. This enmity, which had grown sharper in the 1930s during Warsaw's attempt to Polonize that portion of Ukraine it had acquired under the Treaty of Riga in 1921, was being whipped into warfare by the NKVD. Soon after the Yalta Conference, the new frontier line was drawn. Warsaw announced the repatriation of ethnic Ukrainians to Western Ukraine. Ukrainian villages, pointing out that they had been occupying this land from time immemorial, refused to budge. Often a nearby Polish village would arm itself and attack the Ukrainian village. If a few houses in the Ukrainian village were burned or if someone was killed (this began happening with increasing frequency), Ukrainians would retaliate by attacking a Polish village. The Polish government and police units became involved in the local fighting, and Ukrainian villages turned to UPA units in the forests for help and protection.

Thus began the battles between the UPA and the Poles. UPA's leadership saw its units engaged in fighting the wrong enemy and taking casualties. To halt this conflict, UPA's leadership contacted the Polish anti–Communist resistance, known as Armia Krayova (AK). The two sides met and agreed that they had a common enemy and should direct their joint efforts against the Communists. After that, the fighting between Poles and Ukrainian decreased, but not for long.

Toward the end of 1945, conditions began to change rapidly as UPA came to understand the tack that Warsaw would adopt. Anyone suspected of cooperating with the UPA was arrested. As a result of the repression, the activity of the Ukrainian Red Cross was curtailed. Women partisans were released from their units and told to settle in Polish cities and assume new identities. They were also ordered to make contact with foreign legations in Warsaw and send word west about the UPA struggle behind the descending Iron Curtain.

One of the major events that I remember from that year was the appearance in our camp of three couriers who had been sent by the OUN from its newly established center in the American Zone in Germany. Two of the couriers continued into Western Ukraine, while one, after conferring with Orlan, returned west. The network these couriers established would last for several years.

As UPA's activity decreased in the *Zakerzon krai*, Orlan and I for the first time since our marriage found ourselves living together, albeit with others, in a hideout outside the city of Peremyshl. Because of the cramped space that allowed no privacy, our relations remained for the most part platonic. I soon understood that the life as a partisan and life as a married couple were mutually exclusive. Orlan was very careful to maintain his reputation as a dedicated revolutionary, and his private life was firmly placed in second place, behind his partisan activity. I did not like to be a shadow, a person in the background, and only his explanations and innate tact prevented me from rebelling publicly. In any event, what was happening around us, the constant vigilance and threat of capture, prevented us from focusing on and developing our own private life.

3. Marriage and Motherhood

In the fall of 1945, when Orlan was creating an underground route to the West, he asked me to relocate to western Poland where I would create a link on the route. He specified that this link should be as close as possible to the Czech border, in the so-called "gained lands," the territories that were ceded by Germany to Poland at the end of the war. I was to establish myself there by getting a job and an apartment, which would legalize my presence. Those traveling along the underground route would use the apartment.

I set out, after trading my partisan boots for heeled city shoes and my pistol for false documents. Thus equipped, I crossed Poland from east to west. As instructed, I settled in Yelena Gura, a former German city not far from the border. Finding an apartment turned out to be not too difficult; in fact, it was easy. I found it when I decided to "citify" myself further and went to a hairdresser. There I instructed the stylist to cut off my long hair, which I wore in braids, and then perm my new hairdo. Since this was a long process and I was bored, I started talking to a woman next to me who was also having her hair done. I told her I was looking for a place to live.

"You can have my place," she said. "I'm about to leave town." She thrust a key at me and I took it gladly.

I soon discovered that she was one of those new arrivals in the ceded territories who took full advantage—and more—of the new law that permitted Poles to evict Germans from their homes. All a Pole had to do was register for an apartment with the local housing authority and then find one to his or her liking. This is exactly what my acquaintance at the hairdresser did, as did a number of other Poles. But there was a further twist that I soon discovered. After acquiring an apartment, the new owner would strip it of furniture and any other possessions the Germans had left when the local militia summarily evicted them. Soon thereafter, the new owner would abandon the apartment, as my acquaintance had done, move to a new area and acquire a second apartment and repeat the process of stripping it bare. The stolen possessions would then be sold on the black market. Some people did this several times until they found an apartment to their liking or had accumulated enough stolen property to set up housekeeping. My acquaintance had forced an elderly German couple out of their spacious apartment and then had the militia help her cart away the couple's possessions. What she left behind was an iron bed, a scarred table, and a few kitchen utensils. I heard this account later from the two elderly Germans, who were relegated to one room that had its exit into the hallway. The other two adjoining rooms became mine, although I had to share the kitchen with the German couple. I registered myself with the housing authorities and started looking for a job.

I read in the local newspaper that a certain government agency was looking for a typist. Since all agencies by then had become governmental entities, I did not give the designation a second thought. When I went to apply for the job, I found a man at the address who turned out to be the agency's director. He looked me over carefully and then told me that he had not identified the governmental agency in the advertisement, but that this was the Polish Security Service, whose branch was just being established in Yelena Gura. My blood turned cold as I realized that I had applied for a job at the Polish equivalent of the Soviet NKVD. I tried to keep the conversation going while my mind searched for a way out. Soon, this director noticed my speech and asked me where I was from. I said I was from Lviv, where there had been a sizable Polish population before the war. He was not surprised, since many of the newcomers in the regained territories were from eastern provinces. He was actually pleased that I was from Lviv and was soon reminiscing about the time he had spent in Western Ukraine working for the Communist underground during the German occupation. In the meantime, I was being consumed by fears. What if he or someone else examined my false papers more carefully? What if someone decided to run a security check on me? What if I were questioned about my background before being given the job? I listened to him talk with a smile on my face, and even succeeded in musing enthusiastically about "our beloved Lwow."

My guardian angel was with me that day. The director told me to come back in three days after office furniture and typewriters were delivered. Of course, I did not go back, and when I started looking for a job again, I was more careful in responding to advertisements.

For the first few days at the apartment I slept on a mattress without bed sheets or a blanket, since I had none. The German woman noticed this and gave me sheets and a blanket. Over the next few weeks, relations between the German couple and me became increasingly friendly. They saw that I was polite and did not demand anything from them. Yet, one afternoon when I returned earlier than usual, I found the man looking through my things. I was as embarrassed as he was, and we pretended that he had gone into my rooms to stoke the fire in the stove, since the day was chilly. After that I gave the German couple a duplicate of my key, although I knew they already had one, and the woman would light the stove each afternoon before I returned from work. I had found a job as a typist in the social services agency, whose offices were not far from where I lived.

As fall turned into early winter, I developed a routine but still felt out of place. One of the problems was the language. I had studied Polish in school, and most Western Ukrainians were bilingual, yet I thought in Ukrainian and would find myself using a Ukrainian word when I could not think of the Polish one. I was lucky in that many of the people I worked with were from western or central Poland and they looked at my accent as a "Lwow" accent, which was okay, since being from Lviv—Lwow to the Poles—was a heroic place to be from. I also found it difficult to acclimatize myself to the secular, largely uninhibited life of single people. I had been brought up strictly and was taken aback when the young women I worked with freely discussed their love affairs and lovers.

Two months into my new life, I obtained permission from Orlan to meet him in Peremyshl, where we spent Christmas together. I learned from him that General Perebyinis, who debriefed me when I delivered the UPA reports to Western Ukraine a year earlier, and Taras (the name was a popular nom de guerre), who was Dmytro Maivskyi, a member of the OUN central directorate, had passed through Peremyshl on their way along the underground route to West Germany. Orlan told me that both men were given my address and that on their way back to Western Ukraine I might be called upon to help them.

I returned to Yelena Gura and lived there without incident until March of 1946, when I received an urgent letter from Orlan ordering me to abandon my apartment immediately. I did as I was told. I took the train to Peremyshl where I met a messenger who took me into the Carpathian mountains to Orlan.

The journey was extremely difficult. The snow was deep, and it was exhausting to stumble through the forests, sinking up to the armpits in snow drifts and plodding on and on, day after day. Once we reached Orlan's bunker, additional precautions had to be taken. We could not approach it directly but had to actually jump from tree to tree, or to black patches where snow had blown away or lay in a thin film, in order not to leave any tracks. Orlan's bunker was in a small forest on the bank of a stream. Because it had been dug at the beginning of the winter after the ground had already frozen, it was so small and low that it was practically impossible to stand upright. Because of its proximity to the stream, the bunker had a small interior well. It was equipped with a bed, a table, and a small stove that was lit only at night to cook a meal. Above ground, the chimney pipe was hidden in a bush.

Soon after my arrival, Orlan told me the reason why he had so urgently recalled me. My address in Yelena Gura may have been compromised. Soviet agents had learned of the courier route to West Germany and had infiltrated it in Czechoslovakia, where the NKVD set upon Taras and General Perebyinis. In the gun battle that followed, Taras was wounded and finished himself with—I discovered to my horror—the very pistol I had left behind when I had left to settle in Yelena Gura. Orlan had given my pistol to Taras because it was small and could be easily concealed. General Perebyinis had let himself be taken alive so that, once jailed, he could pass through the prison grapevine the news of Taras's and his fate. Before he could be questioned extensively, he hung himself in his cell.

◆ ◆ ◆ ◆ ◆

Soon the two men who had been living in the bunker with Orlan left on missions and Orlan and I found ourselves alone. We were very happy for the first few days. We had much to tell each and to learn about each other in the unexpected solitude. I told him how lonely I had been in Yelena Gura, how not a day had passed that I had not thought of him and worried about his safety. He, in turn, told me about what had happened in the OUN and the UPA during my absence. Most of what he told me was sad, since there had been many deaths.

A week passed, and we had not gone above ground. The entrance to the bunker had been masked when the others had left, and it could not be opened until they returned. The problem was that there was no one to mask the entrance if we went outside and then wanted to return underground. Only later would UPA bunkers have entrances that could be masked from the inside. (A popular method that came into use later was to have a small conifer planted in a tub to disguise the entrance to a bunker. The conifer could be lifted from below into the hole that served as the entrance.) In any event, such refinements were in the future and we had to wait until the others returned before we could venture out. I became bored and claustrophobic and could not type, while Orlan kept on working on his projects. The smoke from the kerosene lamp irritated my eyes, which turned red. I thought that I would rather be above ground in the cold forest than underground in this bunker that seemed like a cage. I felt fatigued, I had a headache, I missed daylight, I missed the sun. Even Orlan's presence could not counteract my growing restlessness and depression.

"I could give almost anything to spend an hour above ground," I blurted out one day. "I haven't seen daylight in a week."

"I haven't seen it in three months," Orlan said quietly.

I felt ashamed of myself.

In April, when the snow began to melt and the forest floor around the bunker emerged in soggy black patches, Orlan and I began to spend an hour a day aboveground. The first time I went out, I discovered something was wrong with my eyesight—the sky was green, my skin was green. I sat for an hour in the sun, and slowly my vision corrected itself.

A UPA bunker became both a place to escape detection by the enemy and a deadly trap when unmasked. The best place to dig a bunker was on a stream bank. A stream provided a safe access route to a bunker. A partisan would wade into the stream far below the bunker and make his way through the water that hid both his tracks and his scent in the event the enemy came with bloodhounds. Bunkers were first used by the leaders and only later by the remnants of partisan groups. In 1946, UPA still commanded companies of one hundred men who lived in camps above ground, often in the same forests where the bunkers of the leaders were located. However, only the company commander would know the existence of a leader's bunker, but sometimes even he was not informed. It was imperative that the location of bunkers remain secret. When a new one was to be built, partisans from a different district were brought in to do the work. This was done in order to ensure the secrecy of the bunker's location. Local men were not used since they knew their area and would recognize where the bunker was being located, even if they were brought to the site blindfolded.

A bunker was built by excavating a deep hole, then building one or more underground rooms with logs that lined the wall and supported the ceiling. A bunker had two entrances, air vents, and an outhouse. After it was built, it was covered with earth, and the ground above it was replanted with grasses and shrubs so that the bunker's presence could not be detected in a cursory search of the forest. Bunker building was a difficult and extended endeavor. The construction was usually done in spring following the thaw or in late fall when the forest was in the process of seasonal change. All work was done with shovels and large amounts of the soil had to be carted away in wheelbarrows for long distances for disposal, since you could not leave telltale piles of dirt near a bunker. I lived for a time in one of these well-constructed bunkers. It had two large rooms connected by a corridor. The corridor led to two entrances, which were about a hundred meters apart. One was in a gully, while the other one was in the forest on the far slope of the hill. This bunker had a small kitchen and an outhouse. The walls had been lined with planks that had been whitewashed. An icon of the Blessed Virgin, as well as portraits of UPA and OUN leaders, hung on the walls.

◆ ◆ ◆ ◆ ◆

I became pregnant and expected the child before the end of the year. I had not been careful. Orlan blamed himself. We both knew that I faced a difficult life. I would have to leave Orlan to have the child, and I might be fated to raise the child alone. Yet, unlike Orlan, I was happy. I wanted to have the baby. I knew several women, wives of partisans like I was, who were living alone with their children. I decided that I would get a job in some small town in Poland, legalize myself, and have the baby. Occasionally I would visit Orlan, or, at least, correspond with him and see what life would bring. I was twenty and all of life lay before me.

My pregnancy was already showing when one night, Myroslav Soroka, whose nom de guerre was Ptakh, came to the bunker to report the arrival of a visitor. Ptakh was Orlan's closest friend and assistant. He variously served as a bodyguard and a secretary. He was a mild, smiling man, seldom to take umbrage, but the visitor had gotten him annoyed. He described her as a "Cossack woman with a carbine slung across her shoulder" who "liked to give orders."

Myroslav Soroka, whose nom de guerre was "Ptakh," was Orlan's and Maria's bodyguard and friend.

The note she had given Ptakh was signed "Bystra."

"Bystra?" I cried. "I know her. She was one of my early OUN instructors."

"Well, show her in," Orlan told Ptakh, who eventually returned with her.

We had not seen each other in years, but she immediately noticed me sitting to one side in the back. She also noticed my condition.

"Maria," she cried and ran to me and began kissing me, her military stance forgotten.

She told us that Taras Chuprynka (Roman Shukhevych), the commander in chief of the UPA, was sending her along the courier route to make contact with the UHVR in West Germany. The note for Orlan from Chuprynka asked that he assist Bystra in her passage through Poland.

She assured me that she would be back and asked that I wait to baptize the baby until her return so that she could be the baby's godmother. I agreed. When she left, I told Orlan about my promise.

"Baptize the child at once," Orlan said.

"Don't you think she will come back?" I cried.

"We'll see," Orlan replied and shrugged.

"You don't think she will come back," I said, surprised.

I realized now that Orlan's attitude toward couriers going west was similar to that of the rank-and-file partisan. It was suspicious and ambivalent. Occasionally I had overheard partisans asking a departing courier, "Are you really going to come back?"

Since the route through Czechoslovakia had been compromised, Orlan did not know how to send Bystra, and she stayed in Peremyshl while Orlan tried to arrange something. In the meantime, I had to make a trip to Krakow, where I visited Father Hrab, one of the priests who had officiated at our wedding. His parish had been dispersed when the peasants in his area were deported to Western Ukraine as part of the population reshuffling following the drawing of the Curzon Line. Father Hrab had managed to stay behind and had relocated in Krakow where he had become the pastor of a Ukrainian Catholic Church. The church was on the ground floor of a two-story building, while Father Hrab and others lived upstairs. When I called on Father Hrab, I met a Ukrainian priest who was from Czechoslovakia but was sympathetic to our cause. I asked him if he would take a woman who needed to get to West Germany along with him on his return journey, and he agreed. Orlan approved the plan, and Bystra prepared to leave with the priest. Orlan then suggested that I go with Bystra. I considered the suggestion, then said I would stay. I stayed for two reasons. If I went west, my child would never know his father. Going west also meant that we would part forever. Besides, I reasoned, my pregnancy was advanced, and I did not think I could make the long and difficult journey.

Father Hrab and the Czech priest were typical of the Ukrainian Catholic clergy. Although the priests generally sympathized with the partisans, they nevertheless seldom understood why we continued to fight in the face of the overwhelming odds. "Children," they would say, "you will all die and be lost."

The partisans, however, were annoyed that the priests did not comprehend why they persisted in their struggle. They told the priests that they understood that they could not gain a sovereign Ukraine in the political conditions of post-war Europe, yet they could not abandon what they believed in. They argued, "If a nation cannot stand up for itself and challenge the invader, then that nation will not rise out of slavery even when conditions to do so present themselves." Also, the partisan belief was that to struggle was to negate the fatalism among the populace that believed it was the fate of Ukrainians always to be under the heel of the invader. By resisting and trying to get the news of the Ukrainian resistance to the West, UPA and OUN leaders believed that the partisan war would demonstrate to European (and American) leaders that Ukraine could not be erased forever from the map of Europe.

As I look back over the years, I will argue that Ukraine would not have become independent in 1991 had it not possessed the memory of the bloody and bitter UPA war. However maligned and discredited the UPA and the OUN had been at home and in the West by Soviet propaganda in the intervening forty-five years, nonetheless the memory of resistance remained ingrained in the national memory. It counteracted the fatalism of the Ukrainian Slav and helped him make the move for freedom when *perestroika* and *glasnost* collapsed.

There was one more reason, in addition to that of national pride and ideology, for the partisan war. Resistance to the Soviet regime by peasants who were supported by the UPA delayed for at least two crucial years the forced collectivization of land in Western Ukraine and probably prevented a famine. Forced collectivization had caused the Great Famine in Eastern Ukraine in 1932 and 1933. Collectivization that was implemented in Moldavia and southern Ukraine in 1946 and 1947 brought with it famine in which tens of thousands starved, although Moscow attributed the failed crops to the ravages of the war. In any event, what was a young man to do if he had the misfortune to come of age and live in Ukraine between 1939 and 1945? During the German occupation, he would have been conscripted for slave labor in Germany if he did not escape into the forest. During the two Soviet occupations, he would have been inducted into the Red Army if he did not seek shelter in the forest. He knew that if the Red Army took him, he would not be trained or given weapons but would be sent to the front for "cannon fodder." Whether he wanted or not, this young man would die fighting for Stalin, for collectivization. Is it surprising, then, that many young men chose to fight in the resistance, in the UPA? At least then, they believed, they were fighting for their nation, for their land, not for the Soviet empire.

Bystra went west alone, while I settled in the town of Gnezno where a friend from my school days and her husband lived. I gave birth to a son on December 15, 1946. I followed Orlan's advice and had the baby baptized immediately. I named him Zenon, after his father's first nom de guerre.

Later, Ptakh would confide to me that when Orlan received my letter with the news, he raised his head and shouted so that everyone in the bunker looked up. He shouted only one word, "son." And he had assured me that he did not care whether the child was a girl or a boy.

I gave birth in the Gnezno hospital and news quickly spread that the baby's birth certificate did not list a father. Gnezno was a conservative town, and people began looking at me askance. I was in a ward with six other new mothers. I watched as their husbands came to visit them, brought them presents, and marveled at the newborn babies. No one came to see little Zenon and me. I would watch the happy faces of the new fathers, and my eyes would fill with tears. "Stop that," I would tell myself. "You are a revolutionary." But the tears came anyway, when the women whispered to their men about my bastard and me, and the men would look speculatively in my direction.

There was no way to arrange a meeting with Orlan in the winter. He spent winter in a bunker, and I received letters from him sporadically, only when partisans delivering food and mail visited the bunker. I looked forward to each letter with enormous longing, and I could experience no greater joy than the moment when I discovered a letter in the mailbox.

In February 1947 the UPA killed Polish General Karlo Sverchevski, and the antipartisan outcry filled all Polish newspapers. The antipartisan anti–Ukrainian agitation grew, and the Polish government mobilized troops to sweep through the territories inhabited primarily by Ukrainians. In March, I received a letter from Orlan informing me that he and his men had been ordered by General Taras Chuprynka, commander in chief of the UPA, to leave the *Zakerzon krai* and cross the frontier into Western Ukraine. Orlan would be assigned to another post.

The news devastated me. If Orlan went into Ukraine and I stayed in Poland, I would not see him again. I saw the orders as a death sentence for our marriage. Orlan also wrote that he would like to see his son before his departure, and he asked me to come and bring the baby with me. Thus, just before Easter, I took the baby and boarded a series of trains to Peremyshl. The trains were overcrowded and unheated. Windows were broken, and no one would help the baby and me. I have heard people say that suffering ennobles the human spirit, but I don't think that it is true. It was not true in postwar Poland. People were crude and rude, as if the finer nuances of civilized and helpful behavior had been erased during the war. I saw a young father slip the conductor money for a place in the wagon that carried the mail. I followed the conductor and the couple to that wagon and, as I tried to climb in, the young man pushed me so hard that I fell off the stairs onto the platform, the baby in my arms. I don't know how I did it, but my rage at his lack of civility gave me enormous strength. I jumped up and, clutching the baby and his little pram, I pushed my way in somehow.

Ptakh met me in Peremyshl and took the baby and me by cart to an outlying village. That night Orlan came to see us. I was disappointed by his reaction; he stood in front of us and could not say anything. He would not touch the baby. He just stared at us as if he were a simpleton. Finally, he blurted out, "He looks like me." He was right—Zenon was a copy of his father.

Eventually, Orlan regained his composure and took the baby from my arms. We spent the rest of the night talking. He left before dawn,

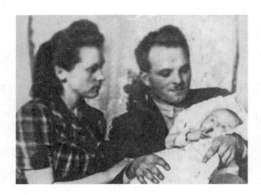

Maria and Orlan with their first son Zenon in May 1947.

and neither he nor I had the premonition that he would not see Zenon ever again. In the morning, the baby and I returned to Peremyshl.

Orlan and I arranged to meet one more time on May 15 on the outskirts of Peremyshl. I was not to come to the rendezvous myself but send the woman escort I would be traveling with. She would then leave me and report to Orlan, who would arrange a meeting. In the meantime, I returned to Krakow, where I thought the baby and I would be safer than if I remained in Peremyshl.

4. Loss of the Firstborn Son

In Krakow, I stayed with Father Hrab, although I was aware that I was endangering the baby and myself. But I had nowhere else to go, as I was waiting for a courier whose name was Gena. She had found a family that was willing to take in the baby and me. She was also going to arrange transportation for the baby and me to our new home. I had expected her to contact me earlier, but she had not, and I became increasingly agitated as the meeting date with Orlan approached and I had not settled on my future location.

Conditions in Krakow were becoming increasingly precarious for Ukrainians. The police were hounding Ukrainians who had fled to Krakow from the *Zakerzon krai*. Local Ukrainians as well as those living in Katovice and other cities came to Krakow to learn what was happening in the *Zakerzon krai*, since newspapers, already under Communist control, were silent about the unfolding Polish offensive against the UPA. Word had spread that Father Hrab had excellent connections and would know the latest news. I was sure that Polish agents had also heard about Father Hrab.

I wanted to leave the parish house, yet I had nowhere to go. I knew two families in Krakow, but I thought they were also under surveillance and were afraid to take the baby and me in. I had no other choice but to wait for Gena at the parish house.

The first inkling of the impending disaster came with the news of Father Hoza's arrest. Father Hoza was a personal friend of Orlan's and had been the second priest who had officiated at our wedding. A few months earlier, Father Hoza had confided to Orlan that he had obtained documents he planned to use to book passage on a ship bound for

America. He was arrested in Gdansk, just as he was about to board the ship. I knew that, to some extent, Father Hoza had brought the arrest upon himself, because he had not been circumspect in his movements or his comments. He had divulged his plans not only to Orlan but also to others. Father Hrab said that Father Hoza's entire parish knew his intentions. I recalled that Orlan had warned Father Hoza about the consequences of loose talk, but he must have disregarded the warning, since he was a talkative man by nature. Still, there had been an arrest, and others would follow. I grew increasingly more worried.

Early on Monday, May 11, 1947, four days before the scheduled rendezvous with Orlan, I was standing at the window of my second-story room when I saw four men in civilian clothing crossing the street and carefully studying the windows of the parish house. I jumped away from the window, but there was no time to get the baby and flee. The four men were already in the house. They immediately arrested Father Hrab. There were two other boarders in the house at the time of the raid. Both were clerics—Father Mykola Denko, who was ill, and a nun from eastern Poland who had fled here to escape Polish persecution and now did all the cooking. The agents arrested them also. When my turn came, I presented my new documents. One of the plainclothesmen asked what I, a Pole, was doing here. I said, "I'm on my way to western Poland to look for a job and stopped here only for a short time."

For the next two days, the parish house became a "mousetrap." Whenever visitors came to the door, one of the agents would open it and invite the unsuspecting victims inside. The agent would immediately lock the door behind the visitors. The plainclothesmen would identify themselves, question the victims, and put them under arrest. By late afternoon of the first day, fifteen people were being held in the house. Among them was Liudimila Kot, who was from Peremyshl and was now living in Krakow. She and I had been classmates, and when she learned I was in town, she came to visit me several times. She had come on such a visit now and was caught. Even people who came to the house on parish business were arrested.

Everyone was kept in the house until evening, and only when it became dark did the police remove the prisoners in unmarked cars. Left behind was Father Denko, who was in bed, the nun, and little Zenon and I. During the day, I had asked if I could go out to buy milk for the baby, but I was told no. Instead, one of the plainclothesmen took my money and went and bought the milk. Three plainclothesmen stayed at the house all night, and lights were left on in every room.

I didn't know why I had not been taken away with the rest. Was it because they believed my documents or because of the baby? The agents stayed most of the time in the large front room, but every so often one of them would come to see me and we would talk. He treated me as if I were Polish and seemed to say that once the "operation" was over, I would be let go. The only thing he did not understand, he said, is why a "Polish woman would stop in a Ukrainian parish house." Of course, from the beginning I had conversed with the agents in Polish.

For two days and two nights, I lived with my nerves strung to breaking. I saw an unavoidable tragedy unfolding. I knew that at any moment I would be discovered. Among those arrested were at least five people who knew who I was, and I was afraid that during interrogations one of them would betray me. If I were discovered, the consequences were extremely grave. At this time, the Communist-controlled government dealt harshly with captured Ukrainian partisans. They were tried quickly, invariably were sentenced to death, and several had already been publicly hanged in Peremyshl. As I waited, I did not actively look for a chance to escape. If I tried to break out, I would have to do so without the baby, and I would not leave the child as long as the possibility existed that no one would reveal my identity and I might slip through the police net.

Early on the third day, a sedan pulled up in front of the parish house, and three men in ill-made suits came into the house. From their dress and their conduct I knew they were Soviet intelligence officers. I also knew who they were after. They came directly to see me, a savage glee in their eyes.

"Well, hello, Marichka. How are you?" one of them said to me in Ukrainian. He was blond and wore a gray suit.

"I don't know any Marichka," I replied in Polish.

He laughed and asked me who I was then.

Although I knew that my false identity no longer protected me, I clung to it anyway and gave him the name on the documents.

"But we even know the names of the two priests who officiated at your wedding," he chided me. "So why are you being stubborn?" He and his two companions were in a good mood, openly pleased with themselves.

The agent in the gray suit ordered the other two to search my room. Then he turned to the baby who was watching everything with large, curious eyes, and said, "How are you, little Orlan?"

Soon the agents found several photographs of Orlan, money, and my real documents. I now realized that my worst fears had come true and that I would soon be separated from my baby and taken to prison for interrogation. Everything was over. I looked at the baby and a sharp pain seized my heart. "What will happen to you, my angel?" I cried to myself. I sat down by the pram that also served as the baby's crib and could not take my eyes off the child. For the first time since his birth, I castigated myself for wanting to have a child. "How dared I in such circumstances?" I reproached myself. My heart cried and demanded my rights as a mother, but reality, like a she-wolf, taunted me. I knew these were my last moments with the boy. I knew he would be taken away from me. Where would they take him when they threw me in prison? Who would look after him? I went numb. I sat with the baby and could not make myself think or move.

The man in the gray suit went to the door and called to the three agents. When they filed into the room, they looked at me with new interest. This is when I realized that they had not known until now who I was. So, I reasoned, I must have been betrayed last night when someone among those arrested broke under interrogation. My fate was sealed.

The man in the gray suit told me to get ready.

"And the baby? What will happen to the baby?" I cried, starting up.

"That's not for you to know," he said. "He will be taken care of."

His words sent an electric shock through my body and my heart. I think this was the first time I realized the full gravity of the situation. I had to act.

"Before we go, I have to give the baby a bath," I said calmly and stood up. I didn't ask them if I could, I simply said I would and headed for the kitchen to heat water. To my surprise and relief, they did not stop me, although the man in the gray suit motioned to one of his men to follow me.

I had only a few seconds to put my plan into action. Next to the kitchen was a small room where the sick Father Denko lay on a cot. He was very pale and looked up at me with fright when I stepped into his room. I knew that the room had a window that overlooked a busy street. Just outside the window were electric cables for the trolley. This was Vistula Street. I turned to the sick man and whispered, "I'm going to escape through this window."

"It's impossible," Father Denko began and was about to add something else, but at that moment the agent that was told to follow me came up and I continued on to the kitchen. I heated some water and brought it back to my room. I put the pot down and picked up the baby who had begun to cry when I left the room. "Now, now," I cooed. "I'll give you a bath. Don't cry, darling." I placed the baby back in the pram and went back to the kitchen for the wash basin.

I knew that I would try to escape. I was ready to die if this is what it took to elude imprisonment and interrogation. I knew the police would torture me to get information about my husband. They would try to force me to betray him. But the baby? How could I abandon him? But he was already being torn from me and I would not see him ever again. Perhaps in a few days they would bring him to me to weaken my will and my resolve, to get to his father. They would use the child to bargain with me: the child or the father. They would promise me a pardon if I betrayed Orlan and the partisans. I could not go through such torture, make such a choice. Even if they broke me, even if I chose the child, what assurances did I have that they would reunite me with my baby? These thoughts raged in my mind as I went through the motions of preparing the baby's bath. Every alternative my brain proposed, my heart negated. Only the realization that long years of imprisonment awaited me, perhaps even a sentence of death and certain separation from my child, kept me thinking, planning, and functioning. I knew I would risk death to avoid prison.

On my second trip to the kitchen, the agent did not follow me. Again I stepped into the little room and said sharply to Father Denko, "Open the window. Now."

I then continued on to the kitchen where I turned on the faucet and knocked the basin hard against the sink so that the men in other room could hear what I was doing and where I was.

On the way back, I looked in on Father Denko again. "Not this way," he whispered. "You'll either fall and be killed or they will capture you." He glanced over my shoulder toward a door that led to the back corridor, which was seldom used. "There," he said and gestured with his head.

Yes, he was right. I had not thought of that escape route. The back corridor opened on a flight of stairs that led up to a garret. In the garret there was a window and not too great a drop to the courtyard.

Instantly, I put down the basin and ran into the corridor. I dashed up the stairs, opened the window, and jumped through it. I found myself in a rectangular courtyard surrounded by the rear facades of other houses. I ran to a gate that led to a house directly in front of me, but it was locked. I knew that at any moment the agents would discover my escape and either come after me or start shooting through the garret window. I looked up at the building in front of me and saw a woman looking down from a window.

"Lady, please help me," I cried. "Open the gate."

"Run to the next gate," she called to me and pointed in the direction I should take. This is when I realized that the courtyard also served an adjoining building. I dashed across the courtyard, passed through the gate into the other building, and in another moment found myself on the street. I began to walk quickly.

I refused to think about the child I had left behind. I concentrated on what I had to do next. It was imperative that I get out of Krakow and return to Orlan and the partisans. Peremyshl was two hundred and fifty kilometers east of Krakow. How was I going to get from here to there? I needed money for transportation, but I had nothing except the dress I was wearing. I should have stuffed some money in my brassiere as soon as the raid began. But I hadn't. What should I do now? Both the Polish police and the MVD (the Soviet Department of Internal Affairs that was operating in Krakow at this time) knew that I would try to go east and would be looking for me on buses and trains. Yet I had to risk discovery—there was no other way of getting to Peremyshl on time to rendezvous with Orlan. Money. I slowed down to a brisk walk while my mind kept repeating, "Money, money. You need to get money."

Suddenly I had the answer. I remembered that last fall I had left behind with a Polish acquaintance in Krakow Orlan's best suit, the one he had worn at our wedding. I also knew that clothing was scarce and very expensive in Poland and the suit was of a fine material and in good condition. In fact, Orlan had given it to me to sell and use the proceeds to live on if my circumstances became difficult. The time had arrived to sell the suit.

Using side streets, I reached my acquaintance's apartment. She was at home. We talked a bit, I said I was short of money and offered to sell her the suit. She bought the pants for 500 zlotys, which was half what they were worth, but I did not care. I decided to keep the jacket. I would put it on to hide the dress I was wearing and by which I could be recognized and identified. I tried to conduct myself normally, chatted with the woman for a few more minutes, then said good-bye and left.

Now that I had money for a train or a bus ticket, I considered the alternatives. I could take a bus, but that was not a good idea, because the police often stopped buses and checked the documents of the passengers. This had happened when I had returned to Krakow after seeing Orlan. If the bus was too risky, then I had to take the train. Okay, I would take the train, but not from Krakow. By now the train station would be under surveillance. I would leave Krakow on foot and board the train at a depot east of the city.

Using side streets and alleys, I made my way to the bridge across the Vistula near Wawel. I crossed the bridge and, keeping to side streets and alleys, again headed east through Zavislia. I had no map, but I had been to Krakow several times to deliver partisan mail or to meet with couriers and had memorized sections of the city. Although I did not know exactly where I was, I had a general idea in which direction to go.

By late afternoon, I had reached the outskirts of the city and found myself on the main road going east. Although I was hungry and tired, I did not stop. I reached the first train station after Krakow at dusk. By now, I had worked out a plan. I was not going to buy a ticket for a direct train to Peremyshl, because the police would be looking for me on such a train. Instead, I bought a ticket for Rzeshov. Later, I would catch the train from Rzeshov to Peremyshl. At the station, the clerk told me that I had missed the evening train and that the next train was not until the morning. I was disappointed because I had hoped to take the night train, which was never well lit, and hide in the shadows from prying eyes.

Several people sat in the station's waiting room and I found a place near them. I was alone not for long. A railroad guard came over to talk to me. With typical Polish naïveté, he started to pay me compliments and court me. I feigned interest in him, since it was better to be seen talking to someone than sitting by oneself. I had glimpsed several policemen at the station, more than was normal. The railroad guard talked and talked, and I listened with a smile on my face. Only the Lord knows what kind of mental torture this was. Now that I was sitting down and not planning, the catastrophe of what had happened overwhelmed me. I had lost my baby son. I could hear him wailing. I had heard him wailing when I ran up the back stairs and jumped out the garret window. My heart was bleeding and breaking, and I had to keep on smiling at the foolish guard babbling away before me. Also, my body was beginning to ache. My knees, on which I had fallen while jumping out the window, were bruised and the bruises were swelling. My feet hurt from the long trek in sandals. Yet I made myself listen to the railroad guard with a sympathetic expression. He was now pouring out his innermost secrets. He confessed that he had a girlfriend with whom he had lived, but she left him and he did not miss her any more. Then he told me that he found me attractive. In fact, he said, this could be love at first sight. He swore he was not lying and that his intentions were serious and honorable. He insisted that he would visit me on Sunday and asked for my address. I gave him one. Let him look me up on Sunday. He finally went home, and I fell asleep.

In the morning, I boarded the Rzeshov train and without incident rode until the stop outside the town. Here I got off and walked to the town on foot. On the way, I passed a Catholic church and stepped inside to pray. Only the Lord could help me out of the predicament in which I found myself. I did not stop at the railroad station where I could board a train for Peremyshl and where, I was certain, local police were checking documents. Instead, I walked through the town. I bought an ice cream and ate it as I headed east.

I was aware that the closer I came to the frontier, the harder it would be to escape notice and arrest. I was approaching an area where the police routinely monitored the movements of people and were especially interested in those traveling on transportation lines. Shortly after noon I reached a rural train depot outside a village. I learned from the clerk on duty that the daily train to Peremyshl would arrive in midafternoon. This was the train from Katovice to Peremyshl that went through Krakow, a train I should avoid. But I had no choice. Tomorrow night I had to keep my rendezvous with Orlan, and I was still too far from Peremyshl to attempt to walk the distance in one day. I would risk taking the train.

When the train came, I got on and tried to act normally, although I was on edge. I knew my fate would be decided in the next few hours on this train. I would either reach my destination, or I would be spotted and arrested. The train was a freight train that took passengers. The wagons were not divided into compartments. Instead, benches were nailed around the perimeter of the wagon. This arrangement would make it easy for me to examine my fellow passengers once I sat down. I made my way past a group of men standing near the door and headed for an empty place in a dark corner at the far end of the wagon. I sat down and tried not to look around. However, I was tense and soon felt someone eyeing me. I raised my eyes and saw that two men in the group by the door were examining me carefully. "It's only my imagination," I reassured myself. "I'm tired and edgy. But why did they turn away as soon as they realized that I had noticed that they were watching me?"

In a few minutes, the two men left the group and began whisper-ing to each other. At the next stop, one of them got off. "Thank God," I said. But my relief was short lived. At the following stop, the man who had gotten off, got back on together with two companions. Plain-clothes police. Now there were four of them. They examined me care-fully, but when they saw me looking at them, they immediately turned away. I kept trying to calm myself by reassuring myself that I was imag-ining their interest in me, but the longer I watched their behavior, the more I became convinced that I had fallen once again into police hands. The train wagon had a door on either side and now, as we neared each stop, the four men in two pairs would take up positions in the two door-ways. They would come back into the wagon only after the train started moving again. At first their movements seemed natural, since many passengers, especially those that appeared to be traveling from a great distance, would come to the doors when the train stopped and some would actually get off and walk around on the platform to stretch their legs. However, only the four men who were interested in me repeated this "dance" to and from the doors at every stop.

I was now convinced that the police had recognized me. For the time being they did not bother me, only watched so that I would not escape when the train stopped. I had no doubt that these men were Pol-ish intelligence agents, or perhaps even Soviet agents. I knew what would happen. As soon as the train reached Peremyshl and I tried to get off, they would arrest me. They probably looked for me on last night's train and, when they did not find me, they staked out the next eastbound train from Krakow. They were sure that I would try to reach Orlan, and it was not too difficult to pick me out from the other pas-sengers. Not only was I wearing the same dress, but after all my mis-adventures, I hardly looked either relaxed or normal.

The more cognizant I became of my predicament, the more I despaired. I knew I would not let them take me alive. I would commit suicide or be shot. I desperately looked around for a way to die. I stud-ied the man sitting next to me. Perhaps I could ask him to lend me his razor. I would take the razor to the toilet and cut my veins. But that was stupid. How did I know the man had a razor? And even if he did, how would he respond to my strange request? No, suicide was stupid. I would try to get away at one of the frequent stops, but that, too, was not wise. This would only hasten my arrest, and I should try to remain free for as long as possible. What I had to do was act before my fate was decided for me.

Since the day was warm, the doors of the wagons were left ajar even when the train was in motion. Many of the passengers sat in the doors, their legs dangling over the side. The openings were crowded and people only moved to the side at stations to permit new passengers to get on. I suddenly had an idea: Why not jump off the train as it rolled along? I got up and made my way slowly to the door as if to get a breath of fresh air and admire the countryside. Once at the door, I looked down and recoiled. The train rode high above the ground on rails that ran along the edge of a steep railroad bed. If I jumped, I would probably bounce off the escarpment and roll down its side. I would get hurt, if not killed. Nonetheless, I sat down in the doorway, my legs dangling over the side of the train car. After a few moments, I glanced casually over my shoulder and saw the four plainclothesmen hovering behind me. They were watching me keenly. I pretended I did not notice their interest in me and turned around again. I examined the familiar countryside, the expanse of sandy fields where the wheat had sprouted. In the gentle afternoon light I glimpsed distant villages and homesteads under the pale green canopies of budding trees. My life passed before my eyes as if it were being projected on a movie screen. My second wedding anniversary was coming up, but I would not be alive to celebrate it. I remembered the day before my wedding. I was with Orlan and we swore to each other to remain faithful until death. "Lord, please watch over my son," I prayed. "The most holy Virgin Mary, intercede on his behalf, act as his guardian since he has no one else."

"Don't die. Live!" another voice screamed inside my head, but I knew I would not listen to it. The train passed the last rural stop and was nearing the town of Yaroslav. I saw the outskirts of the town in the distance. I could not wait any longer.

"Fall forward on your face so you will die instantly," I said to myself and edged forward. Then, another voice said, "Jump, but do it in the direction in which the train is moving." In that final split second before I jumped, I saw a glimmer of hope: "If I jump forward, perhaps..."

In the next instant I was falling through the air, a blast of wind stung my face and the roar of the metal train wheels on the rails reverberated in my head. I realized I was lying face down next to the rails, but I did not remember the impact of my soft body against the hard ground. Nothing hurt. I felt very calm and relaxed, almost on the verge of sleep. Fragmented thoughts whirled through my mind. So this is death. I can rest now. Soon, after the train is gone, it'll be quiet. It's not even as scary to die as I had imagined.

Next to me, the last wagons of the train roared by and the draft they created blew the skirt of my dress over my head. I think that the strong, cold draft brought me back to consciousness. After a few more seconds, I realized I wasn't dead. I experimentally moved my body. I was alive! The instinct for self-preservation took over. I had to get away, but in the next instant, I was consumed with fear. What if I could not get up? What if my legs were broken? I was afraid of that more than of anything else. I forced myself to sit up. Then I stood up cautiously. I was whole; I had not broken any bones. The only thing that was wrong was that I could not see out of my right eye. But that didn't matter at the moment. I was alive and I could run.

"I'm alive!" I whispered to myself as I looked around. In the distance, the train had come to a halt and men were running from it toward me. They were about a kilometer away, far enough for me to have a chance at outrunning them. I took my bearings and decided on the direction in which I should run. My mind was working now. I scrambled down from the escarpment and began to run. When I saw a culvert, I dodged into it and climbed out on the other side of the tracks. Then I took off in earnest. I plunged into a wheat field and ran with all my strength. When I looked over my shoulder, I was far from the tracks, but I had nowhere to hide. The ground was flat, and the field was covered with pale green shoots, recently sprouted. The ground offered no depressions, no groves in which I could find shelter. I ran on, my dismay growing, toward a lonely farmstead some distance ahead of me.

"Run, run faster. They're gaining on you," several farmers, working in the fields and observing my flight, shouted at me as I ran past them. This made me accelerate although I was barely able to catch my breath. I finally reached the farm, but it offered no shelter. Dogs were barking furiously and would not let up. I began to run again along a path that cut across a field of oats that only reached up to my knees. I stumbled, stopped, then fell face down. "Let the Lord decide my fate," I told myself. I had exhausted all my physical resources. I was winded and couldn't move. Something was choking me. I gasped and gasped, gulping lungfuls of air. When I raised my head, my sight turned black and the ground spun.

I must have passed out. I only remember that I lay in the fields of oats for a long, long time. I knew that if the police found me, I would not let them take me away. I would dig myself with my nails into the ground and they would have to use shovels to pry me loose. I would never let go, and they would have to kill me before they could move me.

Not too far from the field ran a major road I had recognized. This was the road that the Polish army used to transport Ukrainian peasants to the holding concentration-type camp near Rzeshov prior to their resettlement in the new territories in the west. Every time a truck approached the field where I lay, it seemed that it would stop and its occupants would come for me. But I had no strength even to crawl away

An hour or more passed before I came to myself. Still lying motionless face down, I took inventory of my body. The right side of my head, the side that I had hit when I jumped from the train, ached dully. I still could not see from my right eye, and I wondered if I had gouged it out. My knees, injured in my escape from the parish house, had swollen, and now the skin had ruptured. I had scraped the skin on my elbows when I fell from the train. I would discover later that the fine soot from the train had worked itself into the torn flesh on my knees. This black reminder of my escape from Krakow, ground into the raw flesh, would remain with me for the rest of my life.

Thus, I lay on the ground, face down, until evening. When dusk came, I began to think about what to do next. How was I to get to Orlan? As I mapped out my course, I suddenly heard a man's voice above me. Someone was touching me with his foot. I did not move, did not respond. The police had found me after all.

"Well, why are you asleep?" the man asked in Polish.

"What do you want from me?" I retorted, but did not move. "I'll not move." I spoke in Ukrainian. I did not feel like pretending I was Polish anymore.

"Oh, so you are the woman who jumped from the train," the man said, surprised by his find. "I thought it peculiar that my neighbor Hanka went for a walk in the fields and went to sleep in the oats. Don't be afraid," he tried to reassure me, "I'm not the police. They were in the village questioning people, but no one told them where you ran."

I sat up immediately.

The man took me to a house that stood alone at the edge of the field, a good distance from the road. He asked the woman to let me sleep in her house. She was a widow, a Baptist, very poor. She had no food to give me except for a pitcher of sour milk. I drank it, although I was not hungry. I spent the night on the floor on some hay because the woman did not give me any sheets or blankets. At daybreak, I left. In the fields I began to pray, "Lord, please help me today. You had helped me to escape twice, don't abandon me on the last day of my way of the cross." Today was May 15, a religious holy day for remembering the dead and visiting gravesites, and the fields were deserted. I still had about thirty kilometers to go to rendezvous tonight with Orlan. I decided to walk this distance. Both trains and buses would be closely guarded and, in any event, I had no money. The zlotys I received in Krakow were still in the pocket of Orlan's jacket that I left in the corner of the train wagon. I made my way across fields, which ran between the railroad line and the road. I was following the railroad line toward Peremyshl.

When I came across a farm, I stopped to ask for something to eat. I was given some coffee that was sweetened with honey and a piece of bread. The people asked me what had happened to my right eye, and I said that a horse had kicked me. They asked no other questions, and I soon left.

I walked the entire day. The day turned out hot; the sun beat down mercilessly. I was thirsty and looked for ditches along the way. Whenever I found one, I fell into it face down and gulped the muddy water to relieve my parched mouth and throat.

I reached the outskirts of Peremyshl in the evening and circled the town toward the Sian River. All day I had worried how I was going to get across the river. The Sian bridge had been dynamited during the war, and people used boats and rafts to cross. It would not be wise to hire a boat, and, in any event, I had no money for the fare. I wished I had learned to swim as a child. If I had, I could have gotten across in several places. I remembered that there was a ford somewhere above the town, and when I passed the last of the houses, I stopped a boy and asked him about it. He pointed toward the crossing with his head. It was already getting dark, and herders were moving cattle across the river from pastures on the other side. I memorized the location and waited until dusk. I had noticed that the ford was knee deep and knew that a wrong step could mean drowning. The Sian was gorged at this time of the year with runoff, which made the water run fast and deep.

I forded the river at dusk without any difficulties and sat down on the opposite bank in relief. My trek was almost over. All I had to do was go up several hillocks to the burial mound that had been erected in memory of Ukrainian soldiers who fell in World War I. That mound was where we had agreed to rendezvous. I reached the mound after dark, sat down off the path in some brambles, and waited. The night dragged on, and soon I was worried. Had something happened to Orlan and his group? Where were the scouts who were to rendezvous here?

When we made our plans initially, a courier whose name was Hanna would come to the rendezvous with Orlan and report where I was staying. Now I looked around for her but saw no one. Some time around midnight, I heard a movement, then the hoot of an owl. This was the signal. I cupped my hands and hooted a response. I left my hiding place and saw Ptakh and Liuty. In a few moments, Hanna and Areta, another partisan courier, emerged from the shadows. Areta said she had come by train with mail for Orlan. The two women had arrived at the rendezvous earlier but had not looked for me because they had not expected me. They had lain nearby under a blanket while I had sat shivering in the brambles. The two men were late because they had become lost, although both knew the countryside well. They had gone so far north that they reached the cemetery and only then discovered that they had gone too far and had to double back.

"What are you doing here?" Ptakh asked me in alarm "What's happened?"

I had run up and hugged him, overcome with relief that finally I was among friends. I didn't know where to begin my story and told it haphazardly, blurting out my escape from Krakow, my plunge from the train, my agony about the baby I left behind. They listened to me in silence, in dismay, in alarm.

When I finished, Ptakh hugged me again and said, "I'm proud of you." He took off his army jacket and gave it to me. Then we set out toward the forest.

But I could no longer walk. I had forded the river and reached the meeting point on sheer willpower, but now an incredible tiredness enveloped me. I tripped and fell every few steps. Finally the two men took me under the arms and carried me to the edge of the forest. Here we waited for Orlan. As we waited, Ptakh told me about the battles the group had fought in recent days and about the growing shortage of food that was beginning to plague all partisan groups. There had been many deaths as well as many heroic acts.

Orlan came before daybreak.

"Where's the baby?" he cried.

His was a reasonable question, but it cut me to the quick. Whenever I had a moment to remember, I reproached myself for abandoning the baby, and in Orlan's first question I heard censure and rebuke. I wanted Orlan to ask me about what had happened to me, how I had been injured, how I had reached him, before going straight for the deepest and rawest wound in my heart.

We waited until dawn before we entered the forest. We did this in order to be able to see and mask our tracks. Orlan was convinced that the forest would be searched after daybreak and, if the enemy found our tracks, they would follow us to the hideout.

We reached the hideout almost at once. Orlan had located it in a large thicket of brambles in a field overgrown with thick underbrush, some distance from the forest. Strategically, it was both a good location and a bad one. No one would dream that there was a hideout so close to town in a thicket of brambles, and, thus, the area would not be searched thoroughly. Yet, if discovered, this would be a very difficult place from which to escape, since it offered no real cover.

Once inside, Orlan and I sat apart, and I told him in detail what had happened. Orlan listened to me silently and in shock. When I finished, he hugged me and kissed my swollen face. The salty tears that fell from his eyes mingled with mine and burned the wounds on my face. We were overwhelmed and stunned by the loss of our child. Orlan told me not to blame myself, kissed me again, and promised to use every avenue at his disposal to find the whereabouts of the baby and perhaps rescue the child. He said the partisans still had contacts in Krakow.

"Look around," Orlan said to me. "We are not the only ones who lost loved ones. A day does not pass without a new disaster, a new atrocity by the Poles."

Quietly he told me about the battles in which he had fought and the friends that we had lost. I listened, and my aching heart filled and overflowed with anguish. It seemed that our tragedy merged into the river of grief and agony of the entire nation. Although this realization did not ease my anguish, it helped me live with it. I knew that Orlan and I, as his wife, could not permit ourselves to be prostrated by our personal tragedy. Orlan, especially, had to remain strong and focused. He had become the leader of all the remaining partisan groups in the southern territory of the *Zakerzon krai*. People continually sought his advice and encouragement. I decided that I should not worry him with my grief, my wretchedness, my tears. Perhaps because I tried to understand the loss of the baby as a tragedy in a stream of other tragedies, I managed to go on. It took a long time before I recovered, and I am convinced it would have taken longer and would have been even more painful had it not been for the patience and love of the man I had married almost two years earlier.

5. Communist Terror

During 1947, a Polish-Soviet offensive that became known in Polish history as Operation Wisla decimated the UPA in the *Zakerzon krai* by destroying the ethnic Ukrainian community in the area. It had become clear that the UPA could not function without the support of the local peasantry which provided the partisans with both intelligence and food. Thus, throughout the late spring and summer of 1947, the Polish Army and its NKVD reinforcements systematically emptied Ukrainian villages by exiling those Ukrainians who had not agreed to be repatriated to Western Ukraine after the Curzon Line became the new Polish-Soviet frontier in 1945. Now the remaining Ukrainians were loaded onto trucks and taken to holding concentration camps, then shipped northwest to resettle the territories ceded to Poland by Germany after the war. The UPA units coming to a village would find devastation and emptiness. There was no food to be had and no hope of food in the future. As the villages were emptied, Polish army units swept into the forests to confront UPA forces. The enemy's strength was tenfold, and UPA units suffered unprecedented losses. Thus, in the middle of 1947, the UPA High Command ordered its detachments to abandon the *Zakerzon krai*. Several of the surviving UPA groups were ordered to turn west, cross the Czech border, and fight their way across Europe to freedom. Their mission, like that of the many couriers that had been sent in the past two years, was to publicize the struggle of the Ukrainian nation against Stalin and the Soviet system. Months later we would learn that the assignment given these fighting groups had been nearly impossible to fulfill, although the men, as well as their leaders, tried valiantly. Soon after the forced marches west began, Soviet authorities realized what was happening. Not only did the UPA groups have to fight the Polish army that blockaded the country's western frontier, once they managed to cross into Czechoslovakia they were also beset by the Czech Army whose units were bolstered by Soviet reinforcements. The casualties were horrific. Most of the partisans died on their way to West Germany. Sometimes only one or two men survived from a group of two dozen or more partisans. Dozens of partisans, including several *sotnya* commanders, were captured and put on show trials, either in Czechoslovakia or in Poland. A few men, the remnants of entire platoons, did make it through. Only one large group, the one led by Hromenko, reached the West and was promptly incarcerated. This, too, we would learn much later.

The UPA units that remained faced an equally bleak future. They were ordered to fight their way across the frontier into Ukraine, where they would strengthen existing UPA forces. For a time, the *Zakerzon krai* reinforcements enabled the groups in Ukraine to continue to wage a guerrilla war.

As mentioned before, Orlan had been ordered by Taras Chuprynka to return to Ukraine before the devastation brought about by Operation Wisla. Orlan had asked for a delay in carrying out the orders, and now he did not have the heart to leave. He was the primary authority figure in the southern districts of the *Zakerzon krai*. If he left, even under orders, his departure would have demoralized the soldiers even further. They came to him individually and in groups. They were spiritually shattered, their resolve was wavering; they reeled under the impact of constant battles, insufficient food, and near-total exhaustion. Somehow Orlan was able to calm them, reinvigorate their resolve,

Roman Shukhevych, whose nom de guerre was "Taras Chuprynka," was the commander in chief of the UPA.

and re-ignite their patriotic ardor. I marveled as I watched these meetings from a dim corner of our hideout. Besides Orlan, there was one other partisan leader of high rank left in Poland. This was Stiah (Yaroslav Starukh), who operated in the areas north of Peremyshl. As communications became increasingly sporadic, Orlan often was forced to act alone. Almost every night he left to meet couriers or confer with group commanders.

In May 1947 Orlan received a message from Stiah requesting a meeting. Orlan and I, together with Ptakh, set out. A platoon of UPA soldiers helped us cross the Sian River on May 27, a date I remember because it was our second wedding anniversary. We traveled for several nights, sleeping and resting during the day, then marching from sunset to sunrise. Since we carried no food, we detoured at night into newly planted gardens to pick sprouted onions and occasionally potatoes that had been planted as seedlings. We resorted to this petty thievery because we had no other alternative. We had money, but we were afraid to show ourselves in the daytime to buy food from local peasants. It was imperative to maintain our passage secret, since the countryside was filled with Polish army units, which could decimate us. We hid in the forests and only occasionally in hideouts at Ukrainian homesteads. These had been built in the early days of the resistance and were still used by local partisans when they left the forests to come to the villages to obtain provisions. We almost fell into Polish hands while resting at one of these hideouts and escaped capture by sheer luck. As the days passed, Orlan grew increasingly worried so, when we began encountering Polish patrols every day, he halted our journey. He decided to go on alone with a bodyguard he chose from our escorts and ordered Ptakh and me to return to our hideout in the brambles near Peremyshl.

Our journey back, facilitated by changing escorts, was uneventful. Soon after our return we were joined by two other partisans, Shchur and Stepovyi, who served both as bodyguards and as providers. Our existence was difficult. Every second night, one of the men would venture out in search of food. Each trip was dangerous since Polish Army units blocked the roads and paths leading to the city. Not a night would pass without distant exchanges of small arms fire, since we were not the only ones hiding in the Peremyshl area. One night Shchur stumbled on a patrol and was wounded in the hand, and later, Stepovyi was trapped by a patrol in an outlying village and barely managed to escape.

We ate mostly potatoes. Occasionally one of the men would bring back porridge or lard, and sometimes bread. During the day, when it was quiet, we hunted for mushrooms. At dusk, we would creep out of the hideout and make our way deep into the forest where we cooked our meals over a fire that we built in a deep ravine through which a stream flowed. We ate during the night and took whatever was left, returning to our hideout before dawn. During the day we would eat what we had brought with us, but the portions were small and we spent many days going hungry. If the men did not leave the hideout in search of food, then they left to meet with other partisans, and I spent many nights alone. My job was to gather wood, build the fire, cook the meal, and wait for the men to return before first light. I had a small pistol, but no other weapons. I would sit by the fire listening to every sound. The sudden breaking of a twig, the rustle of leaves, or distant sounds of shooting would make me tremble. If the men died in an ambush, I knew my survival would be almost impossible.

Eventually we ran out of places where we could get food. The situation would have become critical if it were not for two women, Iryna Styslo and her friend Lilia, who came to our rescue. Iryna was the wife of Inhul, a UPA commander who came from the same village as Ptakh and was one of Ptakh's best friends. Lilia was also married and had been active in the resistance during the German occupation. Both women were pregnant. They bought foodstuffs at the Peremyshl market once a week, then carried them to a prearranged meeting place. We feared for their safety and begged them to be careful, but they would only say that they would see us a week hence. I think they needed to help us. Iryna said that in helping us she was helping her husband who was commanding a UPA group in the Sambir (Ukraine) area. She would say that she hoped someone was looking after him, as she was after us. Lilia had not lost her fervor and helped us on the sly, never telling her husband about her "excursions." Lilia was also uncommonly beautiful, with a fresh, childlike face. Looking at the two women, no one would dream that they were keeping alive a group of partisans in the forest.

At the beginning of the summer our situation worsened with the news that Vyshynski, one of OUN's regional underground leaders, had either fallen into Polish hands or had willingly gone to the authorities and was cooperating with them. He was seen trying to make contact with partisans who would lead him to the leadership in the Peremyshl area. Although we were forewarned, others had not been, among them Orlan and Stiah. We waited for Orlan's return with growing anxiety. In the meantime, we were joined by Zoya and Malusha, the two couriers who had replaced me in Elena Gura, in western Poland. They had received a letter from Orlan directing them to return to Peremyshl for new orders.

Orlan finally arrived in August. His first words were, "Thank God you are safe. We were afraid that you might have been betrayed." He told us that Vyshynski had reached Stiah before Orlan's arrival, and Stiah barely escaped alive. Several men who were dressed like partisans accompanied Vyshynski. When stopped by Stiah's lookouts, Vyshynski sent a message that he had to meet face to face with Stiah because he carried sensitive news from Orlan. Stiah set the meeting in a forest where he had met Vyshynski a year earlier, but ordered his men to go ahead of him and bring Vyshynski alone to the meeting. Although Vyshynski insisted on taking his "protection" with him, Stiah's men obeyed orders and Vyshynski arrived alone.

"First, the mail from Orlan," Stiah had said to Vyshynski and Stiah's cold voice momentarily panicked the other man.

"I left it with my men," Vyshynski began to explain, and Stiah immediately sensed that something was not right. He asked a few other questions, then suddenly turned to his men and ordered a retreat. In a moment, Stiah and his men disappeared into the forest, leaving Vyshynski alone. Vyshynski then returned to his group and they mounted an attack, but Stiah and his men were able to evade them. When Orlan arrived, Stiah told him what had happened, and both worried whether Vyshynski had managed to betray us also.

Other news that Orlan brought back was equally grave. The UPA units in the north were under constant attack by Polish and Soviet forces. The partisans were starving in the forests, and peasants who helped them or were suspected of sympathizing with the UPA were shot. Orlan also told me that Stiah had learned about what had happened in Krakow from his courier Gena, the woman I was expecting at the time of the raid on the parish house. Gena arrived a day after my escape and fell into the hands of Polish agents still at the house. They questioned her for several hours, but she managed to speak with Father Denko, who told her about my escape. She then told the agents that she needed to go to the toilet, ran up the stairs, and escaped through the same window that I had used. Stiah sent back with Orlan a commendation for me. Orlan also brought back heartbreaking news about our little Zenon. The head of the Polish Secret Service in Krakow, who was childless, had adopted the baby.

The news was like a knife plunged into a fresh wound. My son would grow up in the home of our enemy who was decimating our ranks. I knew that it would be impossible to rescue the child from this home.

Stiah's refusal to move bunkers following the meeting with Vyshynski worried Orlan. Stiah continued to occupy a bunker that had a typewriter and copying equipment; he was working on UPA literature and leaflets that a unit he was sending to the West would carry. He told Orlan he did not wish to interrupt his work. When Orlan urged him to at least live "above ground" for a while, which would make him more mobile, Stiah had said, "I wouldn't be able to continue my work if I'm always on the move. In any event, someone will shoot me from behind a tree, but if I stay in the bunker and am attacked, I can at least fight for a while and take some of them with me."

As Orlan was leaving, Stiah, who knew about our imminent departure to Ukraine, said, "Take my heart home with you." Orlan said that as they shook hands, tears glistened in his and Stiah's eyes.

◆ ◆ ◆ ◆ ◆

By late summer of 1947 only a few UPA units were still actively engaged in armed warfare in Western Ukraine, although the underground network that the OUN had created remained relatively strong. It was augmented by the demobilized UPA soldiers who were returning to civilian life. Further strengthening the underground, as well as reinforcing the existing armed units with men from the *Zakerzon krai*, became one of the aims of the UPA High Command. Orlan and Stiah had spent some time deciding who would stay behind and who would cross the frontier. Soon we all learned about their decisions. Ptakh was coming with us, but Taras and Sviatoslava, the couple who exchanged wedding vows when we did, would remain in the Peremyshl area. Also remaining in Poland would be my good friend and confidant Zoya and another courier, Malusha, whom Orlan, upon his return, dispatched back to Elena Gura with bundles of new partisan literature. Zoya and Malusha would deliver the literature to Warsaw and the port cities on the Baltic. In view of the High Command's decision to publicize UPA's struggle against the Soviets, Orlan supplied the two women with literature in Polish, French, and English. He also gave them several thousand zlotys for travel and other expenses. The two women would maintain contact with and report to Stiah, who was also staying behind. As I said good-bye to Zoya, with whom I had shared my girlish dreams when everything seemed possible, I silently wondered whether I would see her—or the others who remained at their posts—ever again.

Several more weeks passed as Orlan completed his work and as friends came at night to bid farewell. One night Sviatoslava and Taras came, and as we embraced, I thanked Sviatoslava for the support and sympathy she had offered in the tragic days after my escape from Krakow and the loss of little Zenon. She and I wept, our tears mingling as they fell. Then on the very eve of our departure, bad news arrived. A courier who had been sent to Elena Gura with additional literature returned to inform us that Zoya and Malusha had been arrested, and their fate was not known.

And so we left, sad and worried.

Further south, remaining UPA soldiers were being organized into two *sotnyas* which would fight their way across the border, heading southeast as we would do, into the Carpathian mountains.

♦ ♦ ♦ ♦ ♦

There were five of us, Orlan, Ptakh, and I, and two bodyguards for Orlan, Ihor and Bukva. A UPA group led by Orach escorted us to the frontier, and we rendezvoused with a unit led by Sokil, who had grown up in the border area, as had the men in his group. Sokil was in charge of taking us across, while Orach would stand by in the event of trouble. At dawn, we halted on a hillock that overlooked the frontier and the surrounding terrain. Below us flowed the Vihor River, along whose banks ran the frontier in this area. The Vihor was shallow where we planned to ford it and, therefore, did not pose much of a problem. The frontier itself was another matter. On the east bank of the river, a few hundred meters from the stream, ran a wide strip of plowed earth. Beyond it rose the barbed wire fence of the frontier itself. Further east in the distance stretched the village of Viis'ko. We could make out the orchards, houses, and a main street. We spent the day observing the activity in the village through binoculars. Nothing out of the ordinary was happening, although we noticed that the village's inhabitants were dressed in their Sunday best. Someone remembered that this was the feast of the Ascension of the Blessed Virgin and a holiday. Young women stood in the street talking or promenaded in groups. Older women sat outside the houses gossiping. There was a noticeable absence of young men. They had been either mobilized into the Red Army or had joined the UPA. Sokil identified some of the young women by name, since Viis'ko was his native village. I noticed, however, that he was nervous. I knew I was, and I thought the others in our group were also. I kept examining the plowed strip of dirt in front of the barbed wire fence and wondered if we would manage to get across. Finally, I turned to Sokil. "Do you worry when you cross the frontier?" I asked him.

"That depends," he said. "When I'm alone or with my men, that's one thing. But when you are taking others across, the stakes are different, as is the responsibility. Besides, today I have one of our leaders and his wife."

We waited until nightfall, then for the border patrol to pass on its rounds. Only then did Sokil motion to us to follow him. Behind us, Orach's unit, which had kept watch during the day, took its position. If something went wrong and the border patrol saw us or we tripped one of the booby traps, Orach and his men would open fire to draw the border patrol's attention while we tried to escape.

Near the river, we paused to take off our boots and waded across barefoot. The water was cold, but it came up only to our ankles. Once on the other bank, we moved in a single file across the strip of plowed earth. Behind us came two of Sokil's men. They carried rakes with which they obliterated our tracks. We crossed the plowed strip. We were right behind Sokil's men who were bent over searching with their hands for the wires that, if disturbed, would set off an alarm and launch flares into the sky. They whispered to us the location of the wires and we carefully stepped over them. We also were walking bent over to minimize the outline of our bodies. Once he was sure we were past the booby traps, Sokil commanded, "Now run."

We dashed toward the houses and the orchards among whose shadows we would hide in the event a border patrol appeared.

"One down, two to go," Sokil said as we stood panting, wiping the sweat that had dripped into our eyes, obscuring vision.

We now began walking sedately toward the village's main street. Sokil saw an older man he knew and asked him about the situation in the village.

"You would think they would leave us alone on a feast day," the man complained. "But no, they come into the houses demanding meals and drink. What a beggarly nation they are."

We cut across the village and again found ourselves in the open. The terrain here was hilly with low brush and occasional gullies, excellent terrain for guerrilla warfare but difficult for quick passage. After a few kilometers we came to another barrier. This was a barbed wire fence about three meters high and about as wide because of the rolled barbed wire on the ground on both sides of the fence. Our escorts had brought with them two pairs of large pliers with which they cut a hole through the barrier. They worked quickly since guards patrolled this barrier on horseback and made rounds frequently. We crawled through the hole, being careful not to snag our clothing on the sharp barbs.

The third obstacle was the paved road. It, too, was patrolled, and we had to approach it carefully, bent over, across a flat, open field.

We made it.

And now we began to run again. We ran for a long time in order to get as far away from the frontier and from the tracks and the cut wires that would be discovered at daybreak. We ran until we had no breath left, until sweat stuck our clothing to our backs, until we thought we couldn't run any farther, yet we kept on running and running. I don't know where we got the superhuman strength to run and run and forget our tiredness and the weight of our rucksacks on our backs. One night like this cost several years of one's life.

At dawn we reached a village and took shelter in two adjoining cottages. We were tired, but also happy that we had crossed the frontier without discovery or loss of life. We rested, were fed by a friendly housewife, and that evening headed for a nearby forest to rendezvous with a UPA group that would lead us into the Ukrainian countryside.

We rendezvoused and made camp. Shortly after dawn we heard the breaking of twigs and footfalls. Was it an enemy patrol? Had someone betrayed us? But how could they have? There hadn't been enough time to summon an enemy detachment to search the forest. We pulled out our weapons and took positions in the brush. Two men went forward to investigate, coming back in a few minutes but not alone. They brought back two women.

We soon learned that the women had come into the forest to pick mushrooms since this was the season for mushrooms. By nine in the morning there were ten women in the forest. Our men brought them all to us. What to do? We couldn't hold them all day. Their families would become worried by their long absence, would think they had been arrested by a border patrol, would try to find out where they had been taken, and then contact the authorities who would come to investigate. On the other hand, if we let them go, would one or another of them tell about meeting us or report us to the enemy?

Orlan was very upset, as were others from the *Zakerzon krai*. On the other hand, the local UPA men were not worried. "They're okay," Khmara, the commander of the platoon with which we had rendezvoused, told us. "We should let them go. They might even bring us supper. These are good women. Holding them could cause trouble."

"It's senseless to rely on the discretion of ten women," Orlan argued. "One of them is bound to brag to someone, and the rumor will spread. There's no safe way out of this forest in daytime and we'd be trapped." But he could not come up with a different solution. Thus, the women were told to go home, and we made them promise not tell anyone about meeting us.

Khmara knew his people. In the afternoon, the women started coming back. Again they carried their baskets for mushrooms, but in the bottom of each basket lay a hot dish. One brought a baked chicken, another a bowl of borscht, a third one fried dumplings. We ate. No, we feasted, while they stood looking at us and urging us to eat more.

"Eat, you need your strength," they cajoled. "As long as we have something, we will share it with you."

That evening we said good-bye to Sokil and the men in his group who had taken us across the frontier. They would again cross the frontier, while we turned southeast for our long trek to the Carpathian mountains. We would never see Sokil or any of his men again. They died that winter in the village of Viis'ko.

Khmara led us without any incidents to a meeting place near the town of Sambir. Inhul (Dmytro Styslo) and his men were waiting for us. Ptakh, as I mentioned before, came from the same village as Inhul, and they were best friends. Orlan also knew Inhul well. Immediately they started telling Inhul what had happened in the *Zakerzon krai* and related other partisan news. I watched Inhul closely. He listened, but at the same time I could see he was growing impatient, as if he wanted them to finish so he could ask a question. I interrupted the conversation. I took his hands into mine and said. "Let us be the first to congratulate you. Iryna gave birth to a little girl just before we left."

He trembled with emotion. Then he took off his cap and threw it in the air, then kissed each one of us in turn. He was the happiest father I have ever seen. He and Iryna had had two other children who had died in infancy and the new baby was extremely important to both of them. We spent three days with Inhul waiting for a new group of escorts who would take us into the foothills of the mountains.

Again the good-byes would be forever. Inhul died a few days after we left him, never having seen his baby daughter. He and his men were trapped in a house where they had stopped for the day. The enemy surrounded the house and tried to convince them to surrender, but Inhul refused. He and his men fought until their ammunition ran out. Then they killed themselves with their last bullets.

When I heard the news about his death, all I could think of was the two pregnant women, Iryna and Lilia, who risked their safety to bring food to our hideout. I remembered how at each weekly meeting Iryna would look at us, an unspoken question in her eyes that asked, "Is he still alive?" When she read in our faces that we did not harbor any bad news, she would ask shyly if there was "anything" for her. Sometimes we did have a letter from Inhul that had come with other partisan mail. When she received a letter, she would unroll the tight cylinder that had been carried hidden by several couriers. Sometimes the cylinder was darkened with sweat and its edges were torn or ragged. Iryna would unroll the cylinder carefully and read the contents while tears fell onto the paper as she wept. A letter from her husband was what she lived for. It was proof that he was still alive. She would accept any hardship that came her way, if only he would not die.

When we reached our next rendezvous point and made contact, we learned that two *sotnyas* that had broken across the frontier from *Zakerzon krai* were camped in a nearby forest. The two *sotnyas* had brought with them two *Zakerzon krai* couriers, Marta and Mariika. Orlan immediately left to meet with the *sotnyas'* commanders, Khrin and Myron. He spent the day with them and the following night returned accompanied by both men.

When we were alone, I asked Orlan about the two women and how they had come through the constant battles that the two *sotnyas* had engaged in as they made their way forest by forest, field by field, from Poland into Ukraine.

"They're okay, although Mariika is a little depressed. She had hoped to meet Mar here. He was her fiancé."

A little later Orlan said, "I decided to send them West with the mail. They'll go back to *Zakerzon krai* and from there West."

"But it's almost winter," I cried in surprise. "They'll have to cross the frontier again, and then they'll be in an area that is virtually deserted."

"I'll arrange for an escort for them across the frontier," Orlan said. "They told me they know some families who will help them. They might as well go West. Otherwise they'll die here, or it may even be worse if they're taken alive. In any event, they accepted my offer with alacrity."

"He's sending them West because Mar went West," I said to myself.

We learned that Khrin and Myron, like us, had also been ordered to report to Poltava (Major Petro Fedun), one of the leaders of the OUN, and Orlan said that they should accompany us. We started out the following evening. When we rested during the day, both men told us about the hell they had gone through in the preceding month. Not only were they under constant attack, they had to do battle with the enemy to get food and supplies. They were pursued across the frontier and were engaged by Soviet troops once they were in Ukraine. The problem was, of course, that large groups attracted attention because they needed much food, and it was nearly impossible to mask a large encampment.

With the addition of new escorts and the two *sotnya* commanders, our group now numbered fifteen men and one woman. In a few days, we rendezvoused with another escort group that led us through the foothills to the area near the town of Skole. Here we were given over to a group led by Bor, who at age thirty-eight was older than most partisans. He was an even-tempered and careful man. Orlan halted our march and wrote a note to Poltava that he sent by courier. We waited for Poltava's reply.

A response came for us to proceed, while Khrin and Myron would stay behind. We crossed the river Stryi that night. We were met by new escorts and began to climb up into the mountains. We spent the next day in an empty hut in the forest and once again changed escorts. At daybreak the following day, we reached a large bunker that served as the center of UPA's publications and propaganda.

♦ ♦ ♦ ♦ ♦

As soon as I saw him, I knew I had seen Poltava in civilian life, but I did not know where until we fell into a conversation one evening. As we sat outside the bunker and watched dusk envelope the forests and the mountains, I learned that he was from a village near Zadviria and had commuted to Lviv on the same train that many students and I used during the German occupation. He was of middle height and was thin, as were most of the partisans. His eyes were extremely kind and sympathetic and belied his military bearing, which was accentuated by the fact that he wore the uniform of a Soviet officer and belted the jacket with a leather belt that was buckled tightly around his waist. The uniform and a revolver in a holster that hung from the belt contributed to the military aura. He told me that the atrocities and terrorism inflicted on the Ukrainian population by Russians and Germans during the war had convinced him that the only way the Ukrainian nation could survive was to fight for its existence. Thus, he joined the OUN where his journalistic talents were discovered, and he rose quickly

in rank. That intimate conversation established a bond between us
which resulted in a greeting Poltava would append in the future to letters he would write to Orlan. The greeting would always say, "My
respects to Marichka."

Poltava had a clear logical mind and was also an original thinker.
He was able to synthesize a broad array of ideas and weave them into
a whole that was succinct and astute. During the week that we spent
at the propaganda bunker, Poltava and Orlan, together with three other
workers in the bunker, discussed and hammered out the thrust of UPA's
future propaganda activities. Poltava's staff consisted of Stepovyi (Stepan
Kuzma), Dolia (Bohdana Svitlyk), who, under the literary nom de
plume Maria Dmytrenko had authored a collection of novellas entitled
For Death, Not for Life, and Hornovii, Orlan's boyhood friend whom
I met in 1944 when I served as a courier delivering reports on the
Zakerzon krai to a conference near Lviv. Hornovii was one of the edi-
tors with the OUN propaganda center and later a member of the
UHVR.

Most of the discussions centered on the form that UPA's resistance
should take in the years ahead. Demobilization of UPA soldiers in the
hope that they would be absorbed into civilian life was not working in
practice. The Soviets were thorough in checking credentials and more
often than not discovered false documents. Also, if a partisan's documents passed scrutiny, his life as a civilian was so precarious that it was
impossible for him to continue antigovernment activity.

There was also the problem of a dearth of new recruits to take the
place of those that were killed. OUN's and UPA's membership had been
drawn mostly from Western Ukraine, primarily from the generation
that had matured politically during the 1930s and the war years. Oppression and severe punishment by the postwar Soviet regime dissuaded
likely candidates from joining the resistance. In Eastern Ukraine, the
UPA and OUN were less known, and what information was available
was hugely corrupted by the virulent anti–UPA and anti–OUN propaganda by Soviet organizations. During the war, Red Army soldiers were
exposed to propaganda that portrayed the OUN and UPA fighters as
fascists and bandits. This information was carried home by demobilized
Red Army soldiers and distorted the perception of the guerrilla war by
populations far removed from the conflict.

The upshot of these discussions was that the UPA had to produce
information that would counter Soviet propaganda and misinformation
and that the target audience had to be the new generation. In Western

Ukraine, the older generation was well aware of the reasons for the guerrilla war and supported it, even if increasingly tacitly. In Eastern Ukraine, the older generation, decimated by the Great Famine and further traumatized by the Stalinist repressions of 1936–38, had been so cowed that it was not interested in an antiregime struggle.

As a result of these discussions, Orlan would write a brochure that winter on the forms opposition should take in the postwar years. Poltava took on the job of producing a brochure refuting Soviet propaganda and explaining the reasons behind the formation and struggle of the UPA.

These discussions were conducted against a perspective of radically changing circumstance. By 1947, the UPA leadership knew that UPA was no longer capable of open warfare. Although battles with the better-equipped and overwhelmingly stronger enemy were to be avoided, nonetheless armed warfare was necessary in certain cases, particularly where the enemy had committed atrocities. In such instances, the use of force was not only permitted but was also approved, since it demonstrated both to the population and to the enemy that terrorism would not be tolerated. Such punishing raids were necessary not only to maintain the population's respect for the UPA, but also to feed the nationalist fervor among the people.

We all knew that none of us would see an independent Ukraine, but we cared mightily about its future rebirth. We wanted to leave a legacy that, when the time was ripe, would lead to the rise of a Ukrainian state that would be a democracy, one that would protect the rights and dignity of the individual.

6. Wintering in the Carpathian Mountains

Orlan and I left the propaganda bunker to spend the winter in a bunker deep in the Carpathian mountains with four partisans we had not met before. Orlan's three bodyguards, Ptakh, Ihor, and Bukva, were sent to a different bunker. We were separated because the leadership had decided that the *Zakerzon krai* newcomers had to be integrated into the local ranks as quickly as possible. The reasoning went something like this: What better way was there to get to know people than spending a winter with them in a bunker? There was a second reason why our group was split up: We would have a better chance of surviving the winter if we lived with men who knew the terrain well and were friendly with local villagers who would supply the bunker with food.

We left the propaganda bunker at the end of October. Snow had already fallen and lay in drifts in the forest. For that reason we traveled during the day, stepping from one patch of bare earth to another, avoiding the drifts where our tracks would leave a telltale trail for NKVD patrols to follow. We were passed along the route from one set of escorts to another, changing escorts several times, until we were finally met by three of the four men with whom we would live for the next six months. Their noms de guerre were Baida, Chornota, and Moroz. Iskra, the fourth man, had stayed at the bunker. If the men were dismayed that one of their bunker mates would be a woman, they did not show their feelings. They greeted us politely, and we set out. The first test of their—and mine—adaptability came that first night. We had to ford the Opir River half-naked in order not to get our outer clothing wet. The Opir was swift. Semi-frozen chunks of ice tumbled on its foamy crests. The men told us that the bottom was strewn with rocks, and they gave us sturdy staves which we would use to support ourselves during the crossing. Then they went away, undressed, packed their belongings into bundles, and plunged into the river, holding the clothing above the water. Orlan and I followed their example. I never knew water could be this cold and awful. I gasped in agony. Thousands of icy daggers stung my skin, and I felt my body beginning to freeze. I concentrated all my attention on my stave and where I was stepping and carefully began to make my way across. I stepped gingerly over the rocks, using the stave for support. Somehow Orlan, who also could not swim, and I got to the other side without falling or drowning. My fingers were numb and refused to bend. My whole body trembled with cold and relief, and my teeth were chattering. I fumbled with my clothes, but I could not force my fingers to hold them. I do not know how, but somehow I managed to get dressed. When I was done, one of the men came up to me, handed me a flask, and told me to take a large swallow. "This will get you warm," he said kindly.

The liquid was whiskey, and it burned going down. But soon its warmth spread through my body, and the terrible cold and shivering receded.

Other difficulties lay ahead. Soon we began to climb in earnest. The cold gave way to warmth and then to sweat. Our guides climbed without tiring, while Orlan and I concentrated all our resources on keeping up with their easy strides. We gulped air into our straining lungs, while the sweat clouded our vision and stuck our clothing to our backs. We wiped the rivulets of sweat from our faces as we followed the three men ever higher into the mountains. In that twenty-four-hour walk, we crossed several mountain ranges. We had left in the afternoon, walked all night, and when the next day dawned we were still walking. It was almost noon when we reached our destination, where Iskra was waiting for us.

The bunker was well situated, hard to spot, yet commanding a panoramic view of the area. Although I was exhausted, I could not help but notice the loveliness of the view. We were so high that clouds seemed right over our heads. Occasionally one would drift across the side of the nearest mountain and seemingly cut it in half. Far below, the valleys and gorges were marked by deep purple shadows, while, at eye level or just above us, rose granite pinnacles that were already covered with snow.

I had looked forward to reaching the bunker, because that meant I could rest. It turned out, however, that the bunker was still under construction. It did not even have a door, and we had to climb inside through an opening that would eventually become a window. The bunker consisted of one room which had been built by excavating an appropriate hole, then lining it with logs, mostly young pine. The sloped ceiling, which conformed to the fall of the hill, was also framed with logs. After the room was constructed, it was covered with the excavated soil, and the vegetation was replaced. This and similar bunkers in the Carpathians were so well masked that they were virtually invisible from a distance of a few meters. But these bunkers had a feature that made life significantly more pleasant. The short front wall had a window. When the soil was replaced to hide the bunker, a square hole was left in front of the window. Daylight would pour in through the hole and be reflected back into the bunker. As soon as I entered the bunker, I noticed that only two bunk beds stood against the walls. The beds were covered with pine branches on which lay the belongings of the four men.

On that first day, Iskra made coffee on a spirit stove, since the bunker's earthen stove had yet to be built. We ate and drank mostly in silence. Occasionally someone would say something. The four men studied us discreetly, especially me; I studied them in turn. Only Orlan seemed not to be participating in this mutual scrutiny. I did know, because Orlan had told me, that the leadership considered these four men particularly trustworthy and reliable. They had been permitted to be on the direct line that led to the propaganda bunker, and that is why they were selected as Orlan's and my keepers for the winter.

Over the next weeks and months, I would learn more about these men. All four grew up in this area of the Carpathians and as youths had worked as lumberjacks, so they knew the mountains intimately. They were in their late twenties, with Baida, at age twenty-nine, the oldest and the one to whom the other three deferred. He was short of stature, dark, with a broad face that was calm and friendly. We would discover that he was thoughtful and not prone to rash decisions. Before acting, he would think the assignment through and work out every detail. Iskra was also short, but blond with large clear blue eyes. He seemed to be the most daring, if one judged by the escapades he related, although a recent injury had curbed his appetite for adventure. He had broken his leg a year earlier, and the bones had knitted poorly since he had received no medical help. He could walk, but tired easily and seldom went down the mountain, although he was engaged to a girl in the village of Kami-anka. The girl and her parents had been loaded onto the train to Siberia, but the girl had escaped along the way and returned home half-alive. She lived and hid in the village. Moroz was taller than both Baida and Iskra. He was friendly, trusting to the point of naïveté, and easy going. Chornota was the opposite of Moroz. Determined, a doer, he was always going to get food or news. He carried the heaviest load, did not complain, and was the last one to retreat when they met the enemy.

Now, as we sat opposite each other outside the half-finished bunker—they to one side, and Orlan and me together opposite them— I discerned on their faces and in their sidelong glances the question they were asking themselves: How is this going to turn out? What kind of person is she? Is she going to put on airs and make our lives hell? I smiled to myself. I had seen these same questions on other faces and in other eyes. I would see them again in a future bunker with future bunker mates, if God let me live.

Later I would learn that what worried them was not so much my gender, but how they would maintain "proper behavior" in front of an "educated woman" during the long and cramped winter days. They worried that I would become offended if they swore or argued. They were not sure they could be on their best behavior for seven months. Not that they had never before met a woman partisan—there were women in the UPA, but their number was small since the leaders were much more selective in recruiting women. Many of the women who enlisted were assigned to regional partisan centers where they acted as secretaries. These women usually had a gymnasium education, while many of the men, particularly those who came from the countryside, had completed only elementary school. The men, who had matured in partisan ranks, often could not bear the thought that a woman could be regarded as superior to them, even in the area of formal education. They felt that life had been their instructor and that they had developed a certain world view by simply being in the UPA. They were no longer the idealistic and naïve youths who had left their families in 1943 and 1944. What was important was not their level of education but what they had done in the intervening years and how they had treated their fellow men. A woman who could prove herself was accepted, although the scope of the acceptance mirrored the role of women in the society of that day. A woman could and would be consulted, but men did the deciding.

After we rested, Orlan set to work. He took out a pencil and a notebook and calculated how much food we would need for the winter. When he questioned the men, we discovered that they had put aside only half of what was needed. Orlan next prepared a list. Our diet would consist mostly of potatoes, which were relatively easy to get but heavy and difficult to bring into the mountains. We also would need flour and grouts, as well as some lard and meat, probably smoked pork. Orlan then took out his wallet and gave the men money to buy the needed provisions. He warned them to make purchases very carefully and in small quantities in order not to betray themselves. They were also forewarned not to mention our presence to anyone at all, including their underground contacts in the area. The extra provisions were to be bought and transported in small quantities, since the local militia did sporadic checks, and a villager returning home with a large quantity of food, which he shouldn't have been able to afford to buy, was subject to immediate arrest on suspicion of helping partisans.

When the three men departed the following day, Orlan turned his energies to building an earthen stove. Of course we had no bricks, so the walls had to be made from stones that we gathered and brought to the bunker. Iskra, who had stayed behind, helped us. He had remained with us for two reasons. In the event of an attack, we needed someone to guide our escape through the mountains. In addition, Iskra not only had difficulty walking, but he also could not haul a heavy load, since carrying any kind of weight put extra pressure on his bad leg and caused excruciating pain.

Orlan finished the stove before the men returned with the additional foodstuffs. The top of the stove was covered with a metal plate, which the men had brought to the bunker earlier. This stove served us as long as we lived in the bunker. The stove, as well as a window that was eventually installed, eliminated the need for illumination and the necessity of obtaining large amounts of kerosene for a lamp. During the day, we would use the spirit stove to heat what had been cooked earlier.

The men not only brought back food but also several books and reference materials that Orlan needed for his work. These materials came from Poltava. Throughout November, we worked on finishing the bunker, while the men ventured back into civilization periodically for more food. We were lucky that we had a long autumn and snow did not come until late, while at lower elevations it would hardly fall at all that winter.

Toward the end of November, as winter was about to descend in earnest, the men left for one last rendezvous with the local partisan leader, who had not been informed of our presence in his territory. Two days later they returned, worried. They told us the following story: They met with Nechai, the local leader, who had built a large, well-equipped bunker for himself and his four men. They had left the bunker to meet with others for final instructions before the winter hibernation began and to get one more load of provisions. Upon their return, they came across a tree in the vicinity of the bunker on which someone had cut a deep gash. Who had done it? And why? Had it been done by someone who had followed one of them earlier and had discovered the location of the bunker? Or was the mark made by a local villager who had gone into the forest to cut wood? Since the origin and significance of the mark could not be ascertained, it meant that the bunker was presumed unmasked and, therefore, at risk. When Nechai had related this information to our men, he suggested that three from his group attach themselves to our bunker. Baida, who usually acted as the spokesman for our men, instead of agreeing, told Nechai that he had to think about the proposal overnight. Nechai was both astounded and hurt, but Baida did not explain since he had been placed under strict orders not to reveal Orlan's presence in the region.

Now Baida asked Orlan what should he do. The problem was, of course, that our bunker had been built for four people. Now six people were living in it, and there was hardly any space left. If Nechai and two others joined us, we would be squeezed in like sardines and be forced to sleep in shifts. Besides, there was the additional problem of adequate provisions.

Orlan did not even hesitate for a moment. "Let them come," he said. "We'll manage."

There were now nine of us. Nechai was the tallest. When he first walked into the bunker to report his arrival to Orlan, his blond, closely cropped hair nearly brushed the ceiling. He wore a Red Army uniform with a black cotton shirt that had been embroidered along the standup collar. He was accompanied by Slavko and Evhen, also tall and fair-haired men. All three were local men, and Slavko and Evhen were slightly younger than Chornota and Moroz.

After the first heavy snowfall, our contact with the outside world became irregular. The snow covered the mountains and piled high in the valleys. We, as well as other partisans in other bunkers in the Carpathians, settled down to wait for spring. As the days passed and we talked, I learned other details about the men. All had joined the UPA in 1943 and first fought the Germans before facing the NKVD Special Troop units. They had all participated in a training school that UPA had run in the early years of its existence and also had attended a first aid course.

But we did not idle the days away talking. We had a daily schedule that we followed exactly. We worked and we studied. Except for me, everyone took turns at guard duty outside the bunker. The watch was kept from early morning until after dusk. We changed guards every hour and, if it was very cold, more often.

Orlan was working on his brochure, as well as writing a history of the Ukrainian revolutionary movement in the *Zakerzon krai* from 1943 to 1947. Nechai was preparing detailed reports of his and his unit's activities during 1947. He also was required to submit a plan of activities for the coming year.

My job was to type the materials Orlan and Nechai prepared on a typewriter we had brought to the bunker. If I was not typing, I gave lessons in history and literature, mathematics, and geography to the other men. In fact, I shared this work with Orlan and Nechai, lecturing when they were occupied with other tasks.

We cooked after nightfall, so that smoke would not be visible. At first I did the cooking, but to cook for so many was difficult and tiring, and when the others saw my fatigue they would take turns cooking. After supper, we had no organized activities. We took turns playing chess. Some watched the chess game, other read or studied the assigned lessons for the following day. Later in the evening, we would sleep in shifts since there were not enough beds to accommodate everyone at one time.

As Christmas approached, I made plans for a Christmas Eve dinner and a joyous, if that was possible, celebration of the birth of Our Lord. At my urging, the men cut down a Christmas tree for which I had started making ornaments weeks earlier. I used scraps of colorful paper to make stars and snowflakes. Once the men saw my ornaments, they joined in, using whatever was at hand to decorate the tree.

Finding the ingredients for a festive meal was more difficult. We had a little flour, some dried beans, a little honey, several pounds of sugar, as well as some dried mushrooms and apples, meat and potatoes.

I cooked the apples with the sugar to make a filling for a layered sweet bread that I made from the flour, having found a bit of baking powder among our provisions. I also made potato dumplings and borscht, the beet soup that is a traditional first course on Christmas Eve; also kutia, the honey-sweetened wheat kernel porridge that is the traditional Christmas Eve sweet.

Everything was ready as dusk fell on Christmas Eve, but we sat and waited. Taking advantage of a change in the weather, three of the men had gone down to pay a visit to a village and bring back news and more food. They had left two days earlier with the start of the blizzard. Although it may sound dangerous, we left the bunker only during bad weather. During bright and calm days, any footprint was clearly visible on the endless expanse of glistening snow. Thus, excursions on calm days could not be risked, however carefully one tried to mask his passage. During a storm, especially a full-fledged blizzard, the raging wind and blowing snow almost immediately erased all footprints. I secretly liked this turbulent weather. When the wind began to blow, then whistle and finally roar, I would put on my heavy clothing and slip outside. I would take a few steps only, but the wind and the snow were blowing so hard that I immediately felt isolated and alone. I would hold on to a branch of a nearby pine, so that the fierce wind would not topple me over, and stare into the snow and the wind for as long as I could bear the cold. At such moments we were as isolated and safe as if we were on a different planet. The storm lorded over the mountains, cutting them off from civilization, transforming the familiar panorama of peaks into otherworldly vistas.

Having grown up in the mountains, the men could predict bad weather. They would listen to the wind and read other signs and announce that a storm was coming. They also grew excited, because a storm was not something to be feared. They knew their mountains well and every trail in them, and they seldom became lost. A major storm broke two days before Christmas Eve, and the three men had hurried away. They promised to return in time for Christmas Eve supper, but when evening arrived there still was no sign of them. At dusk we looked at each other but could not bring ourselves to sit down to the waiting supper. Thus passed Christmas Eve and night. We sat silent and worried. Next to us the Christmas tree looked forlorn and shabby.

As if realizing the solemnity of the holy feast, the blizzard hesitated, paused, and then ceased. A quiet settled over the snowbound mountains and forests. We knew that with the cessation of snowfall and blowing wind, the three men would not dare approach the bunker for fear of leaving telltale tracks. We began to cheer each other with surmises that the men had left the village and had halted somewhere in the forest. But our festive mood did not revive. We ate, but with little appetite. Then we waited some more, increasingly fearful that some disaster had overtaken the three men.

Christmas Day crawled by. Toward evening, another storm swept across the mountains, and the wind began to roar anew. We immediately became more cheerful. If all was well with them, the men would return tonight.—And they did. They brought joy and sunshine into the dark, cold bunker. How we rejoiced to see them. They told us that they had left the village a day earlier. They had completed half of the journey when the storm suddenly gave out. They knew that they could go no farther for fear that someone would be able to follow their tracks. They were near an alpine pasture where the peasants had left several haystacks. They crawled inside the haystacks and thus spent the day.

We finally celebrated Christmas with laughter and caroling. We had become one family.

◆ ◆ ◆ ◆ ◆

Snow began to melt in April 1948. Nechai and his two men left soon thereafter. The four remaining men began to plan spring activities. I, too, wanted to get moving. I had been sick on and off through the winter and decided to see a doctor. I planned to coordinate the consultation with a visit to my parents. I discussed my plans with Orlan, and one of the men obtained a travel permit for me. Before I left, I took off my boots and pants and put on a peasant skirt and blouse.

I reached Lviv without any difficulties and went to see my friend Nastia, with whose family I had boarded when I went to school. She had married but was living alone since her husband had been imprisoned. She had kept in touch with my parents and said they were still in Zadviria and constantly worried about my fate. The next morning she took the train to Zadviria to get my parents. I waited impatiently— I had not seen my family for two years.

My mother and my sister Stefa returned with her in the evening. Our reunion embraced all possible emotions. We wept with joy. We wept over the deaths and disasters that had befallen most everyone we knew. We worried about the future. Father had been arrested, then released. All their grain had been taken away. Mother told me that other families had fared much worse. Some families had been exiled to Siberia in punishment for having sons in the underground, while men from other families had disappeared after being arrested. Then it was my turn to tell them about my life, about my baby son and his loss. We sat together and talked through the night. In the morning, my father and my sister Lesia arrived. My father gazed at me and tears rolled down his cheeks. He had grown old. "How thin you are, child," he said.

"You all are not looking so well yourselves," I retorted. My mother and father had lost their vitality under the harsh conditions of their lives. On the other hand, Stefa and Lesia had grown up in the intervening two years and were no longer children but young women. Olia had stayed home with Ivanko.

I would suffer one more blow. The doctor told me I was pregnant again. I had suspected that my illnesses were the result of another pregnancy, but I had not wanted to believe it. After the tragedy with little Zenon, I did not want to get pregnant again. I had considered an abortion, but by the time I arrived in Lviv, I knew I would not go through with one. I realized that the reason I came to Lviv was to see my parents and, with their help, find a family who would take the child in after I gave birth. I told my parents about my condition, and we spent many hours discussing what I should do. Those who would have made the best foster parents had been exiled to Siberia, and those who remained were too scared to help me. We did come up with a few names, and my father promised to go see these families and explain my situation. I spent three days in Lviv. Then my father accompanied me back to the Carpathians. My family had never met Orlan, and both my parents and I wanted this meeting to take place. My mother packed a backpack for me with all kinds of good things, using what money she had saved for Easter for the family.

From Skole, my father and I went to Kamianka. An escort was already waiting for us, and we immediately left for the forest. My father, who had no experience hiking in the mountains, became very tired and could not get over the way we easily moved through the forests. We stopped at a prearranged meeting place, and the next morning, Orlan, accompanied by bodyguards, arrived. The three of us spent the day together. In the evening, two men escorted my father back to Skole and put him on the Lviv-bound train. I would learn later that when he returned home, he told my mother and my sisters, "Everything's fine. He's a good man. We have nothing to worry about." But after spending a day as a target of Orlan's charm, he could not have thought otherwise.

The week before Easter arrived. On Holy Thursday, Moroz, Chornota, and Baida went down to the village, where they were to take care of some personal matters, obtain food for the coming holy feast, and pick up mail and newspapers. During the night we heard gunfire coming from the direction of the village. We knew that partisans had stumbled on an enemy trap. We did not know whether it had happened

to our three men or to some other group. We spent the night waiting
for them, our worries growing. By morning we were convinced that
something awful had happened. Only Moroz returned during the day,
tired and pale. He told us that he had been left outside as a guard while
Chornota and Baida stopped at a house. As the two men approached
the house, the enemy opened fire, immediately wounding both men.
They were still able to get way, but the enemy lit up the area with flares
and killed Chornota. Baida, who could not escape because of his
wounds, used the last bullet to kill himself.

In the days that followed we learned that the enemy took the bodies of the two men to Skole. Chornota's fiancée and her friends went
into the forest and brought back blood-soaked earth from the place
where the men fell. A funeral was held, and the bloodied earth was
buried in the village cemetery. That Easter, the village bell tolled mourn-
fully for the dead men.

7. The Toll of Being a Guerrilla

When snow was finally gone and the enemy could no longer follow a trail of telltale footprints into the forest, Ptakh arrived at our bunker with the mail that had accumulated during the months we had spent underground, cut off from communications. As it had become the norm, the mail contained mostly accounts of deaths in our ranks. The most shattering letter was from Taras. The letter said that Sviatoslava had died not long after our departure. She had been living with their one-year-old baby daughter Lidia in Peremyshl. During the mass arrests of Ukrainians that accompanied Operation Wisla, someone had revealed Sviatoslava's identity and whereabouts, and Polish intelligence agents came to arrest her. When the agents told her to pack, she pretended to agree but asked if she could get something from an adjoining room. Once alone, she opened the window and jumped out. She fell three stories, hit her head against the pavement, and died instantly. People gathered around the body, but soon an unmarked car arrived, and Sviatoslava's corpse was loaded into it. The Polish agents took the baby girl with them. Taras had lost the two people he loved most. He did not even know if Sviatoslava had received a decent Christian burial.

As I read Taras' letter, I began to tremble. I remembered how after my escape from Krakow, I had poured out the details of my own tragedy to her. She had sat listening silently, her eyes brimming with tears, involuntary spasms convulsing her body. Finally, she had said, "I don't think I could have done what you did. I don't think I have that kind of determination or courage." How wrong she had been. She had proved she possessed both. She had had the courage and the determination not to let herself be taken alive.

There was a second reason why it was so difficult to read Taras'
letter. By the time we received it, Taras was dead, too. He had been shot
while crossing the frontier a few weeks after he wrote the letter. We
learned about his death from Ptakh.

We also learned about the death of Stiah. His death was partially,
or perhaps largely, due to his refusal to move from his favorite bunker,
although, as I mentioned earlier, Orlan had repeatedly urged him to do
so the previous autumn. Our intelligence had told us that the NKVD
had discovered the general area in which Stiah operated. Stiah pooh-
poohed the warnings and had stayed in his bunker. The NKVD spent
months searching the vicinity and finally found what they were looking for. Stiah had mined the area around the bunker and the NKVD
lost many men, but in the end they got him. We also learned that careful and methodical Bor, who had been one of our escorts on our trek to
Poltava's bunker, had also died.

As communications were reestablished, Orlan was summoned to
a meeting of the UPA's High Command that was to take place near Lviv.
Poltava and Hornovii would also attend, but we did not plan to go in
one group because it was too dangerous. Calling such a conference was
in itself very risky, but the need for a meeting of the leadership was self-
evident. The UPA stood at a crossroads, and decisions had to be made
about what form resistance would take in circumstances where the
Soviet regime was slowly but inexorably solidifying its control over all
Ukraine, including the mountains and rural areas.

We left on May 15, after prolonged and painful good-byes with
those with whom we had spent the winter. I think that when you leave,
you leave part of yourself behind. You shake hands, you mouth plati-
tudes about a next time, but you know that you'll never in your life see
these people again, and your heart breaks a little.

The nights that spring were bright and luminous. The moon illu-
minated the panorama of peaks and made our progress through the
forests easier. One night we passed through the Chornohora Range, the
legendary home of Dovbush, the seventeenth-century Ukrainian Robin
Hood who took from the feudal lords and their wardens and distributed the spoils gained to the serfs. As I was remembering the Dovbush
legend, we came out suddenly onto a moonlit meadow amid the circlet
of peaks. This was exactly the kind of meadow described in the Dovbush
legend. Dovbush would gather his men on a moonlit night before
descending down to the plains and valleys. Then the second coincidence occurred. We saw a cave carved into a nearby rockface. Again,

according to the legend, Dovbush and his men kept their horses in just such a cave. The legend said that to this day Dovbush's faithful horses await the return of their master, neighing and pawing the ground impatiently. I bent down and put my ear to a huge rock at the entrance to the cave. I heard strange sounds, as if the horses, sensing our presence, were striking at the cave walls with their hooves. What if, I mused, we had horses that would take us out of the mountains? We, too, were avengers like Dovbush had been. We were fighting for our people, as he had fought for them. As I thought these thoughts, the past and the present seemed to be linked by a silvery thread, and nothing was impossible.

Once we left the mountains, the forests became sparse and scattered. This had been taken into account when the route was laid out, and we were always able to reach the next forest by dawn where we could hide and rest. We were escorted by changing pairs of escorts. One would lead the way while the other man would bring up the rear. We would spend the daylight hours hidden in the brush. We would eat our meager rations, then sleep or, if we could not sleep, lie quietly awake listening to the life around us. We would resume our journey at dusk. The march was steady but difficult, and often during the nights I would stumble and fall behind. One time, I lagged behind, and the others disappeared among the trees. Suddenly, I found myself at a crossing of two trails, and I didn't know which way to go, to the right or to the left. I remember this moment vividly even after so many years because it epitomized my life: I am standing bewildered at a crossroads as I did as a child, unsure of where the roads lead and which one I want to, or should, follow. At this particular crossroads, I stopped, sat down, and waited. I was actually happy that I had been given a respite from walking on and on. I knew that eventually my absence would be noted; the last man in the file of silent men would realize I was missing. He would stop the others and turn back to find me. This scenario repeated itself more than once. The men were stronger and bigger than I, but they did not reprimand me for my slowness. They knew I was doing my best. They also knew that if we came to a particularly dangerous area, or if we had to hurry to make a rendezvous, I would gather what strength I had left and not delay them or jeopardize our safety. When we stopped to rest, someone would always urge me to eat more or catnap.

We had to cross the Dnister River, a swift mountain river with many eddies and undercurrents that made fording difficult, especially in the middle of the night. Once on the other side, we hurried in order to reach a forest by morning. Once in the forest, we all sat down on toppled tree trunks except for Orlan, who lay down on the ground. During the day, he complained of a headache, and by night he was burning with fever. We started out, but a kilometer or so later Orlan collapsed. We could not stop since we had to rendezvous by morning with Fedir, the head of the resistance in the Lviv area. We had come out on a meadow where several horses were grazing. One of the men caught one of the horses, put Orlan on it, and we continued on our journey. In the morning, we let the horse go, and two men carried Orlan to our meeting place.

Fedir (Zenon Tershakovec) himself and several fighters met us. Fedir was of medium height, with a shaved head and a pleasant smile that lit up his face. He also was overweight, especially when his bulk was compared to the lean, sinewy partisans coming out of the mountains. I soon discovered he was ashamed of his size, and once he got to know you, he would allude to his weight and say that he did not know why his body was the way it was since he did not eat any more than the others. Nonetheless, we immediately noticed that the partisans we met were better dressed and less apprehensive than we were. Fedir wore a neatly pressed, well-fitting uniform. His boots shone from polishing. Next to us, he and his men looked like officers and we like recruits. It became apparent that the life of a partisan was less exacting in the lowlands than in the mountains.

Orlan was taken to a hut where he was given some penicillin, and by evening he was better. Fedir had planned everything meticulously, and I gathered that he was the one who was meeting all the leaders arriving for the conference.

We spent about twenty-four hours with Fedir. The following morning Ptakh, Bukva, and I left with a group of partisans. We had to walk carefully since this was May, and the ground was covered with new growth and spring flowers. I saw Ptakh pause, then lag behind, but I did not put much thought into what he was doing. In a few minutes, he caught up to me and presented me with a bouquet. He was smiling broadly and squeezed my hands as he said, "On the anniversary of your wedding, I want to wish you all the best." I had remembered several days earlier that our third wedding anniversary was coming, but then forgot. Orlan had forgotten also since he had said nothing when we parted, but Ptakh had remembered.

We waited in a new hideout for several days for Orlan's return. In the meantime, Natalka, a courier for Fedir, joined us. She was a cheerful girl who had incredibly beautiful black hair that she wore in two thick braids. We quickly became friends and exchanged information about our lives. Her parents and younger sister had been exiled to Siberia, while an older sister had immigrated west during the war.

When Orlan returned, he was accompanied by Ulas (Vasyl Bei), the head of the resistance in the Podillia region, who had been also at the meeting with Chuprynka. Orlan told me that he had been assigned to Volyn and that he and Ulas would be traveling together, since the route to Volyn passed through part of Podillia. Orlan also told me that I would not be going with him, at least not for the time being. Although I understood his and the leadership's reasoning, I was devastated. The journey on foot to Volyn was not that long. This was unknown territory, where contacts were fragmented and sometimes unreliable. That's how Orlan explained the decision to me. He added that the OUN network would assist me in finding a village where there were trusted people who would take me in for as long as was necessary. After this, he kissed me and we parted.

During our brief reunion, Orlan had said very little about the conference, and I don't know who, besides Poltava, Hornovii, Fedir, Ulas, and Orlan, met with Chuprynka. Neither do I know if they conferred as a group or individually. To hold such a meeting in 1948 was extremely dangerous since Soviet authorities had by then co-opted numerous agents and had placed moles among the population and, possibly, had also infiltrated the resistance. What I did know was that Orlan regarded this meeting as very important since it addressed a number of problems that had arisen with the coming of the Soviet regime. Orlan, as well as the other leaders, realized that such a meeting was long overdue. Yet, the risk of having all the leaders in one place was monumental. However well they were guarded and however circumspect the arrival of various individuals, nonetheless there was always the risk of betrayal and discovery.

What I pieced together over time was this: The first order of business was for each leader to report on the conditions in his territory. Orlan, of course, reported on the *Zakerzon krai* and gave detailed accounts of the UPA groups that had gone to the West as well as about the *sotnyas* that had crossed into Ukraine. I also learned that much of the discussion was centered on how to appeal to and recruit the new generation into the UPA and the OUN. These young people knew little of the prewar nationalistic movement, and it and its ideals had to be explained to them, as well as the aim and purpose of continuing the armed resistance. At the conference, the decision was made to enlarge the potential source of new cadres by carrying the UPA and OUN ideology to central and eastern Ukraine. Sending OUN and UPA activists to live in those areas would accomplish this. The thinking was that these dedicated individuals would slowly begin to build a nationalist movement in parts of Ukraine that had been under Russian control since shortly after the October Revolution.

Orlan had been assigned an additional task in Volyn. Not only was he to reorganize and reinvigorate the resistance there, but he also was to settle an ongoing dispute between two local leaders. The UPA in Volyn faced problems that did not exist in other regions, problems dating back to World War II. When the German army defeated the Russian army in 1941 and 1942, many of the soldiers in the Russian army, especially those who were Ukrainians, fled into the forests and the large marshy areas of the Volyn region to escape German POW camps. Many of these soldiers were absorbed into the UPA, which was being created at that time.

The OUN, which monitored the formation of these armed units, did not agree with the mass acceptance of former Red Army soldiers into UPA ranks. The OUN leaders warned that the influx of unvetted men would carry serious repercussion in the future. My former superior, Mikushka, as the head of the OUN security police, warned against and objected vociferously to this unmonitored swell in UPA ranks. Mikushka predicted that the unregulated influx would offer an unparalleled opportunity for infiltration by Soviet moles and agents and that this would eventually lead to enormous losses. His warning did not have much impact, since the OUN was not as strong in Volyn and Polisia as it was in Halychyna, the area around Lviv.

Mikushka proved to be right. Although there were not many traitors, their number was sufficiently large to nearly destroy the UPA and the OUN in Volyn over the next several years. The NKVD managed to infiltrate the UPA by sending operatives who had military training and could lead armed units. Such skill was prized by the UPA, and these men quickly rose to leadership positions. They became commanders of UPA units, some rising to lead *sotnyas* while other became leaders in the provincial OUN organization. As long as the enemy was the Germans, these men fought with the UPA. But in 1945, the situation changed dramatically. Germans retreated, and the UPA turned its attention to fighting the arriving NKVD Special Troops. Suddenly, these experienced and able commanders started losing battles and incurring enormous losses. One such leader whose nom de guerre was Stal' (steel) was said to have led an entire *sotnya* into a series of planned traps in which almost every man perished. There were other similar instances of inexplicable disasters on the battlefield. These agents also acted in a different, but equally deadly, way. A mole would watch his men and pick out those who were losing their spirit as the fighting grew more difficult and as supplies, especially food, became scarce. Then this mole/commander would seek out a discouraged fighter and confide to him that the outlook was hopeless, then suggest that the man leave the UPA and seek amnesty. If the man hesitated or if he grew angry at the suggestion, the mole would threaten him. He would say that there were many men in the group who shared his feelings about the hopelessness of the struggle, and if the recalcitrant man tried to protest or complain to others he would be dead within the hour. Such tactics sowed seeds of doubt and suspicion in UPA groups and, upon occasion, led to the group becoming dysfunctional, as the men scattered in panic. Reports of such instances became so frequent and so debilitating that they focused the full attention of the UPA leadership and that of the OUN on Volyn and what was happening to the guerrilla war there.

The UPA and OUN leadership had made an attempt at unmasking and expunging the planted agents. The OUN SB security police operations in Volyn were only marginally successful. In several instances, SB actions resulted in tragedies in which innocent people were accused of being moles, were tried by military tribunals, and were shot. This happened when a trapped agent would, on purpose, implicate innocent people during interrogations. Since both the UPA and the OUN were under constant pressure from the Soviet Special Troops, the SB often did not have the luxury of time or the resources to unravel what had really happened and therefore believed the mole's accusations.

Then the leader of the UPA in Volyn, Klym Savur (Lt. Col. Dmytro Kliachkivsky), was betrayed and died in an ambush. Chuprynka replaced him with Smok (Mykola Kozak, also later known under the nom de guerre as Vivchar), who came from Halychyna, had been thoroughly vetted, and was trusted by the UPA and the OUN. Smok initiated radical surgery to rid the UPA of moles and NKVD agents. He was so extreme that even the head of the SB for the northern regions, Daleky (Stepan Ianishewsky), condemned his tactics. The conflict between these two leaders became so serious and so divisive that it paralyzed the underground and the UPA. What emerged were two factions, one on the side of Smok, the other on the side of Daleky, and

each refused to cooperate with the other. The schism was also territo-
rial. The Rivne area was under the control of Daleky, while the Volyn
countryside was under Smok.

When Chuprynka learned of this, he sent his representative to
both men and invited both to meet with him. Smok came, but Daleky
did not, presumably thinking that the leadership would side with Smok,
whom it had sent earlier to the area. The trouble was that the men
under Daleky's control did not realize that he had broken with the UPA
leadership and was acting on his own, not under the jurisdiction and
in conjunction with Chuprynka.

These events and the turmoil they caused did, in fact, pretty much
rid the UPA and the Volyn OUN of moles, but not completely, since,
throughout its war against the UPA, the NKVD tried to infiltrate both
the UPA and the OUN. The NKVD believed that the way to destroy
the partisans was from the inside and through betrayals. Although the
Volyn underground was weakened, it did not disintegrate. Although
both Smok and Daleky carried on the resistance, instances occurred
when one man's group got in the way of the other group. Upon occasion, one group would accidentally stumble on the other in the forest,
and the men, thinking that they had come across a band of the NKVD,
would start shooting at each other.

Thus, the decision was made to send someone totally new and previously uninvolved with the Volyn problem to become the ranking superior officer over both Daleky and Smok. Chuprynka chose Orlan for
the job. Chuprynka had decided on Orlan in 1946 and had postponed
that transfer because of the turmoil in the *Zakerzon krai*. After Orlan
and I crossed into Ukraine in 1947, Chuprynka waited for the opportune time to implement his decision.

As we were saying good-bye, I saw that Orlan was challenged by
his new assignment and was eager to begin working. This assignment
was also a promotion, since he became the leader of the resistance for
all of northwestern Ukraine.

I learned this complicated history of the Volyn resistance much
later, when Orlan and I were reunited. In the spring of 1948, all I knew
was that Orlan had left for Volyn, and I stayed behind. Orlan's parting
present was a set of beautifully forged documents that said I was a repatriate from *Zakerzon krai*. Once I found a place to live, Orlan said, I
would use these credentials to legalize myself. Although I knew the
documents would help and having them was an enormous plus, I realized that my survival depended ultimately only on me.

8. Birth of My Second Son

After Orlan's departure, Natalka and I left the forest and went to the village of Hranky, near the town of Khodoriv. A number of families repatriated from the *Zakerzon krai* lived in Hranky. None of them had Soviet documents, and that is why we had selected this particular village to visit. In the larger towns and administrative centers, the *Zakerzon krai* repatriates had already been issued internal passports. At the village administration in Hranky, I said I was from the village of Brylynec in *Zakerzon krai,* presented the document Orlan had given me that I was a repatriate, and filled out an application for residency. My request was granted, and I received a document that said I was a resident of Hranky. Through people she knew, Natalka also arranged for a document that permitted me to travel. Natalka also gave me a few skirts and dresses, since I had been wearing pants and had no women's clothing. Thus, equipped with papers and appropriate clothing, I set out for Sambir on the train to drop off mail I had brought with me from the partisans. I had to change trains in Stryi. Since the train was not leaving right away, I took a walk in the town. When I approached the gate where I had to show my ticket, a well-dressed young man went up to the militiaman checking documents and whispered something while pointing me out. I noticed this exchange, but did not loose my composure.

The militiaman came up to me through the crowd and said, "May I see your documents?"

As I pulled out my new documents, I suddenly realized I had forgotten my new name. What to do. I drew the document from my bag, opened it slowly, quickly scanned the name and then folding it again, handed it to the militiaman. He read the document carefully and then put me through the drill: "Name? Date of birth? Place?"

If he had snatched my residency document from my hands before I had time to read it, I would have been lost. I learned my lesson well that first day, but, thank God, all turned out well. In a police regime, not only did the authorities check documents but also probed your thoughts.

After delivering the mail in Sambir, I continued on to Lviv, where I met my father. Orlan and I had decided on two conduits for keeping in touch. One was through Natalka who worked for Fedir and thus had access to couriers. The second conduit would be through my family. I told my father that once Orlan had settled in Volyn, he would write to one of my uncles. My parents would retrieve the letters and I would somehow get them from them. Orlan and I left open the question of what I would do after the baby was born. We had two choices: I could raise the child myself by getting a job and legalizing myself in some small town. Or, if I could not find the means to raise the baby myself, I would find a family with whom I would place the child and return to the underground.

I outlined these plans to my father and also taught him how to hide the letters from Orlan, how to transport them, and how to get them to me. I then went back to Sambir and started looking for a place to live. I spent several weeks with different families, most of them repatriates from *Zakerzon krai*, but could not find appropriate lodgings. What I was looking for was a family that was local and was not under any suspicion of having anything to do with the partisans. Eventually, I found what I thought would be a suitable place in the village of Kalyniv, outside Sambir. This was the home of three sisters and a brother whose ages ranged from a little over twenty down to ten years. They had been left orphans during the *Zakerzon krai* repatriations and now were trying to recreate their family. The middle sister, a teenager, already had a three-year-old daughter but no one knew who the father was. Since I was about the same age as the eldest sister, my presence and my condition did not seem out of the ordinary in this family unit.

For a few weeks everything went well. I registered with the village administration and was planning to live with this family until spring when the baby would be a few months old and when it would be easier to travel with the child. I met with Natalka who gave me a letter from one of Orlan's contacts that contained the news that Orlan had reached Volyn safely. The news brightened my otherwise gray existence.

But my plans did not work out. I discovered that a woman whose husband had been pardoned for evading the draft and was now cooperating with the authorities had found out who I was. Eventually, he or she would tell the authorities about me. Thus, two months before the baby was due, I had to move. What complicated matters was that I had fallen ill and missed a second scheduled rendezvous with Natalka in Hranky, the village we had gone to when I left the underground. When I finally arrived at the village, I discovered that Natalka had waited for me for an entire day and left a message that she had found a suitable place for me. I was beside myself. Not only had I missed a chance to find a place for myself and the child that would soon be born, but I also missed receiving news about Orlan. Was he all right? Was he alive? I was discovering how bitter life could be for a wife of a partisan. Even if a man goes to war, he has a chance of returning alive. But a man who is in the partisans has no chance at all.

I decided to stay in Hranky to wait for the next meeting with Natalka, which we had agreed on to be on the same date a month hence if one of us somehow missed the August meeting. During this time—the end of August and the beginning of September of 1948—the special troops of the security forces were combing the forests for the remaining partisan groups. They had also devised a method to turn the population against the partisans. Using Soviet partisans who had been active during the German occupation, the authorities ordered these men to pretend they were UPA. These men would commit terrorist acts, engage in debauchery, and assault people living in villages near the forests, especially villages the enemy knew partisans visited often to obtain information and provisions. Sometimes these UPA impostors would drag people off into the forest to bunkers they had built for this purpose. They would question and torture people for allegedly cooperating with the authorities. Disoriented and fearful, some people told their inquisitors about what they had done for the UPA and also named others in the village who knew about their patriotic activities and could serve as witnesses. Then the authorities would arrest the people who had been named. These Soviet tactics created distrust among the villagers and frightened many people from cooperating further with what was left of the underground.

In Hranky, I lived in a state of readiness and fear. Since houses were searched constantly, I spent a lot of time in the loft in the barn. One day I saw trucks filled with soldiers coming into the village, and I immediately went into the fields. I hid among the grain that had not yet been harvested. The day passed, and the barking of dogs told me that strangers were still in the village. Toward evening, I became cold, since I was wearing a summer dress. Then it began to rain. I spent the night in the fields and did not go back until the middle of the following day when one of the girls came to get me.

Natalka did not come to the September meeting, and I grew increasingly worried. Then we heard the news that one of the partisan leaders and his secretary were killed in a bunker in the forest. The secretary was described as having had long black braids. I remembered Natalka's luxuriant hair and was certain that she had been killed. I think I guessed right, because I never saw Natalka again. Whom had she found for me? The question nagged me, and I was near despair.

At the end of September, I arranged a meeting with my family to which Lesia came, bringing important news. My parents had received a letter from Orlan through the conduit I had established. I was very disappointed when Lesia told me that Orlan had been in touch and had set a time for us to meet. This date had fallen before my prearranged contact with my family, and they did not know how and where to find me earlier. Thus, Lesia had gone to the rendezvous with Orlan. Lesia said that Ptakh and one other partisan met her and tied her eyes with a kerchief, then led her to a bunker. Once the kerchief was removed, she found herself in a small bunker with a very low ceiling. Orlan was waiting for her, and they spent a long time talking. She told him what she knew about my situation. My ill fortune to have missed a chance to see my husband was in some measure relieved by the knowledge that he was alive and well, which made me very happy.

My second son was born on October 18, 1948, in Hranky. I used a midwife who came from Eastern Ukraine and had settled in a nearby village back in 1939 during the first Soviet occupation. I did not want to use her but had no choice. When she handed me the baby she examined me closely, then said, "You have delicate hands." And when she left she added, "You're not a villager, but that is none of my business."

Although I did not think she would betray me because she lived in harmony with the Ukrainian population, nonetheless it became quite apparent that I was different from the people I lived with, however hard I tried to blend in. Eventually, someone started asking questions, and the gossip spread.

This was an extremely difficult time in the countryside since the authorities, having defeated the UPA and pacified Western Ukraine, were turning to collectivizing villages. Villages resisted, but the authorities would torture peasants until they agreed to sign the collectivization agreement, or the authorities would descend unannounced on a village and take away the heads of household for questioning and conversion.

The partisans opposed collectivization because they knew what it would bring, also because they believed that the population should resist the invader. Sometimes partisans punished and drove out men who came to collectivize a village. The population also opposed collectivization vehemently, because everyone by then knew about the famine of 1946 and 1947 in Moldavia and southern Ukraine that had been brought about both by a drought and inhuman collectivization methods. The partisans also knew that collectivization would make acquisition of provisions much harder. An independent villager could always find a little extra, but a villager totally dependent on the collective for his share of food would receive so little that nothing could be spared for an outsider.

I was still in Hranky when the collectivization arrived there. Often, the organizers would stop at the house where I was living and demand food and drink at all hours of the night. An entry divided the house into two rooms, a large one and a small one where the baby and I lived. Often the baby cried and I worried, as did the family, that the baby's crying would attract the attention of the guests, and they would come into the small room and ask who I was. The family let me know that it would be better if I left. I had been thinking since the baby's birth about what to do and decided that I would give the child to my parents while I searched for a family to take the baby in.

My father was waiting for me in Lviv. He asked me about the child, what I had named the boy—Taras—and what I planned to do. I burst into tears and poured out what had happened and the difficulties I had had finding lodgings. Although I was twenty-three, I wanted to tell my father my problems as I did when I was a child. After hearing me out, my father said, "Mother and I had been thinking. I think you should give the child to us."

I was immensely grateful to them. I knew that my mother would take better care of the baby than I would; I also knew that this arrangement was temporary. The probability that my parents would be exiled to Siberia was very real, and I did not want the baby to be caught in the deportation. They would face grave hardships during the exile, and a small child would only compound them. My father and I agreed that I would bring the child to Lviv at the beginning of December.

On the appointed day it snowed and was very cold. The ground, not yet frozen, had turned to mud. I made my way from the train to the trolley depot but knew that I would never be able to climb on with the child and my packages. As I was debating what to do, Stefa appeared at my side. She had foreseen my difficulties and had come down to meet me. With her help we climbed aboard the trolley. We spent the night with Nastia, where I usually stopped when in Lviv. In the morning, Lesia arrived and I gave little Taras to my sisters.

I returned to Hranky, where I stayed for two more weeks. Although the family was less nervous now that the baby was gone, nonetheless neighbors were increasingly interested in me and were curious to know who I was. Then someone began gossiping that I was a partisan, and I knew that the rumor would eventually reach the authorities, who would come to investigate. Thus, I decided to go to Orlan's family, who lived in a small village called Olesyn deep in the countryside. I knew that Orlan's mother, who was a widow, had died when she was exiled during the first Soviet occupation. I also knew that Orlan had a sister, who was married and lived in the village. However, I did not know her surname. It hadn't been important while living in the forest to know the surnames of Orlan's relatives. Perhaps he had mentioned it, and I had simply forgotten. I was sure of his sister's first name, though, since it was unusual. It was Pol'ka. I arrived in Olesyn after dark, stopped at a house and asked directions, and was told to go to a house at the edge of the village.

Pol'ka was not at home, but her three children were. I could see from the furnishings and from the clothes the children wore that Pol'ka was very poor. The youngest child, a boy called Myron, was barefoot, while his older brother had on a torn pair of shoes. When Pol'ka returned, I told her who I was and she, without asking any detailed questions, hugged and kissed me. But this was her nature—she was open, gullible, and kind. To make a living, she ran a still and made *horilka* from the grain that others would bring to her. She, of course, was putting herself and the children at grave risk, since operating a still was illegal. But she had no other way of earning a living. Her husband was arrested during the summer, although he had advanced tuberculosis. He had written once from prison, but that was two months ago and she had not heard from him again.

When Pol'ka made *horilka*, her pay was a liter of the whiskey. She sold this at the local market and used the proceeds to feed the children. The local authorities knew about Pol'ka's enterprise, and whenever they came to Olesyn they stopped at Pol'ka's for a sample, which cut into the small profit she made.

I stayed with Pol'ka until early January. I taught little Myron the alphabet and was amazed at how quickly he learned. Although he was of school age, he did not go to school because he had no shoes.

Word spread quickly through the tiny village that the wife of their local hero Vasyl Halasa was staying with his sister. Since the village was so deep in the countryside and was small, it had not yet been collectivized and was not often visited by the Soviet authorities. But they did come while I was there for a load of timber. Two officials came to Pol'ka's house, probably to get a "sample." When they saw me, they asked for my documents, which I showed them. I told them that I was a seamstress and had come to Olesyn to earn money. I don't think they believed me at all, and they took me to the village administration. As we walked down the main road, villagers came out of their homes and watched in silence as I passed. At the village administration, the agent in charge examined my papers and released me. This was one of the times that fate was kind to me.

But the brush with authorities made it clear that I could not stay even here. I moved to a neighboring village called Helenka, where one of Orlan's cousins arranged a room for me. The people of Helenka were wonderful, honest people, and I remember my stay there as one of the best.

9. Betrayal

My parents and I had arranged to meet again in Nastia's apartment in Lviv on January 20 so that I could get a report on the baby and news of Orlan in the event a letter had arrived in the interim. At the apartment, a disturbing surprise in the form of a letter from Zoya was waiting for me. Zoya knew about my friendship with Nastia, since both of us had stayed with her back in 1945. In the letter, which I opened at once, Zoya wrote that she was in Lviv and wanted to meet with me. She also said that it was my duty to help her and underlined the phrase.

The letter puzzled me, although I already knew that Zoya was trying to get in touch with me. The last time I was in Lviv, Nastia had told me that a young girl, who had said she was the sister of a dear friend of mine, had come to the apartment. The girl had asked Nastia when I would be in Lviv again so she could make contact. When Nastia described the strange girl, I knew immediately that she was Zoya's younger sister.

What troubled me was the girl's assertion that her sister had been in touch with her. As far as I knew, Zoya was still in prison in Poland following her arrest in Yelena Gura, and I wondered how she could have contacted her sister in Lviv. Thus, the girl's visit to Nastia's apartment worried me a little, but not enough for me to forsake news of the baby and Orlan.

Now, as I read Zoya's letter, I sensed that something was not right. Had she been broken by the MVD (Stalin's post–World War II version of the NKVD), and was she cooperating with the security authorities? I theorized that they may have brought her to Lviv, hoping that through me she would again become involved with the underground. I decided that I would ignore the letter. I also realized that Nastia's apartment was probably under surveillance, but I nonetheless decided to spend the night there and meet with my family the next day, as we had agreed.

My sister Lesia arrived with the news that the baby was doing well under mother's care. She also brought a letter from Orlan. I immediately hid the return address in the lining of my jacket since it was my only thread to my husband. After reading the letter, I stuffed it in my pocket since it spoke about ordinary matters. Toward evening, Lesia and I said good-bye to Nastia and got ready to leave. We had our coats on when there was a loud knock on the door, and Zoya stood on the threshold. My first reaction was that of fear, but then I chided myself. This was Zoya, my true friend with whom I had studied for the gymnasium diploma and who had joined the underground with me. She was the friend who had nursed me back to health and who had shared many hardships with me. No one knew me as well as she did; with no one had I shared so many of my most intimate thoughts.

I smiled and hugged her in greeting, then examined her face more closely. It was drawn, and her eyes were troubled. She had also lost a great deal of weight. She suggested that we go for a walk to talk; therefore, the three of us left together. On the threshold I turned around and told Nastia I would be back in a little while. Outside, I said good-bye to Lesia who was catching the trolley to the train station, while Zoya and I went for our walk.

I tried not to show that I was worried and on my guard. I speculated that Nastia knew Zoya and must have somehow told her when I would be in Lviv. The night was cold, and I was soon shivering, since I was wearing a light jacket and a skirt, while Zoya had on a warm winter coat and a large woolen kerchief. She saw that I was cold and offered me her kerchief. I said no, adding that my scarf was adequate, but she insisted. She stopped and took my scarf off and draped her kerchief over my head, knotting the ends under my chin. For a moment it was as it used to be—she and I sharing and exchanging what we had.

As we resumed our walk, Zoya told me an incredible story. She said that following her arrest in Yelena Gura, she was taken to Warsaw and jailed. She said that an Englishman, whom she had met at the embassy while distributing underground materials, somehow obtained her release. He then arranged for her to cross the border and gave her a contact that would furnish her with legal papers. Her story was too fantastic to be believed. I said I was very cold and tried to turn back to Nastia's apartment, but Zoya would not let go of me. She kept insisting that she had more to tell me and held on to my elbow.

Suddenly, a tall man materialized behind us. He pushed us apart while grabbing us under the arms. In the next moment, two more men in dark overcoats appeared on either side of us and also grabbed us under the arms. I tried to yank free, but they held on firmly.

"Take it easy," one said in Russian. "You're coming with us." Then we were pushed into a car that had pulled up alongside us.

Throughout my walk with Zoya I had expected something to happen, but we were accosted so quickly that I did not have time to react. I could not make myself believe what was happening. I was under arrest, but I could not comprehend this calamity. I was thinking, "At any moment now, I'll wake up. Zoya couldn't be doing this to me. This is a nightmare. Zoya couldn't betray me and our friendship."

Then, suddenly, I remembered that I was carrying Orlan's address and letter. This thought brought me back to reality with a jolt. The MVD will find the drop and will set a trap. When Orlan comes, they'll kill him. There is nothing I can do.

We were driven to the regional headquarters of the MVD. The gate swung open heavily, and the car drove into the prison yard. Behind us, the gate closed slowly and with finality. As it clanked shut, I felt it was closing on my life. Only someone who has been arrested by Soviet security authorities can comprehend the terrible terminality of a gate—or a door—closing behind them.

We were led inside and then up three flights of stairs to the third floor. When we halted in a brightly-lit corridor, I abruptly turned to face Zoya. I stared at her and I wanted to ask, "How will you sleep tonight?" but I found no words. We stood staring at each other for a long moment. She was still wearing my scarf. Her eyes were bulging and seemed to be asking for forgiveness. One of the men noticed our silent exchange and stepped between us so that I could no longer see Zoya. Then he led her away. Someone else told me to take off my jacket, which was searched carefully and the letter from Orlan removed. I decided they were searching me to ascertain that I did not carry a revolver. Once they were satisfied that I was unarmed, I was ushered into a room where two matrons made me undress completely. They also told me to unplait my long hair, and they combed through it in the event I carried a message hidden in my braids. Next, they checked every seam of my clothing and, if one appeared unduly thick, they ripped it open. Thus, they found Orlan's address.

After the search, I was permitted to get dressed, then I was led into a large, brightly-lit office. Soon two investigating magistrates entered and asked me who I was. I gave them the information on my papers, saying I was a repatriate from the *Zakerzon krai*. They listened without paying much attention. Then one of them stood up, left the office, and returned shortly with several photographs. One was a group photo of our people from the *Zakerzon krai*. In the group I saw Orlan and myself.

"Why play cat and mouse with us?" the magistrate asked. "We know you're Marichka, Orlan's wife." I realized that to continue denying who I was, was absurd. I had been betrayed by my best friend who knew me and my activities as well as I did.

They asked me where Orlan was hiding. "I don't know," I said truthfully.

That was the last thing I said that night. I did not answer any other questions. They had Orlan's letter and knew that we were not living together. It was ironic that the letter both condemned and exonerated me. I truly did not know where Orlan was.

By then it was very late, and the two investigators realized that they would get nothing further from me that night. They pushed some chairs together and told me to lie down and rest. They then departed, leaving me in the brightly-lit office with two guards standing at the door.

I lay down and closed my eyes but didn't sleep a moment all that night. My head was filled with black thoughts. What will happen to Orlan and those with him, now that the MVD knew where the drop was? Orlan will never learn what had happened to me. He will never know how he was betrayed. I will never see him or my second son again. I have lost two children. Little Taras will be deported to Siberia with my family, or the authorities will take him away and place him in an orphanage. Such thoughts swirled through my mind until daybreak.

A man came to the office in the morning, gave me a sheaf of blank papers, and told me to write my autobiography. I took the papers and the pencil and began to sketch. He watched me and every so often reminded me to write, but I ignored him. I had realized by then that he was not there to question me but to change the guards and keep watch. During the day, several men came and looked me over as if I were some exotic specimen. In the evening, the two investigating magistrates returned and questioned me until dawn. This went on for several days. I was not only interrogated, but they also tried to "reeducate" me. Although they were not pleasant, they did not hurt me. I began to understand what they were up to. They wanted to find a way to use me to get to Orlan. We both knew that they had the letter and the return address and could set a trap. But having this information did not guarantee that they would catch their quarry. He would most likely not come by himself but would send someone else to the drop. Partisans traveled in pairs or sometimes went as a threesome. One would stay behind and keep watch while the other two approached the house. If they were caught, the third one could escape and inform Orlan that the drop had been compromised. Thus, the MVD would again be at a dead end.

One night around midnight I was taken before the head of the Lviv MVD, who had the rank of a general. He did not question me, only told me to think very carefully about my situation and the consequences of my actions. I think he wanted to see me and get a feel for who I was. I had by now realized that the fact that I had recently given birth was working in my favor. My interrogators were not interested in what I had done in the *Zakerzon krai* because they considered that chapter of the resistance crushed and concluded. They were interested in the Ukrainian underground. I could legitimately claim I knew very little since I had spent the winter deep in the Carpathian mountains and had left the underground in the spring when I realized I was pregnant. Thus, they had no witnesses who could say that I had engaged in partisan activities in Ukraine. I steadfastly and logically maintained that my documents had enabled me to return to civilian life. Since there were so many repatriates in Western Ukraine, my explanation that I had been living simply like other repatriates seemed plausible, especially since it was based on fact. I only made sure I mentioned nothing about the underground as I described my life since the winter. After writing their protocol, the investigating magistrates would spend some time trying to "open my eyes" to reality. I should realize, they said, that the Soviet Union was mighty and would soon destroy puny Ukrainian nationalists. I should think about my husband, my son, and my family and conduct myself in such a way that I would be in position to help all of them when the time came.

During one of these discussions, one of the magistrates opened a briefcase and took out a photograph, which he passed to me. "Do you recognize him?" he asked. I glanced at the photograph and my heart broke. It was a photograph of little Zenon. I stared at the picture, committing to memory every feature of his little face, his expression, and his clothing. He was dressed in a winter suit, so the photograph had to be recent.

"He's being well taken care of," the man said.

"Will I get him back if my life returns to normal?" I asked.

"Well, that's a difficult matter. He was taken in by someone who holds a high office in the government, someone who was childless. We're only showing you this photograph to assure you that he's well and being well taken care of."

He was not telling me anything new. We had learned that the head of the Polish security in Krakow had adopted little Zenon. As I listened, my heart broke at the thought that a man whose mission was to exterminate the child's parents was raising my son. The boy would grow up never knowing who his parents were and how and for what they had died. The magistrate, of course, did not tell me the name of the man who had adopted little Zenon.

"You have a second child," they reminded me. "You could raise him, but only if you exculpate yourself in the eyes of the government and repent your past actions."

I was thinking furiously. They and I agreed on one point. It was important for us to reach some sort of resolution. They wanted to eradicate what was left of the underground, and I wanted to do everything in my power to protect Orlan from capture. I knew that if I did not go along with their plans, they would attempt to achieve their goal without me.

"Of course I would like to lead a normal life," I replied. "Who wouldn't?" Then after a pause, I added, "You see from the letter you found on me that I was with the baby and not with my husband. Eventually those in the underground will realize that I have disappeared, and they will cut what tentative contact I have now. At that point, I won't be able to help you in any way."

"We've considered that," came the reply. "We won't hold you too long if we have assurances that you are sincere and are willing to help us."

After this conversation, I was again brought before the MVD general. "From the letter I can see that Orlan loves you very much," he said. "Do you influence his decisions?"

"Depends on the circumstances," I said, "but, in general, I think I do."

He then took out a long thin piece of paper that had been coiled tightly. I immediately recognized the missive as a "shtafeta," an underground letter. He unrolled the paper and showed it to me. "Do you recognize the handwriting?"

I shook my head but I knew exactly who had written the letter. It was from Poltava.

"No, I don't know who wrote it."

The general did not insist. Instead he unrolled the letter to the end and began to read. "This is a letter from Poltava to Orlan," he informed me. "Poltava's courier fell into our hands. There's an interesting sentence here that I think you might like to hear," he added. "At the end, Poltava says, 'Greetings to Marichka.'"

I said nothing.

"Well, then," he continued. "I'm transmitting greeting to you from Poltava."

Although his words rang with irony, he did not realize how the message had renewed my resolve. That greeting from Poltava was like a beacon. I knew the road I had to follow. No matter how the MVD threatened my newborn son, my family, and me, I would never let them destroy the people I cared about. I would not participate in any way in the Soviet government's destruction of what I believed in.

After a few more days, the investigating magistrates completed their work, and I was taken again before the MVD general. He told me that I would be let go if I signed a letter pledging my cooperation and "repent before the authorities." He pushed the letter across the desk toward me and gave me a pen.

"Well, then," the general said, and began to outline MVD's plans. My job was to return to Orlan and convince him to surrender. The general said something like this: "Influence him as only a wife can when she sets her mind to do so. You have a deadline. March 1. We will expect you before that date with Orlan's answer. Since you have a new child, your return to Lviv will not be suspicious. If he agrees, we will develop a plan on how to keep in touch with him. If you carry out your assignment, upon your return you will be given a good apartment and provided a fine livelihood. If Orlan doesn't agree, then you'll probably stay with him, and I expect you'll survive for another year or two, but then we will find you and destroy you. Your child will be left an orphan, and your family will suffer greatly because of you. You must understand that all of you are going to die, and I am giving you the chance to escape that fate."

"So," he concluded, "are you willing to take this assignment?"

"I will do everything in my power, but the decision will be his," I said.

"I know we are taking a risk," he said, "but we'll gain little by imprisoning you. On the other hand, your assignment may net us something. In the worst possible scenario, you two will live a little longer."

This conversation, as all others, took place in the middle of the night. Shortly after dawn, one of the investigating magistrates came for me. He was dressed in civilian clothes (not in the uniform he wore when he interrogated me) and led me out the building, through the prison yard, and out through the gate. The street was deserted; not a soul was visible. He then turned on his heels and started walking in the opposite direction. For a moment, I stood rooted to the sidewalk. I was disoriented. Was I really free? Could I really walk away from here? Once again I looked around, then crossed myself. "Thank you, Lord, for leading me past that gate," I prayed.

◆ ◆ ◆ ◆ ◆

I had been given a month in which to find Orlan. This was not an easy assignment. The partisans went deep into the countryside during the winter and did not emerge until snow began melting. But before I could start searching for Orlan, I had to find a home for little Taras. I knew without even the slightest doubt that neither Orlan nor I would cooperate with the authorities. This meant that after the deadline passed in March, the authorities would take revenge on my family by exiling everyone to Siberia.

When I left with Zoya, I had assured Nastia I would be back to get my things. I had not returned. I would learn that the next morning she took the train to Zadviria to tell my parents I had disappeared. Of course, at home everyone became extremely worried. My mother had sensed something was wrong when Lesia returned and told her about Zoya's unexpected appearance. She was convinced I had been arrested and was about to send my father to Lviv to find out what had happened to me. I learned all of this when I returned to Nastia's apartment that morning to get my belongings.

Since every day was precious, I left Lviv that same morning for Hranky, where I packed my things. From there, I took the train to Zadviria and arrived home in the middle of the night. I was last home five years before. I had also come at night and had crept quietly to the house in order not to wake the dogs. My heart was beating loudly as I approached the house and gently tapped on the windowpane.

Immediately someone moved inside and I saw my father's worried face.

"It's me," I whispered.

"Oh, my God," I heard him whisper and in the next moment the door opened and I was inside. I immediately glanced around and found the crib where little Taras slept. I ran to him and knelt by the crib. "Oh my darling," I whispered. "A day ago, I thought I would never see you again."

Then I greeted my parents, my sisters, and my brothers. I told them what had happened to me.

After the week of sleepless nights, I was exhausted and decided to stay at home for a day. My plan was to take Taras to Orlan's cousin, Nastia Martynovska, whom I had met a few months earlier. Nastia lived in the village of Olesyn. She had only a ten-year-old son, and I was hoping she would agree to take in and raise Taras. The day I spent at home was very difficult. I had to hide so that none of the neighbors would see me. And I read the growing fear in the eyes of my family. My parents and my siblings were asking themselves silently, "What will happen to us now?"

At one point my father began, "If only they would keep us together, then maybe..."

In the evening, I packed my belongings and those of the baby. Stefa was going to come with me to help. As I stood at the door, I knew this was the last time I would see any of my family. I had something very important to tell them, to ask them. I said, "How can I say good-bye and find the words to help you face what lies ahead? Whatever I say won't change anything. I only beg you, don't curse me. I did what my heart and my conscience told me to do. I joined the resistance because I felt it was my duty to do so. And where you have resistance, you will have casualties. Our family cannot escape."

"We're not the first," my father said, while my poor mother looked at my small brothers, at Taras's empty crib, and sighed heavily.

From Zadviria, Stefa and I took the train to Zolochiv, where we were to transfer to the train for Ternopil. The train was already in the station, and we tried to board it since it was heated while the station waiting room was not. A night watchman woke up and made us leave the train. I tried to reason with him by saying that the baby was cold, but he yelled in Russian, "I don't give a damn."

I ground my teeth in impotent anger against a country and a regime whose people had lost the last semblance of kindness and understanding. In the morning, we boarded the train, made one more transfer in Ternopil, and reached our destination shortly after noon. The milk we carried for the baby had long ago become cold and he was hungry, wet, and crying. I had to feed him and change him. Soon after leaving the train station at Kozova, I stopped at a house and asked the woman who opened the door whether my sister and the baby could warm themselves while I went to the bazaar to find the sled that would take us to Olesyn. The woman was frightened because times were uncertain and she had no idea who we were, but she was too kindhearted to turn us out into the cold. I left Stefa and little Taras and went to the bazaar. Of course, no one was waiting for us, and I did not meet anyone I knew. So I started walking toward Olesyn. The day was bitterly cold and in the late afternoon it started snowing. The wind blew in my face and through my clothing and tried to topple me. But I stumbled on as if endowed by superhuman strength. Tears froze on my lashes. The tears were not only brought on by the biting wind. These were tears I shed because of the great injustice done to me and others like me. My heart was breaking. In this great land among so many people I could not raise my own child or find a place to hide him from the enemy.

It was dusk by the time I reached Nastia's house. When I entered, she and her husband were dumbfounded by my appearance. I think they realized from my condition that a great misfortune had brought me to them. I knew I had to go back immediately and get Stefa and the baby, so I told them at once why I had come to them. "My parents are going to be deported to Siberia. I need to find a place for the baby," I said. "Please take him in."

After a moment, Nastia's husband said, "We won't desert the child. We raised one boy. We will raise another one."

He went out to get the sled ready while Nastia began to dress for the journey back into town. I was terribly frightened that the people where I had left Stefa and the baby would turn them out or report them to the police. But I found Stefa and the baby still at the house. I picked up the baby, wrapped him in a warm blanket that Nastia had given me, and took him outside to the waiting sled. I could not hold back my tears any more, and they rolled down my cheeks as I kissed his little face and whispered, "What fate awaits you, my darling?" I kissed him again and pressed him to my breast, then placed the baby in Nastia's arms.

For a moment I held her hand in mine and said, "Nastia, when his father and I are dead, please tell him about us when he is old enough."

"Don't say such things," she answered. "A time will come when you'll take him back and raise him."

But we both knew that it would not be so.

Stefa and I stood in the road and watched the sled disappear into the night. I felt drained of all strength and will power. I was very glad that Stefa was with me. We made our way back to the train station and traveled together back to Krasne. Here we parted forever. For helping me, Stefa would spend ten years in a concentration camp in Magadan.

My next assignment was to find Orlan.

10. Return to the Underground

I took the train north to Rivne in Volyn, where I was able to get a ride to Tuchyn with several other people in the back of a flatbed truck. In Tuchyn, I asked directions to the village of Pustomyty, which had been given in the address of Orlan's letter, and set out immediately. I walked for hours through barren, snow-covered fields without once coming to a village. In the distance, I saw solitary homesteads and on the horizon, a dark streak which was the beginning of the forests of Polisia. Partisans lived in those forests, I thought, and the landscape and the distant forest acquired a secretive aura. If my directions were correct, I should have reached the village by now, but there was nothing in the vicinity except a few sod houses and the remains of several burned-down houses. As I was debating what to do, a woman who must have been walking behind me came up, and when I asked her directions to Pustomyty, she told me this was it. She said that the Germans had burned the village down during one of their engagements with the UPA and, instead of rebuilding houses during the war, the inhabitants dug sod shelters in which they continued to live. I approached one of these dwellings and inquired for the man whose name had been given in the address. The people in the house replied in some surprise that this was where the man lived, but under further questioning categorically denied any knowledge or contact with any partisans. Perhaps they were telling the truth. Someone else in the village may have given the man's name, and had a letter arrived, only then would he have revealed himself to claim it. I begged them to let me stay a few days and tell their neighbors about me so that if anyone was in contact with partisans, they would learn about my arrival.

On the third night, I was awakened by someone bending over me. I opened my eyes and saw a man wearing a Red Army uniform smiling down at me. I could feel the cold that he had brought with him into the house.

"Don't you know who I am?" the man asked as I sat up, frightened.

It was only then that I recognized Ptakh.

When I was dressed, Ptakh gave me a leather holster with a revolver that I buckled around my waist. He told me Orlan was well and was waiting for me. But I couldn't hold back asking Ptakh what he thought about my returning to the underground in the middle of the winter.

"Ptakh, aren't you surprised to see me now?" I asked, and before he could answer I poured out the news about Zoya's betrayal, my interrogation, and the deal I made with the MVD general. "Be careful," I concluded. "Orlan's letter fell into their hands and they have this address. That's why I hurried us out of the house. It's possible that they have set a trap."

Ptakh looked around carefully, then adjusted his stance slightly and fingered his rifle in readiness.

"What did you do with the baby?" he asked.

"Took him deep into the countryside to Orlan's village and placed him with Orlan's cousin," I said, adding, "Aren't you worried about standing with me like this? You understand the MVD didn't let me go until I signed a confession."

"What are you saying?" Ptakh burst out. "You did what you had to do. I would trust you even if you had signed ten confessions."

After a moment, he continued, "You picked the least of the evils. If you hadn't obtained your release and come to warn us, the MVD would have probably set a trap, if not now, then in the spring."

We were waiting for a horse-drawn sled that had brought Ptakh and two other partisans to the village where they were dropping off a courier. When the sled returned, I put on a thick fur coat that the courier had worn and had left behind, and we set out across the snow-covered fields as if in a film. The only sound in the silent, moonlit night was the crunch of snow under the hooves of the horses. An hour or so later we arrived at a homestead, where we spent the day in a bunker Ptakh shared with three other men. The next evening Ptakh took me to Orlan's bunker in a nearby village.

As soon as I walked in, Orlan, after glancing at me, asked, "You were arrested?"

"Yes," I said.

Only then did we greet each other. I told him what had happened. A little later he called in Ptakh, and we spent some time discussing the new situation and what reaction we should expect from the MVD when I ignored their March 1 deadline. There was no question that MVD troops would descend on this backwater and would search the villages and homestead thoroughly for bunkers. It was agreed that Ptakh and the men with whom he was living should move into the forest before the March 1 deadline that the MVD general had given me.

When everyone went to bed that night, I sat up with Orlan and told him all that happened to me and to our child. We both wept. He felt guilty that he had not helped me when I had needed him most, blaming himself partially for my arrest because his long silence had made me return repeatedly to Lviv until I was caught. I assured him that I did not reproach him; I knew what being in the resistance entailed and how difficult life was in hiding. Yet, the tragedy brought about by the collision of the two worlds I inhabited—the world of a mother and the world of the partisan—broke my heart.

Orlan was surprised by my naïveté concerning Zoya and made me write a detailed report which he later sent to headquarters to Taras Chuprynka with the first spring mail. He also wrote to Poltava about what had happened and about Poltava's intercepted letter.

We soon learned that the tactics the MVD had used in my case were being implemented with other women who were married to partisans but who lived semi-legally "above ground." Often they were arrested and released after an interrogation if they promised they would try to convince their husbands to surrender. In cases where the women were not arrested, the authorities kept a close surveillance on them, knowing that a husband would not leave his wife destitute. This happened, for instance, with Fedir, the Lviv UPA leader. By watching his wife constantly, the MVD found the thread that led their operatives to Fedir, whom they killed.

I spent the next few weeks with Orlan and his three companions, two local underground leaders and Chmelyk, who had replaced Ptakh as Orlan's bodyguard. Orlan had decided that Ptakh would live that winter with three local partisans in order to get to know them better, also to conduct with them the necessary ideological training that was required of potential leaders.

Ptakh visited us twice as March approached, and each time Orlan and I reminded him to leave his bunker. He said he was going to, but the weather had turned bad and forced him to postpone the changeover to the forest bunker. Although we worried, we could not blame him too much. A great deal of snow had fallen, and it was impossible to move under such conditions. The bunker that Ptakh and his two companions were to use temporarily was not stocked with food, and to deliver provisions to the forest without leaving tracks was not possible at this time of the year.

I also worried about our bunker since I knew that the MVD general would do his utmost to find us when he discovered I would not keep the bargain I had struck with him. I kept proposing our return to the forest despite the snow. I was afraid we would be found during one of the thorough searches of the area. Ptakh and Orlan thought differently. A well-masked hideout, they argued, was difficult to find even in a meticulous search. On the other hand, tracks in the snow were hard to mask and easy to see and follow. Besides, Orlan would add during one of these arguments, escape through deep snow would be very difficult, if not impossible. Thus, Ptakh decided to wait a little longer, until the spring thaw, and so did we.

As expected, new searches began in the second half of March. These searches were conducted by special troops of the MVD. They searched every house and every homestead, wrecking the earthen stoves, ripping out floorboards, and demolishing root cellars in their furious search for us. They mostly searched around houses or outbuildings, leaving the orchards and the yards for only cursory inspection.

We learned about the results of each search in the evenings from the people who were hiding us. It became increasingly obvious that we were courting grave danger, but because of the heavy snow, we had nowhere to go. Snow kept falling and falling, and we again postponed our relocation.

One morning, we heard the pre-arranged signal that meant that a MVD platoon was approaching the homestead. Soon we heard the barking of an unfamiliar dog. The barking was followed by voices cursing in Russian. We immediately stuffed rags into the three air intake holes so that the dog would not sniff us out. From the noise and the thumping, we realized that the search was focused on the house and the out buildings, the barn yard, and the root cellar. Eventually, we heard steps above us and someone actually stepped on the masked entrance to our bunker. We froze, but after a moment he kept walking on. The search continued for more than an hour. During this time, we sat without talking, barely breathing, on the threshold between death and life. But that day had not been destined to be our last. When the MVD left, I again urged Orlan to move as soon as possible. I pointed out that Ptakh had finally left his bunker.

Sunday, March 23, 1949, sticks in my mind. It was a terrible Sunday. That Sunday night the widow at whose house we had our hideout came to the bunker and said to us in a quavering voice, "Dear Lord, what a tragedy. In Mativci, in a yard, the MVD found a bunker. Four partisans killed themselves when the MVD tossed in a gas bomb. Before they died they sang a UPA song. The enemy wasn't sure they were dead, so they forced the man who owned the house to crawl down in there. Only then did the MVD go in and pull the bodies out. They took the corpses to town."

As we listened, thunderstruck, she added, "Those were the boys who came to see you. Oh, dear, dear, what a shame."

And so we learned that Ptakh, our dear friend, Orlan's faithful bodyguard, was dead.

We discovered later how he was betrayed. We supposed that someone had known Ptakh was coming back for a meeting and informed the MVD. But the answer turned out to be much simpler. The woman who bought food for the men betrayed the hideout. Once, during the winter, they had brought her to the bunker but had tied her eyes with a kerchief so she would not know at whose house the bunker was. While in the bunker, she heard the dog bark and recognized where she was. When the MVD arrested her, she caved in under questioning and told the MVD about the barking dog. Unfortunately, the bunker was raided when Ptakh was again using it temporarily.

We knew that once Ptakh's corpse was identified, the MVD would know that Orlan was nearby. Within days of Ptakh's death, new searches began. The hunting was so intense and thorough that we had no choice but to leave. We decided to move into the forest since snow was melting and it was possible to mask our tracks. We left before dawn, carefully stepping from one piece of bare earth to another in order not to leave a trail and spent the day in an empty bunker we knew about, then continued on into the depths of the forests.

We were not the only ones hiding in the densely forested area. Other groups had left their winter bunkers to escape the furious searches by the MVD. As we waited for spring and warm weather to arrive, we began to reestablish contacts with other partisan groups. Orlan sent his report about my arrest and how I managed to free myself. In due course, instructions came back that stated the conditions of my remaining in the underground: I could not venture among civilians or contact anyone.

Woodcut, August 5, 1949, by UPA artist Nil Khasevych, who illustrated the magazines and newsletters that Orlan published in the 1940s and 1950s. The lettering reads, "For a Ukrainian independent sovereign nation."

As letters and orders were exchanged throughout spring, Orlan continued to work on two publications which he edited during our stay in Volyn from 1948 to 1953. One was called the *Young Revolutionary*, to educate the teenage reader about the true history of Ukraine, as well as about the nationalist resistance, and contained short memoirs by partisans. The other magazine was *For the Freedom of the Nation*, a more serious and literary journal in which the ideological basis for resisting the Soviet regime was analyzed and discussed. This magazine also contained partisan poetry and memoirs of higher literary quality.

News began to arrive with couriers in mid–April. One of the couriers came from Ulian (Anatoliy Maevsky), who commanded the southern Rivne district resistance and had switched allegiances from Daleky to Smok. In his letter, Ulian wrote that Smok, who had become Orlan's deputy in Volyn, had been killed in February. Smok's death necessitated a reorganization of the Volyn leadership, and Orlan had to meet and consult with Ulian and the Volyn district leaders before naming Smok's successor. Thus, Orlan and I set out, escorted by guides that changed several times until we reached Ulian's bunker. We also met with Dubovy, who had been the commander of UPA units in Volyn. When I say "we," I sometimes mean only Orlan, since I did not meet all the district leaders. For reasons of security, we would never go directly to a leader's hideout. We would stop at a hideout that was used for guides and couriers, and Orlan would send a message that he had arrived with Marichka. If the leader invited both of us, we would proceed together to the meeting, but if the leader said he would meet with Orlan and did not mention me, I would stay behind and wait in the guides' hideout until the conference was finished.

I remember that summer as one during which we spent the nights marching from bunker to bunker, hideout to hideout, and the days underground in hiding. On the few occasions that I did go above ground during the day, the beauty of the Volyn countryside charmed me. These occasions above ground were few, because the MVD was continuing its activities in the area and was constantly raiding outlying homesteads which partisans tended to visit to get information and supplies. The enemy also set traps at known trails and river crossings.

During one of our marches we were almost caught in one of these MVD ambushes. Since we knew the route was dangerous, five partisans, three in the lead and two bringing up the rear, accompanied us. As we neared the ford, the three men in the lead went ahead while Orlan and I waited a short distance behind.

Without warning someone shouted in Russian, "Who goes there?" and the sky was lit up with flares until it seemed that day had suddenly dawned. The shout was followed by a burst of machine gun fire, which the three men ahead of us returned to draw the enemy's attention to themselves and away from us. We knew they were doing this in order to give us an opportunity to retreat to safety, but we could hardly move since the gunfire around us was so intense.

This was the first time I had fallen into a trap, and I could not move from fright. I thought every bullet was directed at me. Every time I tried to get up, a new volley made me fall to the ground again. To make matters worse, I was wearing a pair of army boots that were much too large for me and, as I tried to follow the others to safety, I kept stumbling and falling. When the flares again lit up the night and we fell to the ground to avoid detection, I shook my feet and the boots simply slid off. The next time we got up to run, I ran barefoot and made some headway.

Orlan decided it would be foolhardy to try to make the crossing, so we retreated to the bunker where we had spent the previous day. On the following night, we made our way to the hideout we had agreed upon as rendezvous point in the event we became separated or something went amiss, as it had. The hideout belonged to Nazar, who had been a platoon leader in the UPA and had been in charge of the men who had accompanied us on the attempted crossing.

Two days passed before Nazar and one of the other partisans came to meet us. Nazar had a flesh wound in his upper arm where the bullet had gone through without touching the bone. His companion was unhurt, but the third partisan had suffered a more serious wound, and they had taken him to a nurse who helped partisans before making their way to us. Since every woman in the resistance was required to take a first aid course, I had been trained to dress wounds and immediately ascertained that Nazar's wound had become infected. Using the first aid kit in the hideout, I began cleaning the wound. I had to pass a disinfectant through the "tunnel" created by the bullet, and as I worked I saw the pain in Nazar's face and almost fainted myself. Orlan had to finish the job. But in the following days, I saw that the cleaning of the wound had been successful, and the wound began to heal. During this time I got to know Nazar better and liked him very much. He was quiet and reserved and could be depended on to carry out the orders given him. He had several duties in the underground and executed each well. He acted as the principal contact point between the leaders, supplied the leaders with food, and even made monetary collections among the population for the underground. He was markedly successful in the latter effort since he was good looking and knew how to make people like and trust him.

Our stay with Nazar following our encounter with the MVD had one positive end result. One day, a courier brought a letter that was addressed to the "Leadership of the Volyn Resistance." It was written by Zinko, a unit leader loyal to Daleky. At the outset Zinko stated that he was writing on behalf of all unit leaders who recognized Daleky's command. He said he and the others had become aware of the breach between Daleky and the leadership headed by Taras Chuprynka. Since he, Zinko, and the others respected Daleky, they had felt they could not change allegiances. However, now that Daleky was dead or arrested, Zinko and the other unit leaders wanted to reestablish contact with the UPA-OUN leadership and become subordinate to it.

We had not heard about Daleky's fate before or about his men's knowledge of the rift. Orlan immediately replied to the letter, in which he introduced himself and explained at some length why Taras Chuprynka had sent him to Volyn. Since we subsequently heard rumors that Daleky had been betrayed by someone in his ranks, Orlan decided that it would be best not to meet immediately with Zinko or the other unit leaders. Instead, he ordered that the Daleky partisans and the UPA-OUN units cooperate in the future but not intermingle. This was done in the event there were more MVD moles planted among Daleky's units who, if the units were merged, would be able to infiltrate the UPA-OUN resistance.

As we waited for further developments that summer, Orlan continued to work on the journals he was editing and on new propaganda materials that would be distributed in Volyn, with some sent by couriers to the eastern provinces.

We spent early fall in the area around Lutske, where economic conditions were significantly better and national awareness was more developed. Resistance members dressed and ate better here, since both food and clothing were more readily available. In the space of a month in the Lutske (Polish *Lutsk*) area, I met three, newly wed couples, where both the man and the woman were actively engaged in the underground, the women acting either as typists of brochures and journals or as couriers. I think these couples were convinced that they would not live to see a better day and decided that, despite the hardships of life in the resistance, they would spend together what time was allotted to them.

Woodcut, Nil Khasevych, December 31, 1949. The flag reads, "Freedom for Nations! Freedom for the individual!"

However difficult our lives were, we who were members of the resistance did not subscribe to the cult of death. To the contrary, we valued every moment of life. Although once cornered or wounded and about to be taken alive, we chose death by self destruction, such a decision was made only if there was absolutely no escape possible from a tragic situation.

Toward the end of September, Orlan left for several weeks of conferences with district leaders. In October, a guide took me to a hideout at a homestead in a rural area where I found Orlan hard at work on new propaganda materials.

It was a newly constructed hideout where Orlan was planning to spend the coming winter, but I did not like the hideout at all because of its entrance. The hideout adjoined the house and could be accessed through the floor of a small storage room that was part of the house. The floor of the storage room was part dirt while the other part was raised off the dirt with loose floorboards on which grain could be stored for the winter. The entrance to the bunker was beneath the floorboards. In the event an enemy search was feared, the floorboard could be nailed to the walls. This would not only make escape impossible in the event the air intakes in the yard were discovered, but also MVD was now routinely prying up floorboards and looking for hideout entrances under them.

The owner of the house was a widower by the surname of Korecky, whose wife was killed during the war. He was raising their three daughters alone. One of the girls, whose name was Olha, had a beautiful, clear soprano voice and would have likely made a career as a singer if she had lived in different circumstances. Orlan managed to acquire a short-wave radio for the hideout and a good supply of paper for our winter work. Obtaining paper on which to print the underground journals had become very difficult, since a paper purchase required a permission slip from local authorities. Korecky was well read, and everyone in the nearby village knew that he read newspapers. This enabled Orlan to purchase and receive a subscription to *Soviet Ukraine* without arousing any suspicions. During the ensuing winter months, we listened to news programs from Kyiv and Moscow and to Voice of America dispatches in Russian. We read newspapers and Russian journals and worked on publishing underground materials. What Orlan wrote, I copied on the typewriter that always traveled with us. I made a specific number of copies, usually twelve, depending on where the written work was to be sent.

Then one evening, while listening to a Western radio program, we heard that Voice of America would begin broadcasts in Ukrainian. We were overjoyed that we would hear our native language on the airwaves. On the appointed night, Korecky, our host, and two of his daughters came down to the bunker, while the third girl kept watch in the house. We were in a festive mood and listened breathlessly to every single word of the broadcast. The resonance of our language was like music to our ears, but we found nothing memorable in the program's content. We told each other that beginnings were always difficult and that the content would improve. Orlan used information gleaned from subsequent broadcasts to augment news in his publications, although the level of the broadcasts did not improve markedly. Many of the programs contained interviews with immigrants who had settled in America earlier in the century and who talked about the material gains they had made since then.

11. The Deaths
of Comrades

During the final years of the 1940s, the conditions under which the underground existed in Volyn became extremely difficult. Yet, the propaganda work that Orlan and others were producing began to pay off with the beginning of the second half of the twentieth century.

As gay Russian songs and promises of prosperity flowed from the radio with the arrival of the 1950 New Year, we made our own reckoning. The year just ended had seen enormous losses in the underground, mass arrests and deportations to Siberia of OUN sympathizers, and ever-increasing terror in the Ukrainian population. But we had made some impact. We had printed and distributed thousands of leaflets explaining our cause and our reasons for waging war against the enemy. These leaflets were carried for dispersal in the eastern provinces, scattered near the camps of Red Army recruits or handed out in front of schools in Western Ukraine. As we greeted 1950, we realized that this year would be even harder than those before, since the Soviet empire was mobilizing its resources to destroy us once and for all. We wished each other only one thing: strength of mind and soul to carry on the work. We would be gratified in the months ahead by an influx of recruits, primarily from students who learned about us from the leaflets and pamphlets we had distributed in front of schools. These young men replenished our ranks, and the Volyn underground kept on working for another year.

Several days after the New Year, one of the Korecky girls climbed down the ladder to bring us news. Her face was white and her lips were trembling.

"Earlier today a platoon of the MVD found a bunker in which

Gravure in celluloid, Nil Khasevych, 1948. The caption reads, "We have risen in defense of freedom."

three partisans were hiding," she said. We listened to the frightful story in mounting horror.

"The bunker was in the yard and had two exits, one in the barn and one outside. The enemy found the exit in the barn. As they were digging to get in, the men tried to escape through the other exit. Soldiers that had surrounded the house saw them and opened fire," she said, tears rolling down her cheeks. "The third man got away, but they chased him down later and killed him."

We learned more details over the next few days. Two of the partisans were shot dead as they tried to escape on foot. The third partisan, named Dorosh, caught a horse and made his escape. He was trying to get to the forest, but the MVD figured out where he was heading and gave chase in trucks. One of the trucks blocked the road and, when Dorosh saw the truck, he swerved into the fields but not before he was mortally wounded in the stomach. Holding on to the spilling entrails, he managed to get to a homestead where he fell from his horse which had also been wounded. He killed the horse to end its suffering; then, before taking his life, he turned to the woman who had run out into the yard and said, "This is the end," and shot himself in the temple.

As we mourned the three men, I kept remembering Dorosh, whom I had liked very much. He had been only in his twenties. His infectious grin had added to his dark, romantic good looks. How sad, I thought.

In the uneven struggle with the powerful enemy, losses of young, dedicated men like Dorosh became an increasingly frequent occurrence. Yet, it was not possible to become accustomed to death's visitations. Every death filled the soul with sadness and pain, not only mine but everyone else's. The quiet bunker became even more silent. We hardly spoke to each other.

We knew that the death of Dorosh and his two companions would carry serious consequences. The family who had hidden the three men was arrested, interrogated, and tortured. Someone in the family remembered under questioning that a woman had stayed in that bunker on one occasion—and described me. By now, the MVD knew in detail what Orlan and I looked like. If I was in the vicinity, then he was too, and they desperately wanted to get him.

We did not have long to wait. On January 18, a very worried Korecky came to tell us that several trucks filled with MVD troops had pulled into the village and that several cars had also arrived. The presence of automobiles meant that high-ranking officials would direct the search. The troops brought along a kitchen and several dogs. All this indicated that the search for us would be long and thorough.

The searches started at the other end of the strung-out homesteads. Each day, Korecky and the girls reported the enemy's progress. The searches were extraordinarily thoroughgoing. Earthen stoves were demolished in almost every house. All floorboards were ripped up. Every root cellar was dug up. What worried us most was the entrance to our hideout, which I failed to describe earlier. It was under floorboards, and the hideout had only one exit. Besides, the family was getting increasingly nervous about our presence. One of the daughters, whose name was Halia, actually became ill from her apprehension. We worried that once the MVD troops began searching this homestead, Halia's transparent anxiety would make the enemy suspicious, or, perhaps, even give us away.

At this particular time, a local partisan whose name was Tymish was living with us. He knew of another hideout in a nearby village, and Orlan decided that we should relocate until the danger passed. The night was clear, cold, and quiet. We had put on white overcoats that made us nearly invisible against the snow-covered fields and reached our destination without any difficulties. We woke up the family and asked if we could use the hideout. They told us that their place had been searched two days ago. That news convinced us to hide here.

The entrance to the hideout was through a shed in which the family kept a wagon and other farm equipment. Since the hideout had not been used in a long time, the entrance was frozen solid. We had to use pickaxes to break the ground, and the thumping echoed in the silent night. We eventually opened the entrance and climbed in, only to discover another problem. The air intakes were covered and frozen solid. Again, the thumping with the pickaxes. We worried that a sentry would hear the noise and report it in the morning.

The family gave us some bread and water and we got ready to spend the next few days underground. Orlan instructed the family to cover the entrance again with dirt, then pour water over it so the ground would freeze by morning.

The air in the hideout was stagnant and cold. We lit a candle, but after a time we noticed that the flame was wavering and was getting smaller and smaller. Then the candle went out. We knew there was not enough oxygen in the underground room. If we did not do something to stir the air and begin the exchange of outside air with the heavy inside air, then we would suffocate. We took turns trying to move the

Top: Woodcut, Nils Khasevych, January 30, 1949. UPA recruits assembling in the forest. *Bottom:* Woodcut, Nil Khasevych, March 1, 1949. Ukrainian insurgents marching through the hills of Volyn.

stagnant air. Two of us stood under one intake flapping newspapers, while the third person stood under the second air intake and blew hard upward into the hole. This was exhausting work since we worked in oxygen-depleted air. Eventually, our efforts paid off. It became easier to breathe. When we lit the candle, the flame did not go out. We watched that candle all night. As soon as the flame flickered, we started flapping newspapers and blowing again. We did this until morning.

The stagnant air that we encountered was a dilemma that plagued many hideouts. The entrance could be covered with dirt a meter deep, but the air intakes had to stay open. Above ground, a variety of means were used to mask the existence of air intakes, but they could not be completely hidden. The enemy knew this and searched for ventilating holes that led to underground hideouts. Often, the searchers used specially trained dogs to sniff out the ventilators. Air intakes posed other problems. If the air intake was out in the yard, it would become covered with hoarfrost during a cold night and someone from the family had to remove this telltale evidence each morning. Hideouts that were in constant use were equipped with a fan that was oscillated by a wheel that the inhabitants took turns in turning. Our other hideout had such a fan, and the exchange of air worked well.

We were very worried by the noise we had made during the night and were prepared for the worst. But the day passed peacefully. We told the family through the air intake not to open the hideout that evening. Although we were breathing more easily since our bodies and our lungs had warmed the underground room, nonetheless we hardly ate anything that day and night.

On the following morning, the father of the family came to report on what was happening. As always, Orlan first asked him if anyone was keeping watch. He said "Yes," then started making his report. Suddenly, he broke off, and we heard him hurrying away. We knew something had gone wrong. We suspected that someone had arrived and may have noticed him bent over talking into the ground. Our conjectures were correct, the man later told us. Apparently, his daughter, who was keeping watch, was not in the yard but was standing next to him listening to the conversation and did not notice the arrival of a neighbor who came in through the back yard. Even the family's dog had not barked when the neighbor walked up.

Orlan then asked about the neighbor. "What kind of man is he?" The answer was worrisome: "I don't know. Before the war he was an outspoken communist, but now he doesn't talk much."

There was nothing left to do but leave that night.

We returned to our original hideout and learned that the homestead had been searched twice, but the empty hideout had not been found. We lived in constant tension until early February. Although the searches had moved on to other homesteads and villages, the MVD special troop detachments did not depart from the area.

One day in midafternoon, we heard the agreed-upon signal telling us that the MVD was in the area. Korecky came up to one of the air intakes and told us that troops were searching a nearby house.

"Cover the air intakes with dirt," Orlan said. "Try to stay calm."

One of the air intakes was in a storage room and we knew the family had enough time to at least cover it.

We soon heard the barking of the family dog. Then another dog barked in answer, probably one of the sniffing dogs the searchers had brought with them. We had anticipated that the searchers would bring a dog, so we had already put out our oil lamp and attached a light bulb to the batteries that powered our short-wave radio. Not long thereafter, someone began jabbing with a shovel above us. We heard someone's heavy steps directly over our heads. Then someone was poking and digging near the air intake in the storage room. We also heard something heavy being moved and speculated that the family had placed a barrel of sauerkraut on top of the air intake. Someone began to dig. Clumps of earth started falling into the hideout through the air intake. Immediately we stuffed rags up the hole so that those digging wouldn't hear the echo of the falling clumps. We also wanted to prevent them from throwing a gas bomb through the air intake which would render us unconscious.

Almost simultaneously, someone began to dig near the entrance to the hideout. A rather long underground corridor connected the entrance and the hideout itself, and now the corridor echoed with the thumps of someone digging directly above it. The searchers were bound to find us either through the air intake or by coming across the entrance itself. We knew this was the end and began to prepare ourselves for death.

Orlan placed all important documents on the table, then added photographs, notes, and money. Because the air intakes had been closed, we began to feel the lack of oxygen, so instead of burning the materials, we started ripping them into tiny pieces, which we ground into the floor.

I was destroying family photographs. I looked at my father's stern face, and my heart broke as I ripped his photograph into bits. We worked silently and calmly. Only our ashen faces and jerky movements betrayed our internal turmoil. I knew I did not want to die.

As if he had heard my soul's cry, Orlan said, "We knew this would happen. It has happened to many others. We had been fated to live longer than many of our comrades. Thus, let's try to stay calm."

I looked at the three loaded pistols on the table.

"Do you want me to kill myself, or will you do it?" I asked him.

"However you wish," he replied calmly.

I suddenly saw the scene as it would play itself out after our deaths. The searchers would drag us into the yard. Our bodies would become dirty as they pulled us through the trampled snow. Our corpses would freeze in the back of the truck as it returned to the MVD headquarters. The frozen corpses would be propped up against the wall of the building. People would be brought to look at us and make positive identifications. But maybe they would not display our bodies. Maybe they would recognize who we were. Maybe they would take our corpses to Lviv and the identification would be made there. Here in Volyn people would say that a woman partisan had died, but they would not know who I was, and I would die nameless. If I had died in my own village, people would at least have known who I was.

As each minute passed, I began to feel increasingly alone. Someone had told me that death together with those dear to us is easier, but I don't think that's the case. Each one of us must meet death alone. Moreover, I knew that my husband would be dying with me, and that made me even more sad.

After a while, the digging came to a halt. They must have discovered the entrance and had gone back outside to terrorize the family into telling them who was hiding here. Maybe they will send one of the girls to talk to us and try to convince us to surrender. Or maybe they'll use one of the girls as a shield because they knew we would not be taken without a struggle.

Nothing happened for two hours. We got tired of waiting to die and started wondering what was going on.

Then suddenly we heard movement above us and someone was digging out the air intake.

"Thank God the bandits have left," we heard Korecky's tired voice float down to us.

Later, the family opened the entrance to the hideout and told us in detail about the search. The MVD had dug deep holes in the yard, in the shed, and in the root cellar. They had found the cache of potatoes that the family was hoarding. Everyone except Olha had fled the house during the searches and gone to stay with neighbors. Throughout the search one of the MVD men sat in the house with her to monitor her reactions. She said she tried to stay calm, but inside she was barely alive. She did not leave the house, because she did not want to see where the searchers were digging.

The MVD had learned to dig in places where belongings or equip-

Woodcut, Nil Khasevych, May 9, 1949. Ukrainian insurgents visit a *khutir* (farm) in the forest.

ment had been piled up. That is why they noticed the barrel with the sauerkraut. They pushed it aside and began digging in the spot where it had been standing. As they dug, they covered our air intake with dirt, which had started to fall into the hideout. They had also dug a hole very close to the hideout's entrance. For some reason, they had not pulled up the floorboards that disguised the entrance. Both above ground and in our hideout it looked as if a battle had been fought. But, in a way, there had been a battle, although no cannons had roared.

It was clear from the thoroughness of the search that the MVD was hunting Orlan. We expected the searches to continue until spring, while MVD troops blockaded the villages in the area. We knew the MVD would continue hunting for us, and maybe the enemy would not find us on the second or third try, but eventually our hideout would be discovered. We had been living under the threat of discovery for over a month and could not get any work done. We were emotionally exhausted.

I kept insisting that we leave this region, although I knew a move was not easy. A great deal of snow had fallen in January, and now it was melting. The fields were impassable and, if we tried to escape across them, we would sink in the mud up to our knees. We could not use the roads, because they were blocked by troops.

Orlan hesitated, and I knew his reasons. He had everything here to continue his work. He had a small library, paper, a duplicating machine, a typewriter. To leave this behind meant that we would have to acquire these items again, and such purchases were dangerous to make and cost a great deal of money and effort. Because it was so difficult to create a working environment, most leaders moved infrequently. Orlan and people like him were in the underground to work against the regime, and they had to have the means to function.

I had been urging that we move since the beginning of the intense searches, and during our near discovery I had remonstrated that Orlan had not listened to me. He had turned to me and said that this was not the right moment for reproach. I felt badly that I had complained when we were under such enormous emotional stress, yet, now, I continued to urge him to move. I pointed out that it was our duty to try to survive and not leave the initiative in the hands of the MVD. Tymish, who usually listened in silence to our arguments, took my side in this one.

Orlan made up his mind when water began pouring through the air intake in the yard as the thaw continued. He decided that we would return to the area of Lutske and stay in the hideout of commander

Woodcut, Nil Khasevych, September 8, 1949. The caption reads, "The people are yoked." The driver represents the Bolshevik party.

Dubovy, whom we had visited last summer. Orlan asked the family to go out into the fields and test the mud. The answer came back quickly: The fields were impassable.

"I think we should leave this place," I kept insisting.

Orlan agreed. We packed the most essential items and set out at dusk. As we said good-bye to the family, Orlan tried to leave some money behind, but Korecky wouldn't hear of it. "We'll get along somehow," he said. "You need it more than we do."

We crossed the yard, stepped into the field, and immediately discovered that the family had been right. We sank into the mud with each step. I fared the worst since I was wearing boots that were too big for my feet, and I lost a boot with each step. I became so frustrated that I sat down, took off the boots, and started making my way in socks. Soon my feet turned very cold and, soon after that, I could hardly feel them, since they had become numb. I was bringing up the rear so neither Orlan nor Tymish saw what I had done. When Orlan turned around and saw me holding my boots in my hand, he cried, "You can't do this. You'll be sick tomorrow. Let's go back."

He ordered me to put the boots back on, and I did so when we reached a side road. However, after talking over our situation, we knew that none of us wanted to go back. We decided that we would take the road and only go into the fields to bypass villages. The road was covered

with huge puddles. As we were sloshing through one of them, someone ahead of us flicked on a car's headlights. We dashed into the field
and were sure someone would start shooting at us, but nothing happened. We later learned that one of the MVD bosses was staying at that
homestead and had left his driver in the car as a sentry. The driver
apparently heard us, turned on the lights, but was too frightened (or
perhaps did not want) to raise an alarm.

By morning, we reached our destination. Dubovy told us that he
had heard about what had happened to Dorosh and his two companions and had been worried about us.

Dubovy's hideout would have been discovered long ago were it not
for the simple fact that the MVD could not imagine this kind of family cooperating with the underground and thus never searched the house.
The family was extremely poor; it had been the first to join the *kolkhoz*
when the region was collectivized. The family had no cows or horses,
so it had not minded collectivization.

♦ ♦ ♦ ♦ ♦

Spring arrived very early. We began to get news and make contacts in March. Orlan left for conferences with district leaders, while I
remained in the bunker preparing materials that would be sent out with
partisans for distribution throughout Ukraine. In April, I was taken to
a homestead in a distant village where I found Orlan hard at work.

Sometime that spring, a rumor began circulating that a very senior
leader of the UPA had been killed near Lviv. The rumor disturbed us,
since such gossip usually was borne out in letters that were delivered
subsequently. This occurred in this case. Orlan received a letter from
Col. Vasyl Kuk (Vasyl Koval, Lemish) informing him that Taras Chuprynka had been killed by the MVD on March 5 in the village of Bilo-
horshcha, near Lviv. Lemish, who had been Chuprynka's deputy, was
assuming Chuprynka's place. He also asked that Orlan not share the
news with anyone until a formal notification of Chuprynka's death was
issued by the UHVR, the Supreme Ukrainian Liberation Council.

However, the MVD began to circulate the news actively, since the
enemy felt that Chuprynka's death would demoralize and weaken the
underground. The MVD employed the ruse of leaving notes and leaflets
where it suspected the partisans were hiding. In these notes, they asked
their "brothers" to help them contact the underground, since their link
had been severed when Chuprynka died.

The formal notification eventually arrived, and it had a profound impact on the cadres. Every partisan knew that the underground had received a very grave blow. Leaders like Orlan, who had known Chuprynka personally, took his death the hardest. Rank-and-file partisans, who only knew Chuprynka by name, usually felt the death of their immediate superior more keenly than the death of someone at the very top. Yet no one left the underground in the aftermath of Chuprynka's death, although we began to think more often about the future of the resistance.

Nil Khasevych, whose nom de guerre was "Zot-Bey," was a talented woodcut artist who illustrated UPA literature and Orlan's underground publications.

I spent most of the summer making photostat copies of woodcuts executed by Zot-Bey (Nil Khasevych), a talented artist who had studied at the Warsaw Academy of Art. Zot-Bey was extremely valuable to the underground, since his evocative woodcuts were used to illustrate the journals Orlan was publishing and were also used in brochures and leaflets. That summer a group of former UPA fighters was organized. It marched into Belarus and the Baltic states, where it distributed leaflets illustrated with Zot-Bey's woodcuts that urged other captive nations to join OUN-UPA in opposing the Soviet regime. Similar brochures were scattered near Red Army summer camps, while hundreds of others were taken into the eastern provinces of Ukraine. During this time, we also produced leaflets directed at the nations in the Caucasus mountains and those in the far eastern areas of the Soviet Union. However, I don't know how this material was delivered and distributed.

Toward the end of the summer, Orlan received notification that he had been elected a member of the UHVR. Accompanying this notice of honor was a letter from Osyp Hornovii, Orlan's boyhood friend with whom we had spent some time in Poltava's bunker when we wintered in the Carpathian mountains. Hornovii wrote that he had been in contact with Nastia Martynovska who was raising little Petro, the name she had given our baby. Before we parted, Nastia had asked my permission to change the baby's name to one that was common in the village in order to protect him. Both Orlan and I were overjoyed at the news that the child was well. I had been wanting to write to Nastia to get news of the baby but did not dare do so. We also received sporadic mail and news from the West. These deliveries included bulletins published by the UHVR's representation in the West. From one of them, we learned also about the death of Stepovyi, whom we had also met in Poltava's bunker. He had been killed in Czechoslovakia as he made his way west.

In August, Orlan left for a conference with the district leaders in Volyn. The reason the meeting was called was to try to find a solution for the lack of resistance leaders in the eastern provinces. The Volyn underground was reorganized, and two leaders were sent east to the area of Kyiv to begin building a resistance there. Another Volyn leader was sent to the neighboring southern *oblast*, Khmelnytskyi.

While Orlan was attending this conference, Dubovy's bunker location was betrayed. A partisan by the name of Anton had been caught by the MVD and, under questioning, he broke down. He took a platoon of MVD troops to the bunker, although he knew that Dubovy was away at the conference. Inside the bunker were Dubovy's wife Kateryna and a younger woman, Hanna, who acted as Dubovy's secretary. After uncovering the entrance, the MVD pushed inside the bunker the woman at whose house the bunker was, telling her to convince the two women inside to surrender. Instead, the three women shot themselves, after burning all of Dubovy's papers. When we had stayed with Dubovy in February and March, I had become friends with these women and was devastated by the news. I could imagine their last moments, their decision not to be taken alive, and their despair as they readied the revolvers.

Other potential consequences of Anton's betrayal horrified me. He probably knew about the meeting Orlan had called and could betray the gathered leaders. A partisan by the name of Demian, who had been staying with me, and I left immediately to warn Orlan. When we reached the hideout, I waited while Demian went ahead alone.

I breathed a sigh of relief when I heard no shots. That told me that the MVD had not captured Orlan or the other leaders and then set a trap for anyone else that might come to the hideout. Demian returned with the news that Orlan had found out about Anton's betrayal almost immediately and, after spending a very apprehensive day in the hideout, he and the others left shortly after dusk.

But we had no idea where the men had gone. Demian returned to the hideout and left a note; just before dawn, we ran from the homestead to hide in the forest. The note set a date for a meeting but, as the days passed, it was not picked up by anyone.

Since there was no point of waiting any longer, Demian and I made our way south to a hideout in a village called Rikani Velyki. Here we were told that Anton had not betrayed the bunker that housed the underground's printing press. It was clear that Anton could have done much greater damage to the underground but had refrained. We wondered whether he had taken the MVD to Dubovy's bunker where he knew there were only women and was hoping they would surrender instead of taking their own lives. Some even said that Anton would have not betrayed the bunker if Dubovy had been there also.

◆ ◆ ◆ ◆ ◆

I lived alone in a bunker while Demian searched for news of Orlan. In September, Demian returned, having seen Orlan. He also brought back a letter in which Orlan instructed me to communicate with Nazar, the man who had been shot a year earlier in the arm and whose wound I had treated. I would tell Nazar to meet Orlan at a prearranged spot in the forest.

Two partisans served as my guides on the journey to Nazar's hideout. We had to cross the Styr River along whose banks, and especially at fords, the MVD often set ambushes. For that reason, we made our way up river to where it ran fast and where the area was a wilderness. Since the crossing required a person to be able to swim, and since I could not, my guides prepared bales of straw that they tied to ropes front and back, then floated on the current. I was pulled across the river on one of these bales, as was the literature I was bringing with me to Orlan. On the other side of the Styr, we rendezvoused with Nazar and a group of partisans, then camped in the forest to wait for Orlan's arrival. The day and time of the meeting came and went, but we heard nothing from Orlan. We did not know whether something had happened or whether the men who went to meet Orlan had gone to the wrong place, since the meeting point had been designated on a map.

Since there was nothing to be done and the weather was getting colder, I left for one of the hideouts in Nazar's jurisdiction. This bunker was very well built and well kept, and it had a duplicating machine. In a few days, Nazar came to see me. We had become fast friends during his recovery from his wound, and I was delighted to see him. After his two companions went to bed that evening, Nazar and I sat up telling each other our experiences in the months since we had parted. I watched the broad, dimpled smile on his face and listened to his tales with interest. Later that night he mentioned an incident that was troubling him. A family where there was a hideout told him that a man had come to them and said he had important news, and that the family should tell Nazar to meet him on a date that was coming up. What worried Nazar most was that the man had been a civilian, not a partisan. Nazar speculated that someone was trying to get hold of him quickly with important news that might concern Orlan.

I did not pay much attention to his story, since my mind was on Orlan and the possible reasons why he had missed the designated rendezvous. Nazar understood my worry; he said that the alternate date for the rendezvous was coming up and that he would make sure to be at the meeting place. As I waited for the second rendezvous attempt to take place, I spent my time copying the reports Nazar had left for me to give to Orlan. This was not the first time I was left alone in a hideout, but this time I became so worried and sad, and had such a strong premonition of disaster, that I could not work. I could not sit still either, so I paced in the hideout back and forth until I felt faint.

Finally, the time for Nazar's return and news about the second rendezvous arrived. I cleaned the hideout, washed the floor, changed sheets on the beds, and waited. The night passed, dawn was about to break, and still Nazar had not returned with news. Can anyone who has not been involved in a resistance movement understand the worry and the nervousness of the person waiting for news? The next day was an eternity of waiting. The second night came, but I could not bring myself to lie down. Finally, I heard a familiar knock, then someone was coming down the ladder into the underground room. I was astounded to see Orlan before me. At first, I thought I was hallucinating. I gingerly touched him to make sure he was real, as the apostle Thomas had touched our Lord. When Orlan and I had parted, we thought it would be for a week. Instead, two and a half months had passed.

Two other partisans appeared behind Orlan, but not Nazar.

"Where's Nazar?" I asked after we had greeted each other. "Didn't he meet you?"

"No," Orlan said. "We waited for him until dawn."

We still weren't overly worried, speculating that perhaps Nazar had other matters to attend to and could not make the rendezvous.

"That's not like him," I retorted. "He wouldn't miss an important rendezvous." I had become worried again, as the premonition that something had gone terribly wrong returned with new force. Although the men lay down to rest, no one could sleep. On the following day, the woman who owned the house came to tell us what had happened.

"I have very bad news," she began.

"What is it?" we asked.

"Two nights back, the MVD set a trap in the next village over. Two partisans were killed. The third was gravely wounded and taken alive. Today, the MVD brought him back to the village. First, he took them to the forest to a bunker, but it was empty. Now they're dragging him from village to village. They placed a bag on his head so we can't tell who he is, but so far he has said nothing of any use to them."

We were certain that the three men who had walked into the ambush were Nazar and his two companions. We asked the woman to tell us exactly what she had heard about the bunker that was discovered. When she finished, we were quite sure that the bunker had been the same one in which we had stayed after our close escape last summer from the MVD ambush in which Nazar had been wounded. But we had no idea who the captured partisan was. We knew that Nazar and his two companions knew the location of the hideout where we were now hiding and that if the MVD had broken the man under questioning, we were in grave danger and had to leave immediately. Therefore, we left as soon as night fell.

We soon found out what had happened and who had been seized. The captured partisan was Nazar. He had gone to rendezvous with the civilian about whom he had told me. As usual, only one partisan approached the meeting place, while the other two waited and watched at a distance. Nazar came to the house and was met by a man who said he had brought mail that he had attached to the underside of his wagon for safety. He asked Nazar to help him lift the wagon to get at the packet and, as Nazar was raising the wagon, MVD agents rushed from the shadows and hit him on the head. He fell to the ground unconscious. The other two partisans saw the commotion and realized something was wrong. They began to retreat, but the house had been surrounded by MVD troops, and both died in the ensuing battle.

Nazar's capture carried catastrophic consequences if he talked. He was the head of the courier service in Volyn and was well liked by the rank-and-file partisans. We thought that by showing the MVD one of the old bunkers he was trying to inform us of his identity.

The uncertainty continued for some time; then the MVD changed its tactics. It took the bag off Nazar's head and placed him in a group of would-be partisans. This group went from village to village saying that it was trying to make contact with the underground. We learned about this new tactic when two of the men that were with us left the hideout to get an encyclopedia that was hidden elsewhere and stopped to see a woman who had helped the underground in the past. When she saw them, she became terribly worried, since the group of would-be partisans with Nazar among them had just left her house. She told the men that Nazar had given her a note to pass along. She said that before the group left, Nazar had taken her hand and squeezed it twice in warning and, when he had left, he had looked very sad.

"They must have tortured him until he lost his soul," she had wept, not thinking about the trouble he had brought on her by coming with the MVD men to her house.

Yet, we knew that Nazar had not been broken immediately. He knew that on the following night Orlan was likely to come to the bunker where I was. Betraying the head of the Volyn resistance would have bought Nazar his freedom. He also knew where the underground printing house was, since he had been to that center. Because he was the head of the courier network, he could also have led the MVD to Ulian and other leaders. If he began to cooperate with the MVD in earnest, he would deal a mortal blow to the underground.

12. The Winter of Terrible Losses

By 1950, the MVD was making every attempt to capture partisans alive. If apprehended, the fate of such partisans was regarded both in the underground and by the civilian population as more tragic than death. Those who had caved in and cooperated with the MVD were treated with sympathy rather than disdain or anger. Any one of us could fall into enemy hands the next day, and who knew what tactics the MVD would use to make us talk. Yet, all the partisans I remember being captured did not reveal most of what they knew. They tried to safeguard not only their comrades but also civilians who helped the underground. The MVD did not permit these captured men to regain their equilibrium or come to terms with their changed status. Immediately after capture, these men were dragged through the villages and put on show. I wondered whether these poor souls knew how to respond to such tactics. They had fought the MVD and now, suddenly, they found themselves helpless in the midst of the enemy.

The MVD used such tactics not only with captured partisans but also with civilians who helped us. These people were arrested, tortured, and forced to sign documents pledging future cooperation with the authorities. There were so many arrests and interrogations, so many bits and pieces of information tortured out of people, that eventually the MVD assembled much damaging information about our resistance.

As the tragedy of Nazar unfolded, autumn arrived and passed, and we were still living in a bunker in the forest. At night, I sometimes climbed out to breathe deeply the damp cold air of the autumn forest. However, Orlan was determined not to spend the winter in the forest. The bunker was small and not appropriate for work during the long winter nights. More importantly, we did not have enough food to last until spring. Once snow fell, we would not be able to leave to find provisions. Orlan had planned one more meeting that fall with Viktor, one of the district leaders. When they met and Orlan described our situation, Viktor invited us to share his bunker where he had set up a printing press and where he had been planning to spend the winter. We arrived at the new hideout in the middle of November after the first snowfall, which had not been deep and had begun to melt almost at once.

The new hideout was in the village of Borokhiv near Lutske, with a family whose surname was Polishchuk. The underground room was large, though not completely finished. We spent the winter with Viktor and another partisan, Samuil. Samuil was a local man and had grown up in this village.

Volyn had been completely collectivized by the end of 1950, and this created additional difficulties in getting provisions, since the villagers received meager rations from the collective.

At the beginning of winter, seven partisans died at the hands of the MVD near our hideout. We did not know what was happening in other areas and who had died there.

◆ ◆ ◆ ◆ ◆

Although the winter passed without any large offensives or searches by the enemy, platoons of the MVD did not cease their cursory searches of the villages and homesteads. We did not leave the hideout, and Orlan immersed himself in preparing the two journals he was publishing and in writing reports of our activities during the previous summer.

The attrition of contributors and people who regularly helped Orlan with his work placed an additional burden on me. Not only did I continue my work as a typist, I began to help Orlan prepare materials for publication. He also asked me to critique his articles and urged me to write a memoir of my experiences in the underground. I hesitated, because I knew I could not adopt the tone he wanted me to use.

"Our literature should, first and foremost, train new cadres," he would say more than once.

I did not feel competent to write such articles. Although I remembered details of battles or operations as well as heroic acts of many individuals, I believed that judging an individual solely on his bravery in battle or when he faced death was not correct. A person was brave when he, or she, worked hard despite enormous difficulties and did not lose faith. A person was brave to believe in our truth at a time when few held on to their faith. It was also courageous to believe in the future, especially when you knew that you had no future.

During those winter nights, the four of us discussed these subjects at length. Samuil listened in silence, but Viktor often surprised me with his occasional questioning of some of the tactics the resistance was using. He would postulate that the resistance was teaching people to negate the efforts of authority, to destroy governmental property, and to sabotage governmental planning. If Ukraine were ever to become free, these lessons of stubborn negative action would have to be reversed to build a law-abiding nation. Orlan would argue back that it was not the resistance that was deforming the soul of the nation but the repression of a cruel invader that did not care one iota about the individual, his needs, or his rights. Even without us, Orlan argued, the people would search for a means to save themselves, as would any individual faced with extinction.

We also read many Soviet newspapers during the winter and tried to get books, since we had lost our library. We had people we knew borrow books in libraries, and we discovered that books in Ukrainian were being replaced with books in Russian. Many of the new volumes were classics of Russian literature, and we read them with pleasure. I especially enjoyed the works of the great Russian writers and, over time, I came to the conclusion that there were two Russias, just as there had been a double-headed imperial eagle. There was the cruel and uncouth tyrant who not only enslaved his neighbors but also kept his own people in perpetual captivity. The literature I read gave me a glimpse of the other face of Russia and its rich, old, and noble culture. I began to understand the source of Russia's might. It was not simply due to military power but also to that ancient and distinguished heritage. In particular, I remember being enchanted by Mikhail Sholokhov's *And Quiet Flows the Don* and also the works of Oles Honchar and other writers.

The 1950-51 winter ended quickly with a sudden thaw in early March. Since one of the air intakes was out in the yard, we asked the family to dig a ditch that would divert water from pouring down on us. They did as we asked, but the ditch was too small. One day, we heard a roar and suddenly water began to pour into the hideout. We tried to stem the flow, but it was useless. Soon water began to rise in the hideout. There was nothing else to do except to go above ground. The entrance to the bunker was in the barn. When we went down into the hideout, the family placed a bundle of hay in the hole, then covered it with a deep layer of earth. Since we had no way of communicating with the family unless someone was standing near the air intake, we had no other choice but to push the bundle of hay up until it broke through the layer of earth. We then began to move all our things into the barn.

Since this was mid-day, the husband and wife had gone to the collective farm to work, and only their adolescent son and a grandmother were at home. We told the boy to keep a lookout while we tried to divert the water from the air intake. Suddenly the boy came running to tell us that two armed MVD soldiers were heading for the house. We ran into the barn to wait and see what would happen. The two men went to the house and after a while came out into the yard. If they checked the barn, this would be the end of us. Even if we escaped, the forest was twelve kilometers away, and the MVD would spot us before we reached it.

The two MVD soldiers did not look in on the barn. Later we learned that they had come to talk with the grandmother about "believers." This was the name in current use to denote people who had converted to Baptists or Jehovah's Witnesses. The Soviet intelligence services believed that these "believers" were fronts for American intelligence, so they persecuted and hunted them as they did us. I believe that the reason behind the growth of these protestant sects was the low moral state of the Orthodox Church, which had become a collaborator of the regime. Yet, people needed and wanted religion and thirsted for the word of God. Thus, they turned to Protestantism, especially to the Jehovah's Witnesses, for faith and comfort. In Volyn, there were entire villages of these "believers."

With the thaw came renewed underground activity. Soon mail that had accumulated during the winter months arrived. It contained much sad news, including the details of the death of Dubovy. He was betrayed by the daughter of the family where he had his new hideout. The girl had fallen in love with a militiaman and had told her lover that her parents were hiding a partisan. The MVD threw a gas bomb in through the air intake, and Dubovy, recognizing what was happening, destroyed himself and a recruit he was training with a grenade. The girl and her militiamen were resettled in a different area, while the mother and father were exiled to Siberia.

Dubovy's death, and also that of Smok, who had been sent by the UPA leadership two years earlier to revitalize the Volyn resistance, left the underground without authoritative leadership. Although by this time armed resistance had been abandoned except in very few instances, the underground needed leaders who were trusted by the people and who would be listened to and respected.

As soon as it became possible, we left the hideout for the forest, where we spent most of April. I had lost a great deal of weight during the winter and coughed constantly. We were afraid that I had the beginning of tuberculosis. During this time, Orlan received new woodcuts from Zot-Bey and, to our surprise, a letter from Nazar. Nazar wrote that he escaped from the MVD in February and made his way to the bunker of Zot, one of the district leaders. Zot gladly took him in, and Nazar spent the rest of the winter in Zot's hideout. Now, Nazar was writing to ask Orlan to look into his case and decide whether he could rejoin the underground. Since we had become friends with Nazar, Orlan did not want to handle the case and gave the matter over to Ulian. We later learned that Nazar was readmitted.

◆ ◆ ◆ ◆ ◆

That August, we kept moving, as Orlan wanted to meet in person several leaders in Polisia, an *oblast* north of Volyn. Polisia is a lowland region with many marshes and extensive forests. For a time we lived above ground in a thicket of willows, while our supplies and the literature we had brought with us were hidden in a shallow bunker. We were waiting to be contacted by Krucha, the area's district leader. He arrived with his deputy, Zavziaty. Both were veteran partisans, having joined the UPA at its very creation during the German occupation of Ukraine.

In Polisia, partisan life differed from that in Volyn. Partisans lived in the forests and marshes, not in or near villages. They spent only a few months in bunkers, emerging with the first thaw and not returning underground until late in the year. Perhaps because of this lifestyle, they tended to be stronger and healthier than the partisans in Volyn who spent nearly half of the year living underground. The remnants of UPA units in Polisia, which was difficult to occupy because of its topography, continued to wage open battles against the MVD, whose control of the area was tenuous.

Krucha, who was stocky, strong, and blond, related how his unit ambushed a military vehicle the month before and gained a substantial amount of money that was being transferred from one base to another.

"I like to fight the old way," he said, "and I'm for fighting until we gain our freedom."

Orlan and Krucha spent some time together as the latter gave his verbal report on the state of the underground in his area and its activities.

Subsequently, we rendezvoused with Yaryi, also to obtain his verbal report on his activities. Yaryi had led the 1950 march by UPA partisans into Latvia and the other Baltic states. He was about Orlan's age, which meant that he was about thirty or a little older. He was well read and could describe his work and adventures well. He told us that at first his UPA unit encountered no resistance and moved swiftly through Belarus. The going became more difficult when the platoon reached the area of Minsk, the capital of Belarus. He said that the people they met were patriots and often spoke about their dreams for independence from Moscow. We also received mail from the UPA-OUN headquarters and thus learned that Osyp Hornovii, who had risen to the post of deputy of the general secretary of UHVR, had been killed on November 28, 1950, near Ivano-Frankivsk. Orlan not only lost his dearest friend but also someone who always found the time to learn about our son and the fate of our families, and who sent us personal letters together with the official mail.

After the meetings with Yaryi, we turned west, crossed the Styr River again, this time in a boat, and after being passed through several pairs of guides we were taken to a hideout in the village of Stavok, in the general area of Kovel. Toward the end of the summer, Orlan left to rendezvous with At, who was the head of the northern Rivne region. Orlan did not again return to the hideout. I eventually joined him in the forest. The plan was that At would escort us east. We would cross the region around Zhytomyr and then, hopefully, settle in the area near Kyiv, Ukraine's capital, where the underground had established a base.

At had lost his wife the year before and had not recovered from the tragedy. She had been observed by the MVD, and the enemy tried to capture her. She held off the enemy with a machine gun until it ran out of ammunition, then took her life with her pistol.

As we continued to move east, Orlan received mail that informed us that Zavziaty, with whom we met, and Samuil, with whom we had spent the winter, had been captured by the MVD.

◆ ◆ ◆ ◆ ◆

We were moving eastward, changing guides every few nights. At one of these exchanges we were joined by Kolodka, a quiet man in his mid twenties, whom At, following his departure, had sent to Orlan to act as Orlan's bodyguard. A little later, At joined us, as did several other men.

At believed in dreams. One day he told us that he had dreamt that he was walking down a road, when suddenly a huge hole appeared before him. Just as suddenly, a man came into view from nowhere and pushed At into the hole. We did not take his dream very seriously, since many of us had had nightmares. We also had other things on our minds. Tomorrow was the tenth anniversary of the founding of the UPA, and we were going to mark this day in the Tsumansky Forest where the very first detachments of UPA were formed in 1942. We reached the forest about midnight and camped. We made a small fire to keep us warm since the night was cold. I fell asleep by the fire and woke up when our scouts returned to the camp. They brought with them two couriers who were delivering mail. I decided that I would not get up and fell asleep again. Suddenly a roar and an incredible pain in my legs and hips awakened me. As I tried to sit up, I saw that the men were running into the forest, that the coals from the fire had been strewn about and on top of me, and that my flesh was burning. I groped for the place where the pain was but could not feel anything. When I looked at my fingers, they were covered with blood. I had been wounded.

"What's happening?" I whispered and tried to get up, but I must have momentarily fainted.

"I'm dying," I heard someone moan near me.

An eerie silence descended on the campsite. The only sound was someone's labored breathing near me. I listened as it became quieter and finally stopped. I still had no idea what had happened. Neither did those who had escaped into the forest.

When nothing else happened, the men began returning to the fire. Two people picked me up and carried me away from the scattered coals. We still had no idea what had happened. Someone speculated that perhaps we had built a fire on top of an unexploded bomb from the war and the heat had detonated it. Several of the men examined the fire, but found no crater. Later I learned that everyone thought that we were under attack and thought that the enemy had lobbed a grenade into the fire. Everyone had scattered to escape a second salvo.

We next turned to examining our wounds. Everyone had been wounded by shrapnel, some more seriously, some less so. Everyone also had a hard time hearing. Orlan had a minor laceration. The most seriously wounded was Kolodka, who had been near me. He had been hit in the chest. I was badly injured in both legs.

Then we counted our number and found one missing, then began to search in the darkness. Soon someone found At's mutilated corpse.

His legs and arms had been blown off and his head was partially detached from the body. He had taken the brunt of the detonation. We ascertained this by the deep hole that had been created where he had been sitting. This is where the explosion had occurred. We now began to understand what had happened. At had been unpacking the two packages that the couriers had brought with the mail. There must have been a bomb inside one of the packages.

We also knew that we had to leave this area immediately since the explosion would bring the MVD by daybreak. The problem was that there were two casualties that had to be carried. But first we had to bury At and clear the area so that, when it was searched, the enemy would not be able to determine what had happened. As some of the men began digging At's grave, others went to get water to wash Kolodka's and my wounds.

By the time the grave was dug and the campsite cleaned, the night began to gray. Orlan began a short service, but his voice broke with emotion. The men stood silently around the grave and paid their last respects. Their silence was more meaningful than any words would have been.

The grave was leveled with the ground, then scattered with fallen oak leaves so that the enemy would not find it and dig up the body. As I watched, my soul rebelled. This was not a fitting grave for someone who had worked so hard for the resistance. There would be no marker, no cross. No one would ever be able to find his grave to put flowers on it or say a prayer while kneeling beside his remains. There would be nothing that would say that he had lived, fought, and sacrificed for his friends and his ideals. It was unfair.

We left the grave when it was already daylight. Two men supported Kolodka, while others carried me on a makeshift stretcher. As we walked, we reconstructed the horrific events of the night. The couriers had been brought to the campsite by the scouts and had delivered a bag of mail. In the bag had been two packages, presumably containing literature, and a packet of letters. Orlan had taken the letters to read by the light of the fire, while At had begun to unwrap the packages. He opened one and had taken out the list of the contents that was always placed on top, then checked the list against the contents. Usually I unpacked packages but, since I was dozing by the fire, At had volunteered for the job. Someone remembered that after he had finished checking the first package, At had put it to the side and had picked up the second package. He must have untied the string and opened the package, because he was heard complaining that there was no contents list.

The bomb must have detonated as At put his hand into the package to see what was inside. That is why his body was torn to pieces. Kolodka, who had been standing and tending the fire, had been nearest At, and I, who was sleeping nearby, bore the brunt of the explosion. The shrapnel had cut my boots into shreds, and the worst wounds were above the boots. Everyone else had been sitting on the other side of the fire and not in direct line of the exploding bomb.

We also recalled that both packages had been addressed to Orlan, so that the enemy knew exactly where they would be delivered. They had anticipated that the mail would be brought to a hideout and, when Orlan or I opened the package, the explosion would not only kill everyone in the hideout but also collapse the hideout and bury alive anyone surviving the initial blast.

We marched through the day, prepared for the worst, but nothing happened. That night, our group split up, and Orlan, Kolodka, and I were taken to a hideout that the couriers used. Our plans to make our way east to Kyiv had to be put off indefinitely. What was crucial now was to find a hideout for the winter where Kolodka and I could recuperate.

My wounds were very severe. They extended up both legs from my heels to my waist. In addition to numerous shrapnel punctures I was also burned. Because we had no way of keeping the wounds clean, they began to fester and spread. Each time the men changed my bandages, they removed splinters, bits of dirt, and leaves from the raw flesh, and I was in constant agony. I begged Orlan to kill me with his pistol. Kolodka also suffered greatly. He had been wearing a winter jacket, and bits of the insulating material had been pushed into his wound.

We spent most of November in the small, temporary bunker in the forest. I began to get better but had lost so much weight that I was a shadow of my former self. Eventually I was able to stand up and go outside to breathe the cold night air. At the end of November, we received news that a hideout had been found for us, but we had to travel a good distance to get to it. Since I still could take only a few steps, the men arranged for a cart and pulled me to our new winter home.

♦ ♦ ♦ ♦ ♦

We were taken to a bunker where a nurse, named Zina, began treating my wounds. She found gangrene and had to burn it out, but her care was such that in two weeks I was able to walk again. We spent a few weeks in another bunker before we were taken to a village near Rivne. Our winter hideout had been dug at a widow's house. The bunker was small, low, and damp. The widow told us that the root cellar often filled with water during the spring thaw. This did not make us feel better, since the entrance to the hideout was from the cellar, and the room itself was dug lower than the cellar. But since we desperately needed a place for the winter, we didn't complain. Because the bunker was so small, only three people could live in it. The third person was a woman, Liuba, although Orlan would have preferred a man whom he could send to make contacts and who would have been of help in the event of discovery. Again, we had no choice but to agree to this arrangement. Liuba had been the one who had convinced the widow to permit the resistance to locate a hideout at her house. Liuba came from a family that had been decimated by the MVD. After the older brother Roman had joined the underground, the authorities arrested her father and her 14-year-old sister. Her father was sentenced to twenty-five years, while the adolescent girl received ten years. The mother somehow escaped the MVD and was hiding with friends. Another sister was constantly harassed, threatened, arrested, and released.

Since there had not been sufficient time to equip the hideout with food, we had to rely on purchases, which, we worried, could bring suspicion on the widow when she shopped in town.

The widow had several small children. The oldest was a girl who was in elementary school. Sometimes she came and talked with us and, once during such a visit, Orlan asked her who she thought we were and why we were fighting against the Bolsheviks.

She thought for a moment, then said, "I know you are fighting against the Soviets who came here and took over. You want America to come here." We began to laugh but she continued to look at us puzzled, not knowing what was funny about what she had said.

"No, dear, we are not fighting for America," Orlan said in a serious tone. "We are not fighting to exchange one overlord for another. The authorities might want you to believe that we are American agents, but that's not the case. We are fighting for a free Ukraine that will be ruled by Ukrainians."

The first half of the winter passed quietly. Since we had been traveling so much in the fall, a great deal of work had accumulated, and Orlan sat down to deal with it. Then the new year came and February followed. We wanted to leave the hideout as quickly as possible. The winter had been very mild, hardly any snow fell, but when the cold gave way to warmer weather, water began to rise in the hideout. We had a wooden floor that was like a platform which we usually propped up (so that we could stand up straight in the hideout). Even with the platform down, we began standing in water, and we had to bail the water out with buckets every morning. The cold and dampness had made us all ill, and we had come down with bad colds. We had decided to leave when one morning we heard the widow's voice above one of the air intakes.

"Can you hear me?" she called softly.

"Yes, what is it?" Orlan answered.

"The MVD found a bunker in the next village. We could hear the shooting all the way here. People are saying that there were men and women in the bunker. One of the women escaped and ran to the next house to hide. The MVD followed her and set the house on fire. We don't know if she died inside."

The widow was so frightened that she found it difficult to form words. Orlan told her that she should try to control her apprehension since, if she showed it, she might come under suspicion. He also told her not to open our hideout and to wait until evening to contact us. However, if something unusual happened, she should let us know immediately.

We were convinced that the hideout that fell was the one where I had been treated for my wounds and where subsequently, the nurse, another woman, and three men had spent the winter. It was numbing to realize that five people were dead. We heard that one of the dead was Liuba's brother Roman. The bodies were taken by the MVD to their regional headquarters where they were put on display. There were five corpses, two women and three men. As we had suspected, one of the dead was Zina, the nurse, who had treated me. One of the male corpses was not positively identified as Liuba's brother, and there were rumors that there had been a fourth man who had escaped. We did not believe these rumors. Such a rumor would make it natural for the MVD to start searching for the escapee, although in fact, the enemy would be looking for Orlan.

The discovery of a bunker always carried harsh consequences. First the family was arrested, questioned, and tortured. Arrests of other people followed. The village and adjoining villages were thoroughly searched. We were certain that someone would remember that a few months ago a man and his wife spent some time in the bunker. The man would be identified as Orlan, and the searches would become even more thorough.

We knew we had to leave. We would either drown or be discovered, but we had nowhere to go.

On March 4, the MVD uncovered another bunker. The gossip that we heard said that a man without a leg and two young men were killed. Thus, Zot-Bey was dead also, together with two young artists he had been training.

A few days later we learned that a new detachment of troops had arrived in the area and had camped outside the village. That night we left our hideout.

We had nowhere to go, and Liuba was not a trained partisan. Nonetheless, she was the only one who knew the area and the people. After questioning Liuba at length, Orlan decided that we would go to a homestead where Liuba knew the family. We walked all night and reached the homestead just before dawn. Liuba knocked on the window, but no one answered. She knocked twice more, but although someone moved inside, no one opened the door. Since it was almost daylight, we headed for the barn, which had only a partial roof. Some time in the morning, a woman walked in. She recognized Liuba but refused to let us stay in the house the entire day. She told us to go into the forest and advised Liuba to go to the next village where her mother was hiding. Orlan told the woman that we would not head for the forest in the daylight and asked her to bring us a blanket so that we could stay warm. The day was very cold and we grew numb, but the woman did not return with a blanket or any food.

In the evening she reappeared and brought us some hot food. But Orlan would not touch it.

"I have been in the underground for a long time, but I never met someone like you who would not even give us a blanket to keep warm," he said. "You are not worthy for us to have even set foot on your property."

We knew very well why the woman had not give us a blanket. In the event the enemy raided her house, she would claim that she did not know that we were hiding in her barn. A blanket would make her denials worthless. The woman's refusal to help us had a noticeable effect on Liuba. That night we reached the house of Liuba's aunt. When the woman opened the door and saw Liuba, she almost fainted. Eventually she came to herself and told us that when she heard that two women died in the fallen bunker, she was certain that Liuba had been one of the women. She said that the MVD had been to her house twice to search for Roman, Liuba's brother, who may have escaped when the bunker was taken. She also told us that Liuba's mother was staying with a young woman in another part of the village. Since the young woman was in no way connected with the underground, Orlan decided that we would stay the day at her house.

When Liuba's mother saw her daughter, she went into shock. Then she began to deny that Liuba was her daughter.

"Mother, get hold of yourself," Liuba said in a voice I had not heard before. "You know who I am, and stop being so frightened."

Eventually, the woman regained her composure and started telling us all the bad things that had happened to her since her son had joined the underground and her husband and daughter were arrested. She said that she used to be a respected woman, but now she had to hide and live like a thief. Orlan also talked to the young woman who owned the house. She was an orphan and was soon going to move east where she thought she could find a job. She was so poor that there was not enough food to feed us one meal. Orlan gave the girl some money and was hoping to send her to town next morning to buy some provisions. When morning came we discovered that the day was overcast, and snow began to fall soon. The snow intensified into a blizzard and it was impossible to go outside, let alone into town.

Everything is getting worse and worse, I thought, as if we were really reaching the end.

We spent the day in the house hiding in the loft. In the middle of the storm we heard the door open and someone come in. In another moment, we heard someone climbing up to where we were. Orlan grabbed his weapon. Liuba and I pulled out our pistols. When we saw the man's face, we were astounded. The man was Roman, Liuba's brother. He had escaped from the fallen bunker.

"Darling, brother," Liuba cried and tried to squeeze past us to embrace him.

"Sit still," Orlan ordered, not putting down his weapon. We were not only astounded to see Roman, we were also shocked. Five dead partisans lay frozen in the MVD regional headquarters. Had this one been taken alive and was now being used by the MVD to find others in the resistance?

Orlan began questioning Roman, who had been wounded during his escape and now had come for help to where he knew his mother was staying. I cleaned and bandaged Roman's wound, and he told us that it would be best if we left during the storm since this village was not safe. Therefore, we left in the middle of the blizzard. The going was almost impossible. We sank in the drifts; our feet became wet, then turned numb. We hardly made eight kilometers during the entire night, but toward dawn we reached a village called Khorlupy, where we stopped at a homestead where the people knew Roman. They let us in, and we climbed up into the loft to get some sleep and get warm. The family consisted of a stern husband and a good-hearted, but very fearful, wife and many children. The man, after listening to Orlan explain our situation, agreed to let us stay, but once he told his wife his decision, she began to worry and cry. After a while, he climbed back up to the loft and said we had to leave.

"All right," Orlan said. "Let's talk again this evening."

We knew, however, that it was physically impossible to leave. The roaring wind had driven the snow into deep drifts that made not only the fields but also the roads impassable. Besides, the family was very poor, not much respected in the village, and, according to Roman, not at all suspected by the MVD as sympathetic to the partisans. We knew that this was a good place to spend a week or so, but now we had to convince the family to let us stay. Besides, Roman's wound had become infected, and he had to be looked after before the infection spread.

In the evening, we climbed down and I ascertained more clearly the seriousness of Roman's wound. The bullet had entered below his shoulder and had traveled downward through his abdomen, exiting in the back, near his spine. The entry hole was already scabbing, and I had to open the wound in order to clean it out. The wound was very long, and I had nothing that I could use to push through the long bullet tunnel and clean the wound. Therefore, I tried to clean the wound from both ends, as far as I could. Roman also had frostbitten toes, since he had escaped from the bunker barefoot. The toes had swelled and had to be looked after.

While I was dressing Roman's wounds and Liuba was helping me, Orlan went to talk with the family. The woman still would not agree to us staying. Then Orlan said, "If you are so afraid, go and report us to the village council. You know that MVD troops will arrive, and we will not surrender. You also know that their tactic is to set fire to the house. They will do so to get at us. We will defend ourselves, and your house is going to go up in flames. If we had our way, we would not stay with people who are afraid to help us, but we have nowhere to go and we have a badly injured man with us, so we will stay here until the snow starts to melt and we can get out."

The man and his wife opened their mouth in astonishment.

"What are you saying," she cried. "No one's going to report you to the MVD." Then she added, "We want no harm to befall you. It's only that I'm afraid. So stay until the snow melts. Maybe it'll melt soon and there won't be any searches in the meantime."

We could not stay in the loft indefinitely. We had to build some sort of a hideout. The problem was that so much snow had fallen that the family had to dig a tunnel to get water from the well in the yard.

We decided to dig a hole in the barn where we could hide. We all dug, while Roman kept watch. Orlan dug, while Liuba and I removed the soil. Orlan had dug hideouts before, but neither Liuba nor I had any experience. It took us five days to dig it out. Once it was finished, you could not really call the hole a hideout. It was more like a crawl space in which the four of us could either sit or lie in a row.

We now heard the details of Roman's escape. It was a fantastic story. Apparently some five days before the hideout was unmasked, a partisan by the name of Dub came to the bunker to confer with Buiny, the regional leader who was wintering there. Dub decided not to leave until there was a dark night again. In the meantime, one of the daughters of the family was summoned to the regional center for a team training session. When she did not come home, everyone became worried that she had been arrested. Although some of the partisans wanted to leave that night, Buiny decided that they should wait one more night. Everyone went to sleep, except for a sentry by a ventilator. Toward morning, when the sentry heard the steps of many feet above him, he woke everyone. But it was too late. The enemy had already found an air intake and had begun to dig.

Roman climbed up the ladder to where the house-entrance from the bunker was located. He could hear that a soldier had entered the house and had seen that there was food cooking on the stove. "So you're cooking breakfast for the bandits?" he said. Roman climbed down to report what he had heard. The partisans began to destroy all documents. They heard the MVD chase the family out of the house and knew that the house was surrounded by troops. Nonetheless, they decided to break through the encirclement. Roman climbed up, opened the entrance, and threw a grenade. He then threw a second one and, as the smoke cleared, he began firing at the enemy from his automatic rifle. The others, also barefoot, since there had not been time to put on boots, started firing, while the women brought the rest of the weapons from the hideout. The enemy had placed a machine gun behind a tree and now opened fire. The battle raged until the house was filled with smoke. Some of the weapons would not fire, so the men gave them to the women to clean quickly, while they used other rifles. Dub was wounded first. He quietly sank to the ground, then said, "Good-bye comrades, I'm dying." A few minutes later he died as a puddle of blood spread beneath him. This was the first time that Roman saw a partisan die, and he was amazed at how calmly and nobly Dub accepted death.

The remaining partisans decided to escape through one of the windows. The first one through was Roman, who ran toward a hill behind the house instead of toward a nearby forest where he was afraid the MVD might have set an ambush. His rifle had jammed, and he had only a pistol with which to defend himself. Roman had chosen the right way out. Three other partisans who tried to escape through the window died, two near the house and the third as he approached the forest. The fifth, Buiny's wife, did not leave the house, and no one knew whether she had been shot or took her own life. The second woman, the nurse Zina, may have escaped. Roman had not heard what had happened to her.

We interrupted Roman's story to tell him that we had heard that she had evaded the MVD for two days before being tracked down and killed.

Roman spent the day in the forest, barefoot with only a shirt on his back. His toes and nose were frostbitten, and by night he was running a fever. He was lucky that he heard someone drive into the forest, and he recognized a man who had come to gather wood. The man took him to his house where his wife bandaged Roman's wound. Roman was planning to leave the following night. The family had a small boy who was both talkative and curious and liked to tell everyone what was going on around him. In the morning, his mother would not let him go out to play, but she had to leave to get something in the village and locked the child inside. Sometime in the afternoon, the boy's uncle came to the house, and the boy told him about the stranger who was staying at the house.

Roman listened to the boy tell his uncle how his mother had bandaged the man's wound, also that the man carried a gun—so Roman knew he had to leave. He spent the following days with friends, but since the MVD now knew his identity and was hunting for him, he could not stay in any house for any length of time. His search for a place to stay brought him to the village where he knew his mother was hiding. He visited his aunt several hours after we had stopped at her house, and she told him about our visit. When he was with his aunt, his mother came to visit, and he asked her to go back to us and tell us that he was coming. But for some reason his mother had said nothing to us about Roman.

13. The Last Months of Freedom

Finally the terrible winter ended, to be remembered as the hardest winter we had spent in the underground. We left our little hideout on April 1 and headed into the forest, where we were not the only ones seeking refuge. Many partisans lived in the forests during spring and summer to escape MVD ambushes and the furious searches of the villages and homesteads.

Orlan tried to reestablish contacts, and Roman, whose wounds had healed, was of immeasurable help in doing this.

We spent Easter in the forest and shared what food Roman and Orlan (who had never before had to go searching for provisions) managed to solicit among the villagers. Easter in 1952 was a lovely day, the forest quiet and pensive as if nature itself was observing the resurrection of Our Lord. As we sat eating the gruel and black bread the men had brought back, I thought of all the other Easters in my life, and I grew sad that we had no one else to share the holy day with.

Later that spring, we moved further north where we knew no villagers, and obtaining food became much harder. During this difficult time, I began leaving the forest on market days to purchase as much food as I could haul back. I carried my pistol in my pocket on these excursions and would have used it if the militia stopped me for questioning. Finally, Orlan was able to reestablish contact with other partisans, including Nazar. Nazar told us that Kolodka had been killed in an ambush on Easter.

The mail that Orlan received contained a letter from Lemish that summoned Orlan for a conference. Thus, Roman and Liuba joined a group of local partisans, while we made plans to go south. Just before our departure, we heard the ominous sounds of a distant battle and knew that our partisans were under attack. Late that day, Roman reached us. He told us that the enemy had ambushed his group and, as he and the others tried to break through the encirclement, Liuba had been killed.

♦ ♦ ♦ ♦ ♦

Nazar and two other partisans escorted us on part of our journey south. This was a different Nazar, grave, quiet, and introspective, as if he were constantly looking back on his imprisonment by the MVD. It seemed to me that life no longer mattered to him and that the disgrace he had endured when the enemy dragged him from village to village had left a festering wound on his soul. He may also have believed that he no longer was completely trusted, and this stigma hurt his pride. I think I understood more fully than the others how he felt, since I also had returned from my imprisonment feeling traumatized. The fact that Orlan turned to him for help went a long way toward restoring Nazar's self worth. The change was mirrored in his face, which became less grave, and his conduct grew more assured.

Orlan's position as the head of the resistance for northern Ukraine required him to be aware of what was going on throughout Volyn and Polisia. For that reason, we seldom stayed in one place for any length of time, the annual overwintering in a single bunker being the exception. From the standpoint of safety, our mobility carried both positive and negative consequences. The positive result was that the enemy could never pinpoint our location with any certainty. The negative aspect was that we met many people, among whom there could be a mole who would eventually betray us. Perhaps our mobility and our strict security when we were overwintering enabled us to escape capture for so long.

Since Orlan traveled extensively, many people in the underground knew him and liked him. He had the gift of intuitively understanding what troubled the person with whom he was conversing and was able to find the right words to ease a partisan's deepest doubts, including the question of why he should give up his life for a cause that, by 1952, was lost. Every member of the resistance believed totally in the righteousness of our cause, yet it was easier for a rank-and-file partisan to continue his struggle if he also believed in his leader. When circumstances grew even more difficult, when it seemed that there was no way out, people tended to look to Orlan for both inspiration and a solution.

During the late spring, Nazar arranged escorts who would lead us further south, and we parted with him. Our new escorts took us to the village of Pivche, where we met with Ulian. Ulian had joined the OUN before the war and, during the German occupation, had risen to a leadership post in the SB (OUN's security service). He lived in strict secrecy, so much so that this affected his usefulness. He was surprised that Orlan traveled so much and met with civilians upon occasion. Ulian had developed contacts in the eastern provinces, and we stayed in his bunker so that Orlan could prepare packages of literature that would be taken into the Zhytomyr province for distribution. After this work was completed, we again set out with a new group of partisans. We numbered ten, a large number to be traveling together in 1952.

Eventually we reached a hideout deep in the Kremianets mountains, a beautiful, aromatic region between Podilia and Volyn. We spent several days waiting for a change in escorts. During this time, Orlan and I had one of our infrequent arguments, but this one would affect our relationship for most of that year.

In our unusual marriage, conducted in almost constant presence of other people, we had repressed all personal expressions. We loved each other, trusted each other and were each other's best friend. Yet Orlan also demanded that I accept and care about people with the same wholeheartedness that characterized his attitude toward others. This was done so that the solitary partisans who spent so much time with us, guarding us, helping us, risking their lives for us, did not feel left out or become jealous. To be so open and accepting of others was difficult, but I eventually learned to do so and also to adapt myself to whatever circumstance I found myself in. I think that he and I had a positive influence on those around us, and I think that is why those who were caught by the MVD never betrayed us, although betraying Orlan would have bought them their freedom.

As the final chapter of our struggle neared its end, as people we trusted and respected died around us, we became more dependent on each other for moral support. Yet, because I was his wife, Orlan did not feel that it was my place to have a vote in decision making when it concerned the underground. He would let everyone else in the bunker have his say, but when I wanted to add my opinion, he became annoyed.

"You don't go out to make contacts. You don't build hideouts. You don't carry the largest loads. Since you do none of these things, don't have opinions on these matters," he would scold when we were alone.

At first, I was hurt by his attitude, then annoyed, and finally angry.

He did not leave for work in the morning while I stayed at home. His work was part of my life. It determined my life, and I was completely dedicated to his work. Thus, I felt I had the right to be consulted and have an opinion. These differences came to a head the night before he left.

During the day, Ulian arrived at the bunker. Orlan sent everyone in the bunker above ground and spent the night conferring with Ulian. Only in the morning did we return inside, and then the conversation turned to ordinary housekeeping matters. We had a short-wave radio which had stopped working, as often happened if the hideout was damp. As we discussed how to get it fixed, I offered a suggestion.

"Don't butt into things that don't concern you," Orlan suddenly turned on me. Then, addressing Ulian, he added, "She's become impossible."

I couldn't keep silent. "I guess I'm the only one in the underground whose suggestions don't count," I, in my turn, said to Ulian.

Immediately, I felt ashamed of my retort. I think Orlan also felt ashamed. But we were too angry and could not find a way to resolve our differences before his departure.

When the time came for him to leave, everyone went outside so we could say good-bye to each other alone. Orlan said, "If you are so unhappy with your life with me, perhaps we should part."

I said nothing. He then added that he had already talked with Ulian who was willing to have me spend the coming winter in his bunker.

"Fine," I said. "I'll do that."

We shook hands in parting, as if we were strangers. This was the first time in our marriage that we separated angry with each other. Neither of us knew whether he would return alive, and if he did, whether he would find me among the living. He was barely out of sight, and I still could hear the twigs breaking under his boots, when the knowledge that we had parted in anger became a stone on my heart. I wondered whether, if we survived and saw each other again, we would find a compromise and a common language.

♦ ♦ ♦ ♦ ♦

I spent the entire summer in the hill country. I acted as a secretary for Ulian and cooked for the partisans that came and went. Our biggest problem was the lack of water. The bunker was high in the hills, and the nearest stream was nearly three kilometers below us. Moreover, the MVD often set ambushes by the stream. Rain, the patter of rain-drops, was music to my ears. We would immediately put out buckets and fill them with rainwater.

In September, Ulian and I received mail from Orlan. From the official mail, we learned that Major Petro Poltava had died the previous winter in a bunker near Ivano-Frankivsk. As I heard the news, I began trembling. The most memorable people I had ever known were dead. Poltava, Hornovii, Chuprynka. Here in Volyn only Orlan and Ulian remained. It would soon be our time, too.

Orlan's letter to me cheered me up a little. In it, Orlan asked me to come to the bunker where he would be spending the winter. He also told me what materials to bring, ending the letter with, "Come, I miss you and wait for you." But then, at the very bottom, he added a post-script in which he said, "The decision is yours." I knew him well enough to understand that the postscript had been added to show how open minded he was. The letter said something else; that he missed me and wanted us to spend what days were left in our lives together.

◆ ◆ ◆ ◆ ◆

"I was certain you would come," were his first words when he saw me that fall.

"If the circumstances were different, I would have made you wait," I retorted.

"I realize that," he said, and we both smiled, happy to be together again.

Orlan had met with Lemish, and I was eager to hear him describe the meeting and relate other news. I noticed that Orlan had returned less worried and more assured and knew that the meeting with the OUN-UPA leader had renewed him. Orlan had also been made Lemish's deputy for all of Ukraine. Orlan also told me that Vasyl Okhrymovych, representative of the ZP UHVR in exile, had made his way back into Ukraine to confer with Lemish.

Orlan and Lemish had also decided that Orlan would move his activity to the Khmelnytskyi and Vinnytsia *oblasts* the following year. Resistance in those areas had been developed slowly by Ulas, the head of the Podilia resistance. A year ago, Ulas had gone to the city of Vinnytsia to meet with a contact. As he was approaching the rendezvous point, MVD agents jumped him. Cornered and seeing that his situation was hopeless, Ulas tried to shoot himself but only sustained a wound. He was taken to a hospital in Kyiv and did not die.

Ulas was a very significant catch for the MVD. They treated him well and tried to convince him to return to "peaceful" life. They promised him freedom in exchange for acknowledging his transgressions against Soviet authority. The upshot of these conversations was that Ulas said that the MVD could not convince him that the underground was evil; however, he felt sorry for the people who would die, and he was willing to go and meet with his men and explain his new perspective. To buy his freedom, MVD asked Ulas to kill Lemish. If he did this, he would not only go free but also any men he would bring out with him would be spared. Ulas agreed and was released in the spring of 1951. His first action was to contact partisans under his jurisdiction and tell them what had happened and warned them to be on their guard. Then he set out to see Lemish. He met with the UPA-OUN leader, telling him what had transpired in Kyiv.

When Lemish was relating this story to Orlan, he noted that Ulas experienced great difficulty in accepting what had happened to him and what he had done. Lemish asked Ulas to stay with him that year, and they wintered together. During this time, Ulas wrote two significant pieces of work, one on the development of nationalist activities in eastern Ukraine, the other on the national consciousness of the population of eastern Ukraine. In April 1952 Ulas set out again for the eastern provinces, accompanied by ten partisans. During one of their stops, they were surrounded by MVD troops; everyone was presumed dead, although the MVD may have taken prisoners. What Lemish wanted Orlan to do was to reestablish the links that had been severed with Ulas's capture and subsequent death. He asked Orlan to make contact and meet with the district leader, Skob, in the Khmelnytskyi province.

Orlan also told me a little about Lemish. He said Lemish had aged significantly and was ill, had lost most of his teeth, but was morally upbeat about the resistance. Although Lemish knew that the struggle was ending, he believed that the ideal of nationhood had been spread to the population and one day would bear fruit. He believed that the cause would not die with the death of the last partisan; it would become the yeast that would ferment and be ready when the opportune moment arose again.

We spent that winter getting ready for our move to the Khmelnytskyi province and preparing the subsequent issues of the two magazines Orlan edited and published. Many days we went hungry, since the food that had been delivered to the bunker ran out when the winter was only half over.

In March, we learned about the death of Stalin. "We survived you, tyrant," we shouted in glee.

"Now, Russia's history will repeat itself. Squabbles and executions will follow," Orlan predicted correctly.

Yes, we were pleased that Stalin was dead, but we also knew that his death would have little affect on us. There would be a struggle in the Kremlin. The victor would make overtures to the people, promising an earthly paradise and, perhaps, there would be some changes, but there could be none for us. We knew that whoever emerged victor would not tolerate a people whose goal was to free themselves from his rule. Our attitude toward the new dictator would also not undergo change. Thus, we had no illusions that the death of Stalin would make any difference in our struggle.

The people of Western Ukraine received the news of Stalin's death with open joy. First, they refused to go to work in the *kolkhoz*, then they became more defiant. They gathered in groups on the streets, they laughed. Some joked, saying that if the authorities would permit it, Western Ukraine radio stations would play music for "an international dance fest" and not funereal melodies Yet, just as we did not expect changes for the better, neither did the population. The daughter of the family where we hid delivered the best characterization of the events. She came home from school and announced, "We have a new Stalin, but he has no mustache."

In the middle of March, the frightened family told us that several trucks filled with MVD troops had driven into the village. The enemy had brought sniffing dogs and had camped. We knew what this meant: a new hunt. The searches began the following day. The troops were divided into groups, and each searched very thoroughly in the section assigned them. They dug holes, ripped up floorboard, and excavated root cellars. In one house, all the potatoes that the family had put away for the winter were taken out into the yard. This made our family particularly nervous, since the entrance to our hideout was from the cellar and the entrance itself was hidden under a pile of potatoes.

Searches were also underway in neighboring villages. Villagers returning from town were stopped and their packages examined.

We thought it would be wise for us to go into the forest, but we did not know whether an ambush had been set up there. Since all roads were blocked, we would have to make our way through fields, and a well-trained dog would be able to follow our scent. Thus, Orlan decided that we would not leave.

Our hideout was in an old, spread-out village. We waited, while the searches continued for a week. Then, abruptly one morning, the MVD left without searching the remaining houses, including the one in which we were hiding. It seemed that the MVD's sudden departure saved us from discovery.

In April, Chumak, whom we had met when he served as Ulian's bodyguard, and two other men came to see us. Their arrival signaled the season for new contacts and new work. A meeting of local leaders was planned in May. Meanwhile we, accompanied by Chumak and the two other partisans, set out to rendezvous with couriers coming from Halychyna in a forest massif that was on the border between the provinces of Halychyna and Volyn. I was above ground for the first time since the previous September. My legs had become unaccustomed to walking, and I had a hard time keeping up. We met the couriers, but they brought no letters from Lemish, only a verbal message that he was all right. Orlan prepared his mail, including a letter saying that he was planning to make the move east later in the year. The return mail was given to the couriers, and we returned that night to our bunker. I was glad that we were moving. I knew that life would be very difficult in a province that had been under Soviet rule since the creation of Soviet Ukraine in 1923, yet we both wanted to see that part of Ukraine very much. We also were convinced that work had to be done during this historic time following the death of Stalin.

Toward the end of May, we moved into an old bunker in the forest. Two partisans arrived to assist us, as Orlan prepared to meet with Skob, the contact in the Khmelnytskyi province who was to rendezvous with us. At the appointed time, the two partisans left to meet the group coming from the south, but the meeting did not materialize and they returned to us alone.

Two days later, the MVD put on exhibit in a nearby town the corpses of two partisans. After obtaining more details, we decided that these were the men with whom we had planned to meet. But the death of these two partisans raised more questions than gave answers. For some time now, the MVD had not been in the habit of displaying the corpses of partisans, in order not to reveal whether the disappearance of men meant that they were dead or taken prisoner. When we did not know what had happened to our men, all contacts ceased—and were renewed only after new plans and meeting dates were formulated.

Since we knew that men going to a rendezvous could be ambushed, alternate plans were always made for a second attempt at contact. The

second meeting with Skob was set for June 22. That meeting was successful, and the two partisans that had been sent to the rendezvous with
him returned with Skob and two bodyguards. Orlan had been very pre-
cise in ordering that Skob be brought to him alone, but during the rendezvous Skob refused to go without his protection, and our partisans
had decided to disregard Orlan's directive. They reported this and
explained their reasons for their action as soon as they returned. During
their report, our partisans expressed their concern about the conduct of
the three newcomers, especially their indifference to camouflaging their
movements. Since we had no way of determining whether these three
men were really partisans, Orlan conducted himself very carefully. Lemish had told him something about Skob and had given Orlan a specimen of Skob's handwriting. Orlan used these tools to ascertain Skob's
identity.

As Orlan and Skob held their discussions, I talked with his two
bodyguards. Both were good-looking men, more athletes than partisans.
To be more accurate, they talked and we listened. We were surprised
by how openly they described their work and how trusting they were.
It seemed that life in the east was easier for partisans, but this did not
jibe with reports we had received from our men sent there. Our men
had come back tired, had lost a great deal of weight, and wore old shabby
uniforms. These new arrivals were well fed and well dressed.

That afternoon, however, Orlan called me aside and told me that
he had decided that we would go east. When we camped later in the
day, I heard the newcomers whistling a popular song under their breath.
What a contrast these men from the east were to our men. We were
quiet and watchful, and it would not come into our heads to hum a popular Russian song.

"You are looking at death here," one of them remarked, "while we
are looking at life."

"But we've heard from others that living in the east is very difficult,
and you seem to be saying that you are living in paradise," I remarked.

"We do have casualties, but they are not as numerous as here," they
explained.

We could not leave immediately since Orlan was expecting mail
from Lemish. While we waited for the couriers, Orlan prepared his
report on his meeting with Skob. Since we had to wait several days,
Skob's two companions were sent back to their area, while Skob, Orlan,
and I returned to our bunker.

As we waited, I began to dislike and become untrusting of Skob.

He was thin and almost bald with just a fringe of blond hair. His eyes darted about, never quite resting on any one object. It was his eyes as well as his dandy-like mannerisms and other less definable traits that created my aversion to him. The fact was that I mistrusted him, although I tried to be as pleasant as possible.

Our food was not the best, and Skob declined to eat it, saying that he was prone to stomach troubles. He also urged us to camp above ground, which Orlan refused. Like his men, Skob talked freely about his work, and Orlan reprimanded him for such candor.

Skob carried some unusual items in his backpack. He had a new nylon shirt, and his towel was also new and hand-embroidered. Since Skob had said that his wife had been exiled to Siberia, I wondered who had embroidered the towel for him. He also had a razor. (Orlan used to have one, but that was long ago, since obtaining razors was extremely difficult.) I mentioned this to Skob.

"We encounter no difficulty in obtaining razors," Skob said airily.

On June 6 our men returned with letters from Lemish. I was in the habit of watching Orlan's face as he read the mail. I now saw that the letter carried very bad news.

"What is it?" I asked

"A person could go mad," Orlan replied, then told us that the MVD had captured Vasyl Okhrymovych and had taken from him a list of resistance contacts. Lemish also gave his blessing to Orlan's departure east with Skob, and we got ready to leave.

14. Second Betrayal

I had a dream on the last night we spent in the bunker—the night of July 6. I dreamt that I was inside St. Sophia's Cathedral in Kyiv. When I looked around, I found myself alone up in the choir loft. I examined the frescoes and mosaics but did not find them interesting. The cathedral was dark and somber, more like an empty theater than a church. I tried to remember why I had come here, but could not. My confusion frightened me, but as I tried to leave the church, I discovered something was holding me back. I became so afraid that I woke up trembling.

I don't believe in dreams, but this nightmare was so vivid, and the feeling of disaster so intense, that I could not forget the dream and kept reexamining the images. I wondered whether the church had been an allegory for a coffin—my coffin. Although I could not shake the dream or the premonition of tragedy, I told no one about my dream.

Four of us set out that evening—Orlan, Skob, Chumak, and I. Chumak, one of Ulian's most trusted men, had been selected by Orlan to maintain the contact between him and Ulian in the coming months. Chumak was coming with us so he would get to know his new contacts and the terrain. Once we rendezvoused with Skob's men, Chumak would return to Volyn.

During the first night, two other partisans, who worked under Ulian and whom we had met several times before, accompanied us. When the time came for us to part, I found it very difficult to say good-bye to them. The sadness that I had felt since I awakened from my nightmare seemed to intensify, and I knew that either their or our time was about up.

On the third night of our trek, we became separated from Skob. He had been walking so quickly that suddenly he was gone. Since he was the only one who knew the way, we stopped. Orlan and I waited while Chumak, who was younger and not as tired as we were, hurried ahead to catch up with Skob. Chumak found Skob, and we reached the agreed on meeting point at daybreak.

Skob left us to keep the rendezvous and returned a short time later with three men, instead of the two we had met on the initial encounter between him and us.

"You disobeyed my orders," Orlan said sharply to Skob. "I told you that no one local except the two I had already met were to be brought here." Skob mumbled something. A little later he suggested that Chumak and the newcomer camp separately, because our group had grown to seven people and could be noticed. Orlan agreed to the plan, and the two men left.

Yet both Orlan and I noticed that, despite Skob's concern for secrecy, he and his men were careless in their movements and had not tried to mask their tracks. They just charged through the underbrush and left a trail that the enemy could easily discern.

"You need to be much more careful," Orlan admonished them again. My worries surfaced anew. These men were like no partisans I knew. Something was not right.

The new arrivals had brought white bread for breakfast. What luxury, I thought. Even on Easter we had not eaten soft white bread. Orlan and I sat down and ate with gusto, because both of us were hungry. Almost as soon as we were finished, I felt sleepy. I looked at Orlan and he was dozing off, too. I remember putting my things under my head and adjusting my revolver holster so that it would be within easy reach. As I drifted off to sleep, I remember thinking, "Who are these men?"

Suddenly one of the men was shaking me and telling me to wake up.

I sat up. "Is something wrong? Are we under attack?" I asked in worry.

"You are enemy agents," the man replied, "and you are under arrest."

I was fully awake instantly. I looked at Orlan. Skob was unbuckling Orlan's holster where he kept his revolver. Orlan's repeating rifle lay far away and one of Skob's men was tying Orlan's hands with a rope. I reached for my pistol, but the holster had been unbuckled while I slept.

"Are you crazy? What are you doing?" Orlan was demanding. Apparently he had not yet grasped what had happened.

"Don't you understand?" I cried. "We fell into a trap."

"Yes, you did," one of the men said. "We're with the MVD. Don't try to escape. You won't succeed," he warned as I struggled. "We've been waiting for you several days. This forest is surrounded by troops."

It is impossible to describe such moments. You find yourself awake in what you think is the worst possible nightmare. There are so many feelings that fight with each other, crowd against each other, as you try to adjust yourself to what is happening. You are filled with so much pain and despair that you can barely stand the assault on your self-control. I look back at that moment as the worst in my life, more terrifying than death itself. Yet, even as these emotions swept over me and left me staggering, another part of me was examining the three men whom we had trusted and who had betrayed us. They looked like one would imagine a criminal would look as he was committing a heinous crime. Their hair seemed to be standing at end. Their eyes were bulging as if they were about to explode out of the sockets. They were also perspiring profusely, the sweat trickling in dirty rivulets from their foreheads and down their faces and necks. Their lips, clamped together into scowls, nonetheless trembled. I saw in them the epitome of Judas, and I turned to Skob and cried, "Judas," then spit into his face.

He raised his hand to wipe the spittle from his cheek. "There was no Judas. There was no Christ," he said.

I was now seized with a great anger. I had an overwhelming desire to destroy these traitors, to squash them like a roach. But my hands were tied by then, and the realization that I was helpless made me even more furious.

After Orlan and I were tied up, one of the men left, probably to report that the deed had been done.

"Shoot us," Orlan said, turning to Skob. "Do at least one thing that's honest. You know who we are and what we are. Tell your masters that we tried to escape."

"Oh, no," the man called Oles replied. "Do you think I like doing this? Do you think I willingly agreed to do this? I promised to deliver you alive in exchange for my freedom. You've no idea what it's like to be arrested. After Ulas's departure, we were left alone," he continued as if he were trying to rationalize his betrayal to himself and us.

Yet I think that Skob and Oles clearly understood what they had done, at least in the first few moments when we confronted them. So many "strange" things that I had noticed about them were falling into place: the nylon shirt and the razors Skob carried, his men's disregard for strict security, Skob becoming "lost" earlier that night.

"Our contacts," Orlan whispered to me, and in those two words he conveyed the catastrophic consequences our betrayal carried for those Skob had met and for those in Ulian's district who had been assigned to maintain contact with us. Orlan had progressed past thinking about us. Our lives were over. He was thinking about all the men that were still free and to whom Skob could lead the enemy. The possibilities were disastrous. If Skob's role in our capture went undiscovered, he would remain as the district leader in the Khmelnytskyi *oblast* and would be able to show the MVD the line to Ulian and from Ulian all the way up to Lemish.

I examined my husband more closely. He had lost much weight. He looked exhausted. He had sacrificed his life for the cause. And now he stood here with his hands tied with a rope. His own had tied him up.

"We have been ready to die for a long time," Orlan said. "We are prepared for death. But we want to die from an enemy's bullet, not be betrayed by someone in our ranks." Then he added, "Others have been caught, but no one has been betrayed the way you have betrayed us."

"I was arrested," Skob replied. "I didn't go to them on my own. But I'm not an idiot who's willing to die. It's you who don't understand. Those people who are in the West, the members of UHVR, they've sold out to the Americans. They're getting fat, while back here we're living like animals and dying for a lost cause. I'm no fool to die for nothing. No."

"Scum," Orlan spat at him. "Almost every member of the UHVR who didn't go into exile is dead, and you know it. You say you're not going to die for nothing. Don't you know what the others died for? Don't you know why they're dying in prisons and in the gulag? Don't you know?"

"It's easier in the camps than living underground," Oles said.

But Skob interrupted him. "Yes, it's true that most of the leaders are dead. But..."

I stopped listening to him. I was looking around me, regaining my self-control. The worst was already behind me. I had passed from freedom into captivity and had not gone mad. The moment of realization was behind me. What I had been horribly afraid of had happened; I was no longer frightened. A person is afraid as long as there exists an iota of hope, but once hope is gone, there is no longer any reason to be afraid. I think Orlan's thinking was paralleling my own. Our eyes sought each other. We knew that we were most likely spending our last moments together. Skob and Oles were not worthy of our attention. We looked at each other with love in our eyes and anguish on our faces.

"Be brave, Maria," he said. "Our time had to come."

◆ ◆ ◆ ◆ ◆

The first person to come was a tall man, gray-haired, in his fifties. He was wearing the summer uniform of the MVD, a light-colored jacket and darker trousers. The stripes on his uniform informed us that he was of high rank. He was missing three fingers on his right hand and, because of this deformity, his hand looked like an animal's claw. We would learn that he was the officer in charge of the Khmelnytskyi *oblast*. His deputy who accompanied him also wore the summer uniform of the MVD; he was younger, shorter, and heavier.

"Good afternoon, Orlan," the tall man said in Russian. A victorious smile played on his lips. "We know each other."

"Well, this time you won," Orlan replied.

We regarded the appearance of the MVD officer with studied indifference. Although I was outwardly calm, thoughts were churning furiously inside my head. We had fallen into a pit and would soon be dragging others after us. When we set out on this trip, Orlan had packed his most important documents, including a note pad filled with dates of future meetings and their locations. I knew that he carried several important letters, including the most recent mail from Lemish. I remembered that the day before I had seen him re-reading Lemish's last letter, and I had almost said to him that he should destroy that letter as soon as possible since we were in a terrain we did not know and among people we had only met recently. But I had said nothing because I knew how he disliked it when I interfered in matters he thought did not concern me. Now, I could not forgive myself for keeping silent, feeling that I was partially to blame that Lemish's letter would fall into the hands of the MVD. If I had warned Orlan about the risk he was taking carrying that letter, perhaps he would have listened to me and torn the letter up or burned it. I should have said something, since I had a premonition that something catastrophic was about to happen. Again I remembered the razor blades, the nylon shirt, the embroidered towel, the humming of a Russian tango—why had I failed to pay attention to these signs? "Little things tend to add up in our situation and become large problems," Ulian, who was extraordinarily cautious, had said once.

Why had I never shared my misgivings with Orlan? If I had said something, perhaps that conversation would have changed our fate. Why had Orlan trusted Skob, although he himself had noticed deviations from the norms that governed our lives in the underground? The answer was not overly complicated. I had seen this before: If a person desperately wants to believe something, that person will find an explanation for every unanswerable question. Both of us wanted to work in the eastern provinces. Our desire blinded our eyes to the true conditions in those areas. I had kept silent because I did not want to blot out that illusion. I did not dare examine it with a critical eye, because I knew deep inside that the bubble would burst. The underground line through the Zhytomyr province no longer existed, because all the contact people were dead. The only line left to the eastern provinces was this one, created by Skob after Ulas's death. Lemish had spoken favorably about Skob, but what Lemish thought was based on what Ulas had told him. The very fact that Lemish accepted Skob had protected him from our scrutiny. Orlan had attributed Skob's unusual possessions and freewheeling conduct to the fact that conditions were less difficult in the east. In fact, it was exactly the opposite. Moroz, a courier who had gone east and had barely made it back, had told us the truth, but somehow Orlan had forgotten what Moroz had said.

What had happened to Chumak? I had forgotten about him. The MVD must have done to him what they did to us, or worse. In a way, he was more important than we were. He was the thread that could lead the enemy back, back to Ulian, and from Ulian, back all the way to Lemish. I never saw Chumak again. I think the MVD took him away separately.

Someone exchanged the ropes around our wrists for handcuffs. We were led out of the forest and onto a dirt road where two cars waited. Orlan, the MVD officer, Skob, and another MVD agent got into the first car. I was pushed into the back seat of the second vehicle, where the MVD deputy and two other agents guarded me.

Along the way we saw women, children, and even old men carrying bundles of wood from the forest. These people were skinny and bent over. They wore rags, not nylon clothing that Skob had told us was easily available. When we passed them they looked at us with frightened eyes, as if they had been caught "stealing" the wood. I couldn't keep silent.

"You certainly have created a paradise on earth," I said to the
deputy. "These people look like beggars and they live in Ukraine, the
breadbasket."

"Well, you can't get everything done at once," he replied. "It takes
time after a war to get things back to normal. After reconstruction,
things will start getting better."

"Really?" I said with irony dripping from my voice. "The nation
needs to suffer? Why aren't you suffering along with these poor people?
I don't think you're experiencing the shortages that you attribute to the
war. Look at the thick waists you have. You can hardly walk."

He did not answer, although I saw from his expression that my
words had hit their mark. He was not only short but also round and
reminded one of a barrel. They could tie my hands, but not my tongue.

After passing through a town, the two cars came to a halt in the
middle of a field. Here I was told to get into the back seat with Orlan.
He and I sat in the middle, while Skob and an MVD agent guarded
the doors. The MVD officer sat in the front, next to the driver. Orlan
had been handcuffed so that his hands were behind his back. Mine had
been handcuffed in the front and I was more comfortable. When the
MVD officer noticed this, he told the agent to handcuff me with my
hands in the back.

We again drove on side roads, not on the main highway. Through
the window I saw tall wheat, the stalks heavy with grain, ready to be
harvested. Then we drove through a village. It was so poor that the
contrast between the bounty of the land and the poverty of the people
was striking. The houses were not houses, but huts. None had a yard or
any decent outbuildings. If there was a barn, it was a simple lean-to
against the house. Compared to conditions here, Western Ukraine was
truly the land of the kulaks. The people had tried to make the best of
their situation. The houses were whitewashed and the windows sten-
ciled. A riot of flowers and sunflowers grew around the huts.

Despite our capture, both Orlan and I watched the countryside
unfold beyond the car windows with undisguised interest. I wanted to
greet the people we saw, stop, and get to know them, not merely pass
them in an anonymous automobile. Inside, we were squeezed against
each other so much so that my hands and legs went numb. I glanced
sideways at Orlan and saw that he had regained his normal composure,
although his brow was knotted and he was worried. I thought he was
going over the things he had brought with him and which items would
be used to harm others in the underground. When the MVD agents

began talking among themselves, he whispered to me, "All is lost; Lemish is planning to come here."

He said it quickly, without emphasis, but the MVD officer noticed and told us not to converse. Although he was sitting up front, he had half-turned his body so that he could watch both of us. I think Skob had noticed earlier that we were communicating with each other but had decided not to say anything. He had done his part already.

When Orlan's words sank in, I felt faint. That's what Lemish must have written to Orlan in that last letter I had seen Orlan reading. The MVD will use this information to somehow get at Lemish. For a while we rode in silence, then the MVD officer asked Orlan if he knew where Lemish had his hideout.

"Your appetite's too great," Orlan replied. "No, I don't know."

From the conversations among the MVD agents, I began to piece together how the MVD had been able to turn Skob. They had done so through his son, whom they had taken away from the family that was raising him, as Nastia was raising our little son. When Skob broke and promised cooperation, the MVD returned the child to him. This had happened during the time that Ulas was with Lemish. As a reward, the authorities allowed Skob's wife to return from exile in Siberia. Skob regained his family by destroying the underground, not only in the Khmelnytskyi *oblast* but also in parts of Volyn. It was possible, I soon realized, that Skob was responsible for the deaths of Ulas and the ten partisans that had accompanied him. That suspicion did not surface as we listened to conversations in the car. Only later, when I saw Orlan one more time, did I learn that Ulas had planned to rendezvous with Skob on his return from Lemish.

During the long journey in the automobile, the agents relaxed and began to talk with us informally.

"You'll regain some of the flesh you lost in the underground," the MVD officer said to Orlan. "We'll feed you well."

"They lived in unimaginable conditions," Skob said, as he described our bunker. "I had to eat smelly meat and crackers. They didn't even have water."

Up to now Orlan and I had ignored Skob. But his comment made me furious. I turned to Orlan and said extra loudly, "The dog forgot how he once lived. Now he's surprised. I guess he prefers drinking human blood than nibbling on crackers."

No one answered. I looked sideways at Skob. He was smiling foolishly. Then the MVD officer said quietly, "Dogs want to live also."

At that, Skob's smile became even more stupid.

We reached the city of Khmelnytskyi about noon and drove directly into the city prison yard. From there we were taken to the prison office. Orlan's hands had turned blue because of the tight handcuffs. I, who was not used to riding in a car, became nauseated. The MVD refused to let me go to the bathroom, so I vomited on the office floor.

Orlan and I were separated. In the women's prison, matrons took everything away from me, including my wedding band and hairpins. I was given a prison uniform and slippers without laces. Next, they took me to a bathroom where I was told to bathe. After that I was taken to an empty cell. A guard brought a mattress filled with hay and a toilet bucket. So this is how a cell looks, I thought. Later, someone passed dinner through the small opening in the door. It was a malodorous cabbage soup that I did not bother to eat.

I tried to figure out what was going on outside. I was not certain whether there was a factory nearby, or whether someone was building something just outside the walls. The walls continually resounded with loud heavy thumps. The noise became so insistent and debilitating that I soon felt as if someone was hitting me on the head with a mallet.

When the guard came, I gave him back the uneaten food.

"Why didn't you have something?" he asked kindly in Ukrainian. Later he helped me carry the heavy toilet bucket to the door.

I was exhausted. I lay down on the straw and fell into a heavy, deep sleep.

In the evening, I was given some thin soup and then was instructed to get ready. I had no idea what that order meant since I had nothing except the loose prison coat. It was almost dusk when I was taken into the prison yard where two cars stood waiting. When Orlan, wearing a similar prison coat to the one I had on, was led out of the building, he said, smiling sadly, "That outfit makes you look like a nurse."

A few minutes later, the MVD officer and another man, who was big, strong, and husky, came out of the prison office. The MVD officer had changed to an elegant gray suit, while his companion wore the MVD summer uniform, and his stripes indicated that he was a general. Later I learned that this man was the head of the MVD in Kyiv. Two MVD agents brought up the rear. They all smelled of vodka and were in a good mood. I guess they had been celebrating their success.

"Good evening," they said to us.

"Good evening," Orlan replied, but I said nothing.

Orlan was told to get into one car, while I was told to ride in the other. Both cars were driven to the airport, where we boarded an MVD airplane. "Where are you taking us?" Orlan asked.

"To Kyiv, of course," came the reply.

"Your people dream of seeing Kyiv, of wetting your feet in the mighty Dnipro," the MVD officer said. "Did you ever think that your dreams would come true this quickly?"

Orlan ignored his mocking comment. He turned to me and said, "You thought you would never see the capital."

"And now we will, and then we will die," I completed his thought.

"You should be thinking of life, not death," the MVD officer again inserted himself into our conversation. "Both of you are still young."

The airplane was well furnished and was divided into two sections. The front section was dominated by a large table that was surrounded with upholstered chairs. The aft section was furnished with rows of upholstered seats, and clean white curtains hung at the windows.

They put us on opposite sides of the airplane, saying that we both would want to look out the window at the land below us. Instead, we turned to face each other and could not take our eyes away from each other. We could not talk, but we could look and commit to memory every line on each other's faces. It was only now that I truly realized our situation. I knew that nothing could be changed and that I had to reconcile myself to our fate. I did not want to think about the future, since we had no future. Events had seized us and were carrying us into oblivion and the unknown. Orlan's eyes would not leave my face. I think he was begging me to be stoic, not break, and at the same time he was saying good-bye. I tried to answer him with my eyes. I tried to tell him not to worry about me. I would withstand what lay ahead; I would not betray him. Our abductors saw what we were doing and led Orlan away to the front section. Only then did I glance out the window and saw below me a sea of lights. We were flying over Kyiv.

At the airport, we were put into separate cars and driven into the city. I did not even look out the windows. I no longer cared about my surroundings or what would be done to me. I had only one resolve: I would not break.

They drove us down Khreshchatyk, the main boulevard of the capital.

"Now turn onto the Naberezhna," the MVD agent told the driver. We were being shown the city. I guess they were giving us a taste of what life in this city was like. On the streets we saw crowds of people, but all I could think was, "How many of us had been taken already on this tour? How many more will be after us?"

When we were on Lenin Street, I asked the MVD officer where the Lenin Museum was, since I knew that that building was previously the home of the Ukrainian Verkhovna Rada (the Parliament during the 1918–22 independence in Eastern Ukraine).

But I think he discerned my intent in asking that question. "You'll see that later," he replied. "There's plenty of time."

Then he added, "I heard that Lemish would like to see the museum also. Perhaps you will help him get his wish?"

"No, I won't," I replied.

The car drove slowly so we could absorb the beauty of the city and the river. We then again returned to Khreshchatyk, drove across the plaza in front of the St. Sophia Cathedral, turned near the monument of Khmelnytsky, and drove into the prison yard. Behind us the heavy gate of the MVD prison clanged shut.

Orlan was led inside first, while I was left outside in the car with my guards. We waited in the car for such a long time that I dozed off. I think it was way past midnight and the city beyond the walls had fallen silent. Some time later, someone woke me up, and I was led into the building, then taken upstairs in an elevator. The elevator had a large mirror. I looked at myself in it and did not recognize myself. In the oversize prison coat, with my hair uncombed and falling over my shoulders and my eyes wide and staring I looked like an escapee from a home of the mentally ill. Although I did not care what my inquisitors would think of me, nonetheless I was embarrassed that they had thus "prepared" me.

I was led into a beautifully furnished room. A Persian carpet lay on the floor, and heavy drapes hung on the windows. This was the office of Strokach, the minister of security. He wore a general's uniform and was sitting behind his desk. He was heavy, short and blond, with small facial features, except for a mouthful of gold teeth. Every time he moved his lips, it seemed that the teeth wanted to escape his mouth. Sitting on either side of the desk were the heads of the regional MVD for Kyiv and Khmelnytskyi.

Strokach motioned with his hand for me to take the chair in front of his desk, so I sat down. A moment later someone else entered the room and took a seat behind me so that I could not see his face. I almost turned around, then caught myself, since I really did not care who questioned me or who was in the room. Just as before, these men smelled of liquor and were in a good mood, pleased with the "quarry" they had caught. And why shouldn't they be pleased with themselves, I thought? Moscow will reward them.

"Well, then, you tricked us," were Strokach's first words.

I had been prepared for something like this and had my answer ready. "I didn't trick you. You let me go."

"We didn't let you go. We sent you with an assignment to convince your husband to cooperate with us."

"Well, I couldn't convince him. I told him everything that happened and he made the decision."

Strokach did not reply to this, but asked me if I knew Lemish.

"No," I said.

"Do you know how to contact him?"

"No."

"Do you know how to contact Ulian?"

"I didn't even know the contacts to the next district. Those were not things that concerned me."

"Do you know where Orlan left the archives?"

"No."

His tone changed. "Both you and Orlan must realize your position. You'll never leave this prison. That means that you will not leave as the person that came here, your views and your attitudes intact. Your only chance for survival is to be reborn, become different people. Of course, you would need to make amends to the government, exculpate your actions and the damage you have done. And this time we will not accept your words. You will have to do it with your deeds. You will have to help us liquidate the underground."

When Strokach finished, the man sitting behind me came forward and asked, "Do you recognize me?"

This was the general who had flown to Lviv in 1949 and had observed while I was being questioned by the general in charge of the Lviv region. He was very handsome and therefore memorable, but I never learned his name.

I nodded.

"You changed a great deal," he said. "Lost a great deal of weight."

"Of course she lost weight! How couldn't she have, living in those forests? What did they think they could accomplish?" the MVD officer who arrested us said and laughed.

I said nothing.

Their good mood suddenly evaporated. Strokach picked up the telephone and summoned someone. Soon a guard came in. He had a face as flat as a plate and tiny, evil eyes.

The guard led me to a small, windowless room that was like a cage.

I could hardly fit inside. High above me shone a very bright light bulb. A tiny bench, more like a shelf, was fastened to one wall. This MVD cell was worse than the one in Khmelnytskyi, I thought in dread. I later learned that this cell was a holding cell used to hide a prisoner while another prisoner was being brought up for interrogation. These cells were called "boxes," and I would be held in them on many occasions. There were about ten of these cells in the building. They were bare, without mattresses, blankets, or toilet buckets.

I sat down on the bench. I leaned my head against the wall and went numb. I could not think or move or sleep.

I don't know how long they kept me in that box. Eventually, two guards came to get me and led me to a cell on the second floor. This cell was much larger, clean, and had a polished wood floor. From the marks on the floor, I deduced that this room had once held four beds. Now, there was only one metal bed against one of the walls. On it lay a mattress and bed linens. On the opposite wall was a cupboard for bread and utensils. Above it were two shelves and above them, high up on the wall, a tiny window.

I lay down, thinking I would go to sleep, but could not. The bright electric light bulb was directly above me and shone down into my face. Besides, I had been told that I had to lie in such a position so that the guard could see my entire face when he looked in through the peep-hole in the door. Whenever I turned, a guard would knock on the door and demand, "Turn around. I can't see your face."

♦ ♦ ♦ ♦ ♦

The new day dawned. It was exactly twenty-four hours since Skob had delivered us to the enemy. Daylight barely entered through the small, barred window high on the wall. I stared at the gray fragment of sky, and my thoughts were like swarming black clouds. We would never leave this prison alive. There was no point in asking God's help, since He was powerless in this place ruled by human brutality. "I believed in You," I whispered. "I believed in Your infinite justice, but You did not even grant me the wish to die a dignified death. Hadn't we earned this much? We didn't ask for a long life or a happy life, only an honorable death. Didn't Orlan deserve better? He loved others more than he loved himself. Do You really exist, God?"

Crushed by despair, I was reckoning my score with God, as the criminal on the left side of the crucified Christ had done on Golgotha. I had believed in God, conversed with Him upon occasion, not in formal prayers but in fervent conversations. Until now, my faith had been unshakable. But here, behind bars, I doubted His very existence.

Breakfast consisted of a runny gruel, a little sugar, and one-fourth of a loaf of black bread. Borscht and more gruel came in the middle of the day. In the evening, the guard brought a container of boiling water and a little bit of fish. I could not eat anything.

The first day in prison was a Sunday, a free day for the investigating magistrates, and I spent the entire day in the cell. After settling my account with God, I turned to putting my thoughts in some kind of order. I reordered events and prepared myself for interrogations. Physically I was exhausted and, because I had not eaten for two days, I felt faint. Yet I could not sit still. I paced the cell with nervous energy, repeating under my breath, "Four steps forward, four steps back, forward and back."

My imagination visualized the end of our resistance, an end we had seen coming. Orlan's arrest was the fourth act of a five-act tragedy, yet I could not suppress my anger that he had swallowed the bait and been caught. I tried to imagine what the MVD would do next. In Volyn, the underground had virtually ceased to exist, except for several far-flung groups, including those controlled by Ulian in the south. In Polisia, where our contact had been broken for some time, I assumed the same had happened as in Volyn. In Halychyna, there still was a resistance, and the partisans lived mostly in forests. But they had sustained such tremendous losses that Orlan had been apt to say that there were more partisans in Volyn than in Halychyna. Now the MVD had in its possession Orlan's list of contacts, dates of meetings, and signals. Besides, they had Chumak, the contact man to Volyn, and there was no guarantee that he would withstand the interrogations. The enemy also had Skob, which was the worst problem because Lemish trusted him. Thus, Lemish's fate was almost certain. That left only Ulian, and he was also threatened because Chumak led directly to him. Our only hope was that the MVD would make a mistake, and someone along the line would detect what had happened. But this was not a realistic hope since the men would believe someone coming directly from Orlan.

I was afraid to think about Orlan, and my thoughts tried to circumvent him. Then my thoughts would focus on his fate, the death sentence. Probably, I would get the death sentence also, as a reprisal for what I did in Lviv. But before those events came about, the enemy would try to extract our souls during the interrogations.

I had to take my own life. But how? I would hang myself. I would rip the linens during the night, knot them, and hang myself. But hang from what? What was I going to suspend the noose from? Besides, a guard was watching me constantly through the peephole. I had to think of something else. For the first time in my life, I would have welcomed sudden death.

It was good that it was Sunday. I had plenty of time to review my life. At critical moments throughout my life, my thoughts always returned to my village, to my home, to my parents and my family. I found solace in thinking about them, although I knew that they no longer were living in the house where I was born. I had never stopped thinking about my two children, although I pushed those thoughts away since they were so painful that my heart broke again and again. When I was free there had been a spark of hope—perhaps fate would be kind, perhaps at least one of us would survive to raise the children. And now all I could say was, "Children, forgive me for bringing you into this world. My love has not been able to shield you from the cruelties of life."

15. In KGB Prison

The solitary confinement cells occupied the second floor of the prison. At first, I didn't mind being alone in a cell. I had spent several years living in a bunker or a hideout in close proximity to others. Being suddenly alone was a welcome change, especially since I had to prepare myself for the interrogations. Through the early hours of Monday I waited in nervous anticipation to be summoned, but it was not until late afternoon that the key screeched in the lock.

"Hands behind your back," the guard ordered and led me out into the hall. This is when I first noticed that the guard wore slippers instead of shoes or boots and that we walked on a padded walkway that lay in the middle of the corridor. I would learn that this silence was one of the methods used to isolate a prisoner and thus weaken his moral endurance.

Although I had spent a day and a half reconciling myself to my new situation and preparing for interrogations, nonetheless, this first trip to the offices of the investigating magistrate made my stomach turn in anxiety.

Three men were waiting for me: Ptichkin, Sverdlov, and Klymenko, all in MVD uniforms with stripes that showed they were majors. "We will conduct your case," one of them said in Ukrainian.

They did not, however, begin the questioning that day. They only apprised me of the circumstances of my "new life." Ptichkin put it succinctly: "You're in our hands now, and it's time for you to reconcile yourself to your fate. Of course, there's no situation that cannot be resolved," he added and watched if I had understood the meaning of this aside.

I understood, but I also knew that he had failed to add the salient phrase, that is, "There is no situation that cannot be resolved *with honor*."

The interrogation began on the following day. To my surprise, it was not conducted by one of the three men I met the day before but by MVD Major Beroza. He was in his mid thirties, tall, and had a closely shaved head. I don't know what nationality he was, but he spoke Ukrainian haltingly.

The MVD interrogators conversed with me in Ukrainian with varying amounts of ease, although they talked among themselves in Russian and wrote the deposition in Russian. I noticed again that language is the most accurate gauge of the political situation of a country. Those in power speak the language of the conqueror. Orlan and others had discussed the Russification of Ukraine in the underground press and had stressed the need to resist it. I think my interrogators realized the importance I placed on speaking in Ukrainian and used it for that reason when interrogating me. This much-maligned language did not come easily to them. The words were wooden on their tongues and the sounds stuck in their throats, as if the language itself was objecting to being used in this place and under these circumstances.

Beroza started at the very beginning—at my birth. He asked the questions in broken Ukrainian, then translated my answers and recorded them in Russian. Thus, he had to stop and think for a long time before being able to write the deposition. In this way, we wasted the entire day—except for an hour break at midday—to record only a few pages of my statement. To tell the truth, Beroza was not particularly diligent, and it was clear that he was bored. He was a man with a cheerful disposition and often interrupted the proceedings to place calls to his female friends. He would spend a long time on the telephone, flirting outrageously with the women. In sum, Beroza was a poor investigator and did not possess the intellectual discipline of an investigating magistrate. He probably got the job through connections and achieved his rank, as others whom I would meet had, during the war against the Ukrainian partisans.

I had few illusions about what awaited me during the interrogations and had made certain decisions that I felt confident I could keep. On that first day of prison life I had examined my emotional and spiritual state and knew that I would not cave in under pressure. My physical strength was another matter. I was afraid of physical pain and had been so since my childhood. A slap could upset me, and now I was terrified by the possibility of torture. Yet, I knew that no matter what happened, I would not divulge even one name or surrender one bit of information that could endanger anyone connected with the underground.

As I reviewed my conduct, I concluded that I could be accused of two crimes only: being a member of the resistance and discarding the "agreement" I had made with the MVD general at the time of my arrest in 1949. Yet I felt that my detention in Lviv would ultimately help my case. Thus, I began to testify that upon my return to the underground, Orlan refrained from divulging to me the details of the Volyn resistance. I steadfastly adhered to this version throughout the interrogations. I hoped that this stance would shield me from the MVD's attempts to force out not only what I knew, but also what I did not know.

Beroza not only questioned me, he also spent one or two hours each day trying to reeducate me. Every so often he would get up and walk over to a map that hung on the wall.

"Look, Maria," he would say and begin comparing the size of the USSR to that of Western Ukraine. "It's ridiculous to think that you ever had even a ghost of a chance of victory."

My answer, which I kept to myself, was that might did not preclude resistance, but, then, Beroza did not care about my answer. He was already pointing to two major canals that had been completed under Soviet rule—the Volga-Don canal and the one from the Ukrainian mainland to Crimea—and telling me what enormous benefit these waterways had proven to be. During such times, he would sometimes forget the name of some locality, and I would supply it. My knowledge of current events always surprised him.

"So you read newspapers in your bunkers?" he would wonder out loud.

Once he started talking about Kyiv and mentioned the monument of Bohdan Khmelnystky, the Dnipro Cossack hetman.

"Oh, Bohdan, Bohdan," Beroza began to quote, then stopped, the next line forgotten.

"My unwise son," I supplied the second line of Taras Shevchenko's poem about Khmelnytsky's decision to sign a treaty of mutual aid with Czar Alexis Mikhailovich in 1654. (The Treaty of Periaslav marks the beginning of Russia's domination over Ukraine.)

Beroza laughed. "You nationalists think Khmelnytsky was a traitor for signing that treaty."

"No, we don't think he was a traitor. We only condemn his decision."

From Beroza's comments, I could tell that he had questioned other partisans before me. Yet, his understanding of our program and positions was at best superficial. He knew we opposed collectivization and fought for independence from the Soviet empire. His strongest argument on behalf of the government was the government's might, which made the notion of resistance an absurd gesture. I found nothing new or original in his arguments or in the postulations of the other men who questioned me.

One day, Beroza suddenly asked me, "If we should decide to trust you again and send you to Lemish, would you fool us again?"

This question put me immediately on my guard. Did the MVD have a plan, or did Beroza ask the question simply to observe and record my reaction?

"The present situation is different from the earlier one," I said neutrally. "This time my husband's in your hands, too."

Beroza did not pursue this line of questioning again.

◆ ◆ ◆ ◆ ◆

I was ill during the first weeks of imprisonment. I had cramps, could not eat, and suffered fainting spells, so a guard took me to the prison infirmary. It was located on the second floor at the end of a long corridor. The infirmary occupied a room that was the size of one of the cells. The only difference was that it had a standard window instead of one of those tiny openings that were supposed to be windows. The doctor who examined me was a woman who was also an MVD major and either Russian or Jewish since she knew not a single word of Ukrainian. She was in her early thirties, tall and heavy. Her expression was so self-assured that it bordered on arrogance, but she turned out to be tactful in her examination and conduct toward me. Her weight also was an indication of her position on the Soviet ladder of success. In those postwar years, the amount of weight a person carried was a barometer of his or her success. Local agents, who chased after partisans with dogs, were as thin as the animals they handled. Those who had risen to district or regional posts were much heavier, as were the women who worked for them.

The infirmary was not equipped with any diagnostic apparatus and, after a few days there, I was driven to the municipal hospital. Three MVD agents, two guards, and Lieutenant Ageev, accompanied me. I had met Ageev earlier when he sat in on several of the interrogations. During one of these sessions, Ageev had bragged that he had served as an undercover agent in Halychyna and Volyn. He described how he had posed as a starving peasant and had begged and sought shelter at houses the MVD suspected of harboring (or feeding) partisans. Ageev, without a shred of remorse in his voice, described how the partisans often shared with him the food they received. Of course, Ageev did not mention how many of these men he betrayed or how many died in ambushes he would organize. I gathered that he had executed his assignment well, since he had been transferred to the capital recently.

Ageev was one of several men at the ministry who had made their careers by fighting the Ukrainian underground. These men were sons of Party members and represented the postwar breed of Party careerists. Upon their return from the war, they recognized that the fastest and easiest way to get ahead was to join the security organizations and to make a name for themselves in fighting the Ukrainian independence movement. They realized that there was some risk involved in this career path, but having survived the war, they were used to taking and accepting risky assignments. They also realized that each passing year of oppression and terror weakened the resistance and that ultimately the Soviet system would prevail. Such men as Ageev knew that, despite whatever changes occurred in Moscow, despite who was on top and whose star had fallen, they would be regarded as useful by whoever ascended to power. They masked their cynicism with declarations of duty and service to the Party, but, in fact, their ambition was to achieve a secure and successful position.

At the hospital, Ageev led me directly to the head doctor who was waiting for us. The doctor said that specialists would examine me and after the consultations the doctor himself would render whatever diagnosis Ageev requested.

"Not what we want," Ageev responded sharply. "We want to know what's wrong with her."

I never was told what the specialists found, although I suspected I was suffering from exhaustion, not a flare-up of tuberculosis, which I had contracted when in the underground. After being examined, I was returned to prison, not to my cell but to one directly opposite the infirmary. Here I stayed in total isolation for the entire winter. The cell number was 49, and it was the very last cell in that corridor. For a while, I was alone at the end of this corridor, although later a male prisoner was put in the cell adjoining mine. I would hear him coughing, sometimes for hours on end, and I wondered whether he was a partisan who also had contracted tuberculosis while living underground. I never saw this man or learned his name.

My new cell was much smaller and darker than the first one. The tiny window near the ceiling had been blocked on the outside with a piece of metal that had been painted black. Only one corner of the metal plate was bent back, so that I could not even glimpse the sky, and the flow of air was minimal. I began to feel that I was living in a grave.

The days were divided into a strict regimen. I was awakened at six in the morning by the guard shouting, "Get up," and banging on the door. He would watch me through the peephole until I was sitting up. Then I was taken to the toilet to wash and empty the night bucket. I was given a tooth-cleaning powder, a brush, and a towel, the latter changed every ten days. The washing up and cleaning of the cell ended at eight. After that I was given breakfast. After breakfast, I was taken out for exercise to a courtyard no bigger than four cells. It had high walls that had been plastered with very rough cement, so jagged that if you touched it, you would cut yourself. There was no way whatsoever to leave a mark or a sign on that wall. The ground was also cemented from wall to wall. I was left in the courtyard by myself, although a guard in one of the nearby watchtowers observed my movements.

I never saw any other prisoners. If I was on my way to an interrogation and my guard discerned movement ahead of us, he would push me into one of the "box" cells or into a toilet until the other prisoner passed by. On two occasions the guard could not find a place to hide me. In those two instances, he told me to face the wall until the other prisoner passed.

I was interrogated every day except Sunday. Since I knew what I was charged with, I answered questions without any hope of mitigating my eventual sentence. There was nothing to hope for, since I was accused of armed resistance with the aim of overthrowing the empire and was therefore subject to maximum punishment. It would have been absurd for me to deny my participation in the resistance. Yet, there was a second reason why I was open about my participation in the underground. I wanted to preserve what I had witnessed, even if the means were a deposition written in Russian. At least that is how I looked at my prolonged interrogation. My answers were compiling an archive. I also knew that the eventual defeat of the underground would result in the loss of a portion of our national history. I did not think that any of us would survive the usual twenty-five-year sentence in the Siberian gulag. The archives we had left in the bunkers and hideouts would rot, and the bunkers would collapse, become overgrown with vegetation, and be forgotten. People would forget that we ever existed. I, on the other hand, wanted the memory of our struggle to survive. I did not care about the judgment in my case, but it was very important to me to leave information about the resistance in the archives of the enemy. I believed that history might some day discover and bring my story to light.

◆ ◆ ◆ ◆ ◆

The telephone rang one day while I was being interrogated. When he replaced the receiver, the investigating magistrate told me that "the brass" wanted to talk to me. Soon, Ageev came in and took me from the prison to the top floor of the adjoining MVD office building. The offices were allocated in ascending order of importance, with "the brass" occupying the top (fourth) floor. I was first ushered into a waiting room, then taken into an elegantly furnished office. A blond fat man in his fifties sat behind the desk, wearing a general's uniform.

"Good day, Maria, " he said. "Sit down."

He said he would speak in Russian but he understood Ukrainian, so I could answer in Ukrainian.

"Why didn't you cooperate with us when you were arrested back in 1949?" was his first question.

I gave my stock answer.

"What do you think is going to happen to you?"

"There's not much to think about. I'm waiting for the trial."

This general was interested in life in the resistance. He asked me specific questions about overwintering in the bunkers, about what we did and what we studied, and about our relations with the population. Finally, he wanted to know how the leadership viewed the future and if we were hoping that a new World War would enable us to break free of the Soviet Union.

I had no difficulty answering his questions. In fact, I was eager to tell this "brass" the truth about the underground since I knew my answers would contradict the propaganda that we were terrorists and bandits.

"It's unbelievable that a person can survive for such a long time in such incredibly difficult circumstances," he said after hearing me out, and I think I detected admiration in his voice. "I'm especially surprised that women could exist in such conditions."

At the end of the interview, he turned to Ageev and said, "Get her clean clothing."

I was still wearing the loose coat and the slippers I had been given immediately after my arrest.

I later learned that this general's name was Zhukov and that he had made it a point to talk to Orlan and me on his way from a holiday in Crimea. Zhukov was stationed in Moscow.

A day after the interview, Ageev brought me a dress, shoes, and white socks. He also brought me my underwear and a few handkerchiefs, items he took from my bundle of belongings that had been confiscated at the time of my arrest in the forest.

♦ ♦ ♦ ♦ ♦

In the first stages of my interrogations, the investigative magistrates questioning me changed often. Perhaps this was because of the language problem, since several found it very difficult to converse in Ukrainian. I realized this and answered in complicated sentences that were difficult to translate into their standard deposition format. For this reason, the matter progressed slowly. The interrogations alternated with conversations whose aim was to reeducate me, and I began to suspect that the authorities were trying to determine if they could convince me—and perhaps also Orlan—to cooperate with them. I deduced this not only from their use of Ukrainian during the interrogations, but also from the benign way with which I was treated and from the attention I received when I fell ill. I think the MVD had decided that it could achieve more by treating me well than by applying mental or physical coercion. In any event, if the first method did not work, they could turn to the second one at any time. Thus, my case stalled until I was remanded to Lt. Col. Oliinyk, the head of the first division of the MVD.

Oliinyk was in his fifties and was a Ukrainian who boasted about his Cossack ancestry. He saw immediately through my convoluted method of answering questions. Since he was truly bilingual, all he did was pause for a moment, think my answer through, then record it rapidly in Russian. His predecessors had taken the interrogation up to the time I spent in the *Zakerzon krai*, but Oliinyk interrupted the chronology and jumped immediately to questioning me about the time I spent in Volyn. He said that the *Zakerzon krai* interval "wasn't important." He also increased the number of times I was questioned from once to twice a day. Oliinyk was brusque and posed very specific questions. I began to prepare myself prior to every interrogation; during the questioning, I was very focused on my answers so that I would not divulge any details that could be followed up and be used against those who were still free. For that reason, I returned to my cell after each such session physically exhausted and morally depleted. Oliinyk also increased the frequency of conversations aimed at "reeducating" me.

During an interrogation, the prisoner sat on a chair in the middle of the room with his back to the door. On occasion, someone would enter the room and stand at the door. When this happened, Oliinyk would look up at the visitor and shrug or make some other sign. I always wanted to turn around and look at who was standing there, but I never did. I always told myself that this was just another MVD trick to disconcert a prisoner. Oliinyk must have noticed my refusal to turn around because once after such a visit he said, "You certainly are stubborn. You haven't turned once. Most prisoners can't stand the suspense and turn around."

After this, the mysterious visits came to an end.

Oliinyk also demanded my participation in our conversations and would not let me just listen as I had done with the other investigators. He would also try to provoke me.

"An independent Ukraine is an absurd concept," he would argue, "simply because today's Ukraine is a free nation. It stands in brotherhood with the other nations of the Soviet Union. All the member nations are achieving prosperity, and their citizens are enjoying a better standards of living."

Other times he would argue, "What's wrong with speaking Russian? It's the language of Pushkin and Lenin."

He would then return to the first argument: "Your resistance is ludicrous. To fight the Soviet Union is preposterous. Mighty nations are afraid of us. Even if there was a new war, it doesn't mean that Ukraine would gain its independence. Let's assume that the United States would win this war, which, of course, is not possible. But even if it did, do you think America would care about the Ukrainian question? Do you think Americans know, or care, about Ukraine? I think America would view Ukraine the same way Hitler did."

And then, he would twist his argument again, "What did you think you could possibly achieve by hiding in a bunker for months on end?"

Sometimes his barbs would hit their mark, and I would defend the resistance and its aims. "Let's assume that there is a war and the United States wins it and occupies Russia. Don't you think Russians would defend their homeland? Don't you think that many would go underground to fight the occupant? Of course they would. That's exactly what we did. The Soviet Union occupied Ukraine."

Oliinyk also enumerated the damages the government had suffered fighting the Ukrainian resistance. "You cannot imagine the costs in money and in loss of life," he would say. "Your people killed many valuable citizens, including General Vatutin, hundreds of officers, and thousands of soldiers of the Special Forces. You halted collectivization in Western Ukraine; because of you, thousands of people were exiled to Siberia. Other thousands were imprisoned. The losses were equally severe on your side, I may add. Thousands of talented young men died, men who could have helped us build Communism. Besides, you continue to compromise the Soviet system through the literature you smuggle out and have your nationalist compatriots distribute throughout Europe. A Frenchman or an Italian reads what you write and thinks that Ukraine isn't a free nation." After a pause, he would add, "To sum up, you stand in our way."

Once around midnight, the telephone rang. Oliinyk said nothing to me after he replaced the receiver, but soon Ageev entered the room and both of them led me once again to the MVD building. This time I was ushered into the office of the deputy minister of the MVD, named Slon. He was a short fat man with a steely penetrating gaze.

"What are your plans for the future?" he asked me.

"Plans?" I retorted in surprise. "I'll get the death sentence.'

"Well, maybe not," he said. "You'll probably get twenty-five years."

He asked me about my family and my children and, from his questions, I could tell he knew more about them than I did. "You need to think about your children and help them toward a normal life," he said. "You brought them into the world and then abandoned them."

To this I replied, "You wish you had people who would dedicate themselves to Communism the way we dedicated ourselves to our cause."

Slon look startled and began tapping his fingers on the edge of his desk. As an old Communist, he knew that I had hit the mark.

♦ ♦ ♦ ♦ ♦

Following my interviews with Zhukov and Slon, the food rations I received became larger and better. Sometimes I was even given fresh fruits and vegetables, sometimes allowed to rest during the middle of the day. Rather than rejoicing in these privileges, I became frightened, since I knew that this was being done for a reason that I did not yet know. Also, I felt guilty that I had been singled out for preferences, while others who had fought with me were incarcerated under the strictest regimen. Although my conscience was clear, I knew that I was being given an advance against a future service they would demand of me.

Although I listened to the reeducation lessons with some interest, I soon realized that the arguments that were paraded before me did not make an impression on me in the least. Nothing that was said in any way undermined what I believed. It was a simple question of values. Mine were diametrically opposed to theirs. Perhaps I entered the OUN because of romanticism and a desire to make a difference but, through the years, my belief in the rightness of our cause crystallized and sharpened as I learned by watching the ordinary Ukrainian citizen and came to understand his needs. His life was so difficult and so tragic that any sacrifice was worth making to better his lot. I saw that the Soviet occupant was driving the peasant toward extinction, was robbing him of his livelihood, of his language, and of the customs of his ancestors. Nothing that the generals or the investigating magistrates could say would change my perception of what I knew was the reality of life under Communism.

The autumn months were very difficult for me. This was the time when everyone met for the last time before overwintering began, and the enemy capitalized on this increased activity to set traps and ambushes. Every day I listened for noises and footfalls that would indicate that the enemy had caught someone and was putting him behind bars in an isolation cell.

16. Last Meeting with Orlan

One day while I was being interrogated, a smiling Ptichkin came into the room.

"Your husband sends his greetings," he said.

"He's alive?"

"What did you think? That we murdered him? He's alive and well and is asking about you."

After my conversation with Slon, I was convinced that I would never see Orlan again. Now I began to hope, just barely letting myself believe that perhaps we had a chance to survive. Whenever I thought about Orlan, I would let tears gather in my eyes and run down my face. But I did this only when I thought the guard was not watching through the peephole, because I was too proud to let him see me cry or even catch me wiping my eyes. I knew he would report my weakness immediately to the investigating magistrates.

On September 20, 1953, almost three months after our arrest, I was taken before minister Strokach. He seemed to be in a good mood.

"Your husband is very worried about you and asked us to arrange a meeting. I gave my consent, but I want to know if you want to see him also."

I wasn't sure whether he was joking or making fun of me. "I don't think you needed to ask," I replied.

Perhaps doing a good deed makes a person happy. Certainly, Strokach was in a good mood, although the MVD must have carefully contrived the meeting between Orlan and me. I think Strokach knew how much seeing each other meant to us, and the knowledge that he was doing something kind had put him in such a benevolent mood. Yet his sudden joviality did not deter him from asking several questions. Did I know the whereabouts of Lemish, Ulian, our archives, and our printing press?

My answers were the same as before. I knew nothing.

"How's prison life?" he asked me. "It must be better than living underground."

"A prison will always remain a prison," I said.

"If that's the case, you should think about ways for getting out."

"That depends on you, not me."

I was then taken to one of the interrogating rooms where Orlan was waiting for me. He looked nervous, and I read worry in his eyes. I had expected this reaction, since I knew he was not sure how I had dealt with imprisonment and was afraid that I would burst into tears.

I was nervous also. I came up to him and extended my hand—we shook hands.

"At least kiss each other," one of the MVD agents said.

Yet we could not act otherwise in their presence. My guarded behavior calmed Orlan. I already had had time to observe him more closely. He was thinner and, like me, no longer wore prison garb. He had on a blue serge suit that was of poor quality and a little too short in the sleeves.

"I asked to see you because I want to say good-bye," Orlan said.

"You should talk about your future, not about good-byes," one of the MVD men injected.

Orlan ignored him and continued, but his voice was now trembling, "Forgive me if I ever hurt you. You know how difficult our circumstances were. A person's nerves...," and he broke off.

Although I was in control of my facial expression, my eyes filled with tears.

"There's nothing to forgive," I said. "I remember only that which was fine and good. Everything else was a mere trifle." I stopped and held his gaze for a long moment. "I regret nothing."

I had to let him know that I did not blame him in the least for what had happened to us. My words satisfied him and when he spoke again, his voice had ceased to tremble.

The MVD let us spend some time together. We sat next to each other, and Orlan told me about who had interrogated him and what they had asked. I realized that he was trying to communicate the position he had taken during his interrogations and wanted me to understand his strategy and adapt my own to his.

"They told me that the Soviet system had made great strides in bettering the lives of Ukrainians and I told them that words were useless and that they had to show me progress for me to change my views. Then one of the men became so annoyed that he pounded on his desk with a fist and shouted, 'We will show you.'" Orlan continued, "And then I said, 'You can't do it with books and newspapers. I read them when I was sitting in a bunker, and they didn't convince me.'"

The MVD men sitting nearby listened to our conversation in silence. I also said nothing, since I had understood at the onset why Orlan was repeating the conversations he had with his investigating magistrates. He could not escape his sentence, but he could delay it by having the MVD try to convince him that he had been wrong.

Before our meeting ended, one of the men went over to the desk and removed several photographs. These were snapshots of our two children, Zenon and Taras-Petro. They permitted Orlan and me to each have a photo of Petro, but not of little Zenon, since the man who had adopted him had risen in the Polish government to an important position and was passing the child as his own son. Both Orlan and I were permitted to take the snapshots of Petro back to the cells with us. While we were sitting next to each other, I noticed that Orlan was bending his fingers. I realized that he was telling me the number of his cell. I responded in kind and gave him the number of my cell. I realized that Orlan was also on the second floor in a solitary confinement cell and that I passed his cell every time I was summoned for questioning. After our meeting, he came to recognize my footfall and would cough as I passed his cell. It is hard for someone who has never been imprisoned to understand the joy a prisoner feels when he, or she, can make contact—however minimal—with another sharing a similar fate, especially with someone who is dear to the heart.

My meeting with Orlan reinforced my speculation that the MVD was trying to convince both of us to cooperate with them. Not only did they want to use us—particularly Orlan—to capture or kill Lemish and Ulian, they also were thinking of ways to capitalize on Orlan's position as second in command to Lemish to contact and neutralize the OUN-UPA leadership in the American Zone in Germany. No one knew what had happened to us or where we were. Orlan could resurface, and it would have been shortsighted of the MVD not to try to use him. I also realized that Orlan spoke to me freely and conducted himself without fear of reprisals, because he had no hope of having his sentence commuted. He knew he would be sentenced to death, so he had nothing to lose. Besides, he was immensely talented as a speaker and a debater, and he had the gift of changing people's minds by his sincerity and the strength and logic of his arguments. I learned later that on occasion several of the MVD brass would get together and summon Orlan for a "conversation."

"That husband of yours knows how to argue," they would tell me later. "He knows his politics. We only wish he were on our side."

◆ ◆ ◆ ◆ ◆

In October, Ptichkin resumed my case and brought it to conclusion. Thus, in November and December I was seldom summoned for interrogations, although no one informed me that my case had been concluded. I was not permitted to see Orlan again, but otherwise my circumstances did not change. I began to truly hate solitary confinement. I had not minded isolation in the beginning, since I had to prepare myself for the interrogations, but now, with the case in hiatus, I had nothing much else to think about. Being alone became a terrible hardship. Since my food rations were large, I ate a lot, since I thought I was preparing myself for the harsh life in the Siberian gulag. I began to gain weight for the first time in my life and hated myself for it.

One day, deputy minister Slon summoned me. First, he asked me how I was, how I was being treated, and then he began asking the old questions. Did I know where Lemish spent his winters? What about Ulian? Hadn't Orlan told me how to get hold of them in an emergency? What had I been instructed to do if I became separated from him? How was I told to find my way back into the underground?

I answered as I had before. The risk had been too great to impart such knowledge to me. Orlan had told me nothing.

"If you could only help us get Lemish, dead or alive. Alive would be better," Slon said. "We could use him to make contact with your people in the West."

I suddenly had an idea. It was so outlandish that I almost laughed out loud. But why not test it on the deputy minister? All Slon could do was laugh at my naïveté.

"Since Orlan was Lemish's deputy, he legitimately could contact our people in Europe," I said.

Slon looked suddenly very alert.

"How so?" he asked.

"I'm not sure," I said, "but I know that at one time he considered sending me west to make contact."

I could see that my wild idea had intrigued him.

"Whom do you know personally in the West?" he asked.

I named several names.

"You must understand," Slon continued, "that we are going to destroy what's left of your underground very soon. The people in the West are another matter. They are a real nuisance, going around and talking about a guerrilla war in Ukraine, as if there really was one. They could also cause trouble in the event there's a war. Now, mind you, we don't want a war with America, but one's possible. If there's such a war, we're sure the Americans will parachute in behind our lines those ardent nationalists that are screaming about a free Ukraine. Such agents would stir up the people, and we would be faced again with pacifying Ukraine. You know," Slon added, "Stalin once said that the nationalists are the hardest to deal with, and he was right."

He then stood up and went to a map of the world. "We control everything from the Elbe to the Sea of Japan," he said, "and soon we will extend our control to Indochina. A mortal struggle is being fought in the world today, a struggle between the old and the new order. We represent the new way of life, and eventually we will win. Why do I say this? It's self-evident. The stronger order wins wars. We won the Russian civil war. We defeated Hitler. In fact, we not only won that war, we emerged from it a stronger entity. That's why I say we'll win the next war, if there's one. Under such conditions, the ideology of something as puny as your cause means nothing. It *will* be destroyed."

When he finished his lecture, Slon came around from behind his desk and shook my hand. I was then led back to my cell. As I went over the interview, I wondered why he had taken the trouble to shake my hand.

I knew now that Orlan was using me as a pawn in his chessboard game with the MVD. I realized that it was not I, but Orlan, who would really decide my fate and that he would be the architect of a plan he would offer the MVD. I also realized that Orlan would dangle the following gambit before the MVD. He would agree to send a courier from the underground to the leadership in the West. That courier, I knew, would be me.

I became very agitated. I paced my cell thinking and beginning to hope. Stop, take it easy, my mind told me. Going from an isolation cell in a Soviet prison to freedom in the West was an enormous step. Yet I had come away from the interview with Slon convinced that this impossible turn of events could actually happen.

If only I were let go. If only I could carry to the West the news about the conclusion of our struggle. If I could only have the chance to tell the world about the fate of our martyrs. If I could only be given the opportunity to warn those in the West about the attempts on their lives that the MVD was planning.

Then I looked up at the tiny window that had been covered with the piece of metal that someone had painted black. So much for dreams, I told myself.

◆ ◆ ◆ ◆ ◆

In January 1954 Ptichkin summoned me on several occasions and again questioned me minutely about whom I knew in among the UHVR representatives in exile in West Germany and whom I knew in the OUN that had reformed in the West. I was very exact in my answers and listed those I knew, although the list was not very long.

"Did Orlan have direct contact with the nationalists in the West?"

"No. I'm certain he didn't, since I usually prepared the mail and would have noticed."

"You told us earlier that at one time he had planned to send couriers to the West and that you would have gone with them. Why would he have sent you?"

"I know a number of people in exile, and they would trust what I said. Also, bunker life

Maria's family in Siberia in 1955. From the left, sitting, mother, brother Zenon and father. Standing from the left, sister Nadia, sister Olha, brother Ivan, sister Stefa and brother Bohdan. Photograph was taken after father was released from prison.

affected my health, and I was sick often. That's another reason why Orlan considered sending me out of the country, to get medical help."

It is best to base one's testimony on a kernel of truth. Once, long ago, Orlan did talk to me about going west with couriers and, if Ptichkin asked him about that plan, Orlan would most likely recall the episode.

Lesia, Maria's sister, in 1956 in Siberia following release from prison.

During one of these meetings, I noticed that my depositions now carried the heading, "Very Important Matter."

When I saw Orlan next, Ptichkin left us alone for about fifteen minutes. "How are things?" I asked.

"They thought they would catch Lemish since they had my list of meeting dates, but it didn't work out. They went to the rendezvous, but no one from Lemish showed up."

After a moment, he added, "Now, they're thinking of trying to contact our people in the West by sending a courier who would say that he came from me. I told them that I don't have any active contacts in the West and that my earlier plans had included you."

"I'm supposed to convince you that their plan is a good idea," I said and smiled bitterly.

"Go ahead," he said, then after a pause added, "That's their job, not yours."

Toward the end of the month, Ptichkin informed me that he would be taking Orlan and me to Zaporizhia to show us how the Soviet government had industrialized Ukraine. We were taken to the Kyiv airport and boarded a commercial flight. We had four escorts, one of whom was Ptichkin himself. In Zaporizhia we were met by two cars and were driven directly to the local prison. This was an old prison, built under the czars, and, compared to it, the Kyiv prison was a model of cleanliness and comfort. The cells in the Zaporizhia prison were in the basement, and we were again placed in solitary confinement. We spent about ten nights in that prison. During the days, our escorts took us to see the

Maria Savchyn

metallurgical complex that had been built after the war on the Dnipro River. We went to a steel mill and to an aluminum plant. Although the MVD tried to engage guides who spoke Ukrainian, they did not always succeed. I noticed that all commerce and all signage were in Russian. Russian was also the language in the newly built school we visited and in the state-run day care center for workers employed in the factories. During these excursions, Ptichkin introduced us as a delegation from a collective farm in Western Ukraine.

"You see, I told you," Ptichkin boasted. "I told you that you would be impressed by the factories we built after the war."

He did not add that much of what was produced in these Ukrainian factories was shipped directly to Russia for use there, not in Ukraine.

Both Orlan and I especially wanted to be taken to the island of Khortycia, where the Dnipro Cossacks had their citadel in the sixteenth and seventeenth centuries. We were delighted when we learned that the island's vast complex of greenhouses was on our schedule. We learned that the vegetables grown in these greenhouses were shipped to Moscow and Leningrad.

Wherever we went, I noticed the burgeoning wealth of the government, in marked contrast to the poverty of the people. The goods we saw in the stores were few and of inferior quality. People were dressed poorly and there were many beggars on the streets. The MVD had brought us to this area to convince us that the Soviet Union had done great things for Ukraine, and all they did was demonstrate that they could show us nothing that would change our minds.

Throughout this time, Ptichkin and the others would ask whether I would like to see our son Petro. Of course, I yearned to see the child, touch him, and hug him to my breast. But, at the same time, I was convinced it would be extremely harmful if the boy was taken away from Nastia, especially for the sole purpose of enabling Orlan and me to see him on occasion. Thus, whenever the question of bringing the child to Kyiv arose, I argued against the plan. I said that this was not a suitable time for such a reunion, and the more I considered the repercussions of bringing the boy to Kyiv, the more I despaired.

Then, toward the end of our tour of Zaporizhia, Ptichkin informed us that upon our return to the capital, Petro would be waiting for us. My heart was filled with conflicting emotions that ranged from fear for the boy's safety to delight that I would see my son again. But, when we returned to Kyiv, no one mentioned the boy again. I was summoned to several sessions of additional interrogations, but the child's name was not mentioned. Finally, I could not stand the suspense and asked, "What's happening with the boy?"

"The plan is on hold," one of the agents told me.

◆ ◆ ◆ ◆ ◆

February, March, and the beginning of April passed, and I was not interrogated again. My infrequent meetings with Orlan also stopped, but the special rations I received kept on coming. I began to think that the MVD had concluded my case and that soon I would be sentenced to twenty-five years and dispatched to the Siberian gulag. The interrogations and the uncertainty of Orlan's and my fate emotionally debilitated me. I began to have nightmares, including one in which I was shot in a basement execution room. All I wanted now was the conclusion of my case and a sentence.

Only later did I learn that this hiatus was caused by the trial and execution of Beria in Moscow and changes in personnel in the ministry that his death triggered. The MVD was divided into two ministries. We were now under the jurisdiction of the ministry that had been christened the KGB. In Ukraine, the changes resulted in the ascendancy of the Lviv security organizations, and their personnel replaced many of the Kyiv administrators, including minister Strokach. One of those promoted was the agent in Lviv who had led me out of the prison and left me standing on the sidewalk at dawn. Back in 1949, he had the rank of a major, but now he wore the stripes of a lieutenant colonel. When he saw me, he asked why I had not kept my side of the bargain I had made with the Lviv authorities.

"I've been asked that question so many times that I don't want to answer it again," I said.

"You should understand that I'm particularly interested in your case. I bet that when I left you on the sidewalk you crossed yourself and said, 'Thank you, Lord, for snatching me from the talons of those people.' Am I right?"

I nodded. The fact that the Lviv agents were now in power increased my worry that the old matter would be resurrected and would affect the KGB's decision in the current case. However, nothing happened. With the arrival of spring, the KGB resumed taking Orlan and me to see the city. We viewed the May 1 parade as well as a parade commemorating the tercentennial of the signing of the Treaty of Pereiaslav, which was depicted as the older brother (Russia) stretching out a helping hand to a weaker younger brother (Ukraine). I don't know whether the authorities knew this or not, but one of these excursions fell on May 27, our ninth wedding anniversary.

"I wish you freedom," Orlan said to me when he saw me.

◆ ◆ ◆ ◆ ◆

After the dates of the spring rendezvous passed and the KGB did not change its tactics, I began to suspect that the Soviets had not been able to get a lead to Lemish or Ulian. This is when the investigating magistrates once again began to question me about the possibility of making contact with the leaders in exile. Slon, the deputy minister, conducted most of these discussions. He was forthright in explaining the KGB's interest in the UHVR and the OUN in exile. He wanted both groups penetrated and neutralized. I realized that the exiles mattered, not so much because they were continually attacking the Soviet regime, but because they could be used by the Americans in the event of a new war to mobilize resistance in Western Ukraine. Slon again mentioned the possibility of Orlan sending couriers to the West.

"What do you think of the idea of going with our couriers?" Slon asked me. "Of course, this is just an idea, not a proposal."

"I don't know," I replied cautiously. "I'll have to think about it before giving you my answer."

"Next time you see Orlan, why don't you discuss this idea with him and see what he thinks," Slon said.

In a few days, I was taken to an office where Orlan was waiting for me. Since we assumed that someone was listening in, we conducted ourselves with this possibility in mind.

"We need to do something to get out of here," I said in my assumed role of the dissatisfied wife. "We've been here almost a year."

"You seem to be saying that I like it here," Orlan said. "What they want me to do doesn't hark well for our release. They want me to write letters that would be taken to the West. If this game plan works and they make contact with the right people, they'll let us go."

"They're saying that they'll send someone that won't cave in. Maybe they'll send Skob."

"I don't have much faith in Skob or any other courier they might pick," Orlan said. "I'm not a novice in the underground. No one's going to accept a courier without questioning him closely. And I can predict what will happen. The courier won't be believed, and we'll stay in jail or be shot, having extended our lives a few more months. It's simply not worth it. In any event, I have no intention of getting a reputation of being a traitor."

I had purposefully kept what Slon had told me to the end, after I had performed the role of the unhappy wife.

"What if I went with the couriers?" I asked. "Slon suggested that to me."

Orlan looked inquiringly at me and then smiled, "If that's the case, you're not the one I need to discuss this with. I can't believe that they seriously think you'll make contact on their behalf, but if they do, I can discuss the idea with them further."

The following day Slon summoned me again and asked me about my conversation with Orlan.

"He said that the matter was not for him and me to discuss, but for him and you," I reported.

"I've already talked with your husband. He said he feels you can make contact with the UHVR. Are you willing to give it a try?"

The choice between getting out of the Soviet Union or spending twenty-five years in the Siberian gulag was really not a choice. I would not have thought about it twice if I had been alone. But even leaving hell would be difficult if you were leaving a loved one behind.

Slon had talked to me about the political immigration on several occasions. This time he began discussing not so much the methods the émigrés were using to get the attention of the Western governments, but the fact that many who had contact with the underground in Ukraine had "sold out" to the American secret services. He said that he believed the splintering of the OUN and other political parties was primarily caused by the competition among them as to who would represent the underground back in Ukraine. The reason the various groups wanted to be the acknowledged representative was not because of patriotism, but because the successful group would be able to obtain more money from the Americans in selling its information.

He also told me that I might be dazzled by the prosperity I would see in the West and by the variety of goods in Western stores. I should remember, however, that the standard of living in the West had been built over the centuries, while the Soviet Union had been building its country for only several decades.

He concluded with these words: "Even if you tell them that you were sent by us, they won't believe you. They'll follow you and watch you. You won't gain anything."

When I said nothing, he continued. "We'll trust you one more time. If you fool us again," he paused and his eyes became cold and hard, "then watch out." With this he hit the top of his desk with such force that everything on the desk trembled.

Our gazes met, and I felt as if sparks flew. I knew that I was risking everything. I was fighting my last battle, but it wasn't being fought in the forest or in a hideout but in the office of a KGB minister, and I was winning. If Slon had been a better psychologist, he would have read the triumph in my eyes. I gazed into his face and was again surprised how much it mattered to him and his agency to silence us. They, the eyes and ears of a mighty empire, wanted to gather every last grain that we had sown, not only in Ukraine but also beyond its borders.

But when I thought about my family, I was covered with cold sweat. Once the KGB discovered that I had fooled them a second time, they would take revenge not only on Orlan but also on my family. Yet I knew there was no turning back.

The conversation with Slon took place in late afternoon. As soon as I returned to my cell, the guard came to inform me that I was going into the city. In the courtyard, Orlan and our usual escort of four agents met me. Orlan looked exhausted and spoke in a weak voice, but his eyes were clear and calm, and he looked like a man who had accomplished what he had set out to do.

They took us on an excursion boat on the Dnipro River. As night fell and the lights of the city receded behind us, Orlan whispered to me, "I'm so happy, darling, that I feel like singing."

In front of us, a group of young people had begun singing, and Orlan was humming with them.

I was no longer exulting as I had before. I was beginning to feel egotistic. I knew that Orlan wanted desperately for me to escape, not only for myself but also to carry into the world the news about the final years of our struggle. I knew that without his determination, this would not be happening. On the other hand, I realized that if I stayed, my presence in a nearby solitary confinement cell would not help him one bit. Yet the reality was that he would stay in his cell, while I would leave mine, and this fact broke my heart. For the rest of my life I would think about Soviet prisons and would search through newspapers for news about Orlan. How horrible would this news be?

17. The Dictate of Fate

The KGB did not waste time. A few days later I was taken to the office of Oliinyk, who had interrogated me. On this occasion, he did not take my deposition but instructed me to write my confession. It would be my passport to freedom. As I wrote, my conscience did not bother me. I was not ashamed of writing that I had repented when I had not. In any case, a part of the confession told the truth. I wanted to live a normal life, be reunited with my family, obtain the custody of my children, raise them. All these dreams were true, and I set them down on paper without hesitation.

However, Oliinyk was not happy with my effort. He returned the piece of paper three times for additional comments, and then, finally, began dictating what I should add. He cared about the contents of my confession since it was evidence that he had done his work and achieved his aim.

During my years in the underground, I had upon occasion used false documents, both German and Soviet, to execute assignments given me. I regarded my confession like a false passport, a means to an end. And that end was crystal clear in my mind. I would be the bearer of information about our struggle, and I would spread the word to whoever would listen to me.

I think Orlan had watched me and found me capable of this last assignment. That is why he had agreed to send me to the West. It was my responsibility to tell about what had happened at home and to warn those beyond the border to be careful not to fall into the traps that the KGB was preparing for them. Since he had decided on this course of action, every time we met, Orlan entrusted me with new details that I had not known before. I was to remember this information and take it to those who needed to hear it. I was not going as a courier from the KGB, but as a courier from Orlan. I knew that when the KGB discovered that I had tricked them, my actions would result in severe reprisals against everyone I left behind, but I could not do otherwise.

Yet, despite all these arguments, I found it difficult to keep on writing under the watchful eyes of Oliinyk. This is when I told myself that this confession really did not matter. It hurt no one except my self-pride. So I kept on putting down on paper the words he wanted me to write.

I also wondered why the KGB had decided to trust me again. Did they not understand that I could never cooperate with them? I had seen what they had done to my country, to my people, and to my family, and this sea of injustices made it impossible for me ever to stretch my hands to join with theirs. I could not sell out because, if I did, I would never been able to look my parents in the face if fate ever brought us together again. If I became a pawn of the KGB, I would never be able to create a family unit with Orlan and our son if we were reunited. Constancy to the truth of our cause had made it possible for us to survive the tragedies that had come our way. Treason would destroy what held us together.

◆ ◆ ◆ ◆ ◆

Three weeks before my departure, Orlan and I were given an apartment on Gorky Street. But this was just another prison. We continued to be guarded day and night. A woman cooked our meals and slept in the kitchen. We slept in one room, while our guards occupied the other room. Throughout this time, the ministry and its people were working out the details of taking me to West Germany. The KGB once again raised the question of bringing our son Petro to Kyiv. Both Orlan and I objected, arguing that the child should not be told about us or have his life disrupted. I became so agitated that Orlan feared our plan would collapse if I became ill. The KGB noticed my state of mind and changed its mind. A major who came to see me explained it thus: "The child will cry and you'll focus all your attention on him, while there's work to be done."

The day before my departure, the agents brought us an old issue of a newspaper that contained an article stating that Vasyl Okhrymovych had been shot for treason. The agents who dealt with us had been assuring us for months that Okhrymovych was alive. We decided that we were shown the newspaper because I could not go west carrying information that was contrary to what had been published and must have found its way by now beyond the Iron Curtain.

On the last evening in Kyiv, the KGB permitted us to go alone for a walk. I don't know if they were giving us a chance to try to escape, but escape was not on our minds. We would do nothing to jeopardize a plan that had been so difficult to bring to fruition.

◆ ◆ ◆ ◆ ◆

We set out for Lviv the next morning. Orlan and I sat in the back seat of the car. We were accompanied by two agents, the driver and a Major Petchenko. The day was clear, calm, and surprisingly hot for late summer. When we reached Volyn, I looked out the window, and my heart seemed to be crushed by a vise. I had crossed its forests and field back and forth and back again. I had lived in its quiet rural homesteads. I saw it during moonlit nights, and here I was looking at it for the last time in the brightness of a summer day. Here was the place where we crossed the road one night. Even in a nightmare, I could not have dreamt that I would pass this way one more time in a KGB car.

I glanced at Orlan. His face was impassive as he stared out the window. Only the deep furrows on his brow and the occasional twitch in the corner of his mouth told me that he was thinking along the same lines as I was.

As we neared Lviv, I realized we would pass only a few kilometers from Zadviria. After so many years of absence, I had not thought I would feel the pang of heartache, since what I missed was not the village but my family. Yet, as we drove past and left it behind, I felt something akin to pain, realizing that I would never see this piece of land again. I imagined the house where I grew up, filled with laughter and the voices of children, and how it probably looked now—empty, the yard overgrown, the windows broken and gaping darkly.

And then we were in Lviv, and an abundance of new memories replaced those from along the road. I was again a fourteen-year-old girl who was whispering to my friend Olia the words of the OUN Decalogue, "You will gain a free Ukraine or die trying." It had been so easy to be dazzled by the dream and to accept its alternatives—victory or death. Now when I was twice that age, I knew that the road to achieve a dream is not always straight. My road twisted and turned through forests and the undergrowth that life was. Yet, what I had believed then, I still carried with me today in my heart like a precious gem.

We spent the night in a hotel, and the next morning resumed our journey. Our destination was the village of Hai, near Ternopil. This is where Nastia Martynovska lived. When I gave her the baby in 1949, she was living in Orlan's native village of Olesyn. Since then she had been widowed, had remarried, and had moved to her new husband's village. Her surname was now Suta. On the way to Hai, the agents we had picked up in Lviv told us a little more about Nastia and our son. Apparently, the reason why Petro had never been brought to Kyiv was because Nastia had refused to let go of the child. The KGB had sent a woman agent to Nastia who had said that she had come from me and that I wanted Petro back. Nastia had replied that if I wanted to have the child, I had to come myself to claim him. The KGB decided not to create a commotion that might jeopardize their plans of sending me west, so they did not take the boy. As I heard this story, I silently thanked the Lord for giving Nastia the courage to withstand the KGB. The agents also told us that Nastia loved the boy like her own son, and he considered her his mother and Nastia's first husband as his father.

The KGB had a plan for us to see the child. They would stop near Nastia's house and pretend that they were having car trouble. They would then go to the house to borrow tools. They assumed that since the day was warm, the boy would be playing in the yard and we would be able to see him. They warned us that we could not open the window or get out of the car to speak to him.

The plan worked insofar as that Nastia and Petro were at home, but Nastia would not let the boy go out in the yard when she saw the strange car. She watched the agents work under the hood, and her older boy was permitted to observe the repair, but not Petro. Finally, one of the agents returned to the house and asked the boy directly to help carry some of the tools. Nastia did not want to prohibit a direct invitation from the agent, so the boy came out.

He was thin and shy. He had a round face, delicate features, and dark eyes. He was wearing a cap that was much too big for him, which he had to push up several times. When he saw a woman in the car, he kept staring, and one of the agents grabbed my arms and held me firmly inside. Even if I could have, I would not have moved. I sat staring at my child in stony, agonizing immobility. This episode lasted a very short time, too short for me to overcome the shock of seeing my child in the flesh or to absorb anything except the image of a small thin child in a big cap. When I glanced at Orlan he was staring at the boy also in mesmerizing absorption. He had never seen Petro before.

It was noon when we returned to Ternopil. From there we drove to the Kremianets area from where I would theoretically be starting my trek to the West. The KGB plan was that we would drive along the probable course I would have followed on foot. Thus, we drove along rural roads and stayed away from major highways. We stopped for the night at the town of Kremianets, which a year earlier we had observed through binoculars from a forested hill in the distance.

Orlan and I were being given more freedom on this trip than on the one to Zaporizhia. We stayed alone in our hotel room, and Orlan used our privacy to tell me more of the details about the resistance that he wanted me to repeat in the West.

"I will do as you say," I told him. "I will tell them everything that had happened, and then I will come back."

"Good God, no," he cried. "Don't do any such thing. You must survive. You may be the sole witness who survives the last years of our struggle. You must stay in the West, create a life for yourself there. There's nothing you can do for me by coming back."

"Don't say that," I cried. "Don't be so callous. What kind of life can I have alone if you're here?"

"Our people will help you," Orlan said, trying to placate me.

But later he said, "Perhaps they won't believe you. That's a possibility. If that happens, try to mobilize all your resources and stand firm. You were strong here, don't lose that virtue there."

We spent the last night alone. We did not sleep that night. I wept. I wailed. We sat holding each other and, as Orlan tried to calm me, huge tears rolled down his cheeks. In the morning, Orlan would be taken back to Kyiv by Major Petchenko. Night turned into daylight. Soon the door opened, and Orlan got up to leave. He hugged me, kissed me, then quickly walked to the door and closed the door behind him. I stood there as if I had turned to stone. I don't know for how long I remained standing, staring into nothingness.

◆ ◆ ◆ ◆ ◆

Before we reached the Polish border, a KGB agent who would pose as a courier joined us. His name was Taras but we hardly spoke to each other. In fact, he acted as a courier should act, circumspectly and vigilantly, so I never learned anything about him. The closer we came to the frontier, the more troops we saw. Even the KGB car was stopped several times. In the frontier village of Hrushiv we were met by a Polish security officer who introduced himself as Sasha and by Major

Petchenko, who, after taking Orlan back to Kyiv, had returned to supervise our passage through Poland, East Germany, and on to Berlin. We crossed the border at night, climbing over ditches and earthworks. Just before we were across, I stopped and turned around and stared into the darkness at my homeland that I was leaving forever.

Yet I was not entering a foreign land. This was the *Zakerzon krai*, divided in half by a border imposed upon it by the conqueror. I was back on this hallowed ground alone, without my faithful friends, Orlan and Ptakh. Before me lay Krakow, one more place where I had left a fragment of my heart. This is where I lost my firstborn, Zenon. Although I asked, the KGB had no plans to let me see the boy. He was now even beyond their reach. But because I was so close to him, the old wound reopened and hurt as much as before. Yet, in the ashes of this tragedy glimmered a spark of hope. Perhaps when I was free, I would be able to locate him.

We spent our first night in a third-class hotel in the city of Yaroslav, then continued by car through the *Zakerzon krai* foothills, since this would be the way I would have made my way on foot. The area was desolate and empty. The villages we passed were burned and overgrown with weeds. The only people we saw were living near towns, but not in the countryside.

"Between 1945 and 1947, this area was controlled by the UPA," our driver informed us. He had no idea who I was, since Major Petchenko did not tell any of our changing escorts anything about Taras or me.

"It was a real war," the driver continued. "They killed thousands of our men. And were they determined! They wouldn't yield ground for anything. I served in this area, and every time I was sent back here, I said good-bye to my wife. One time they killed the three men I was with, and I was the only survivor."

Later, Major Petchenko said to me, "You could have told him a lot he didn't know. If he had suspected who you were, he would have kept quiet."

We stopped next at Worclaw, and Petchenko flew to Berlin to finalize our plans to cross the border. Sasha, Taras, and I continued through the forests to the River Nissa that formed the border here between Poland and East Germany. The KGB had arranged that this section of the river would not be patrolled that night. We crossed it by swimming across. I had told them that I didn't know how to swim, but Sasha and Taras assured me that they would help me by holding me up, one on each side. In the middle of the river, a current caught us and started pulling us downstream. For a moment, I thought they would let go of me and thus be rid of me. I screamed.

"Shut up," Sasha spat at me, and the two men pulled me to the other side.

Petchenko met us on the bank with a local KGB operative whose name was Vania. Vania was wearing a wide-brimmed hat, a trench coat, and suede shoes which he ruined in the mud. We made our way out of the forest to a road where a car was waiting for us.

We were driven to East Berlin where we were given directions on how to reach the American sector. We lost our way but eventually found the right bridge. Here I left the others behind. Taras seemed to panic and slowed down as if debating whether he should go ahead.

I did not wait for him. In a few more strides, I reached the American guardhouse. The soldier on duty smiled pleasantly as the group of people, including me, walked past him.

Freedom! I was drunk on freedom. It felt as if I had gone mad. I wanted to shout to every one I saw that, at last, I was free. I wanted to shout so loudly so that all Berlin would hear me. In these critical moments, I thought of no one and of nothing. My entire being was focused on the reality that I was free at last. I felt like a caged animal that is able to break through the bars and disappear in the tall grass of the savanna.

I kept on walking. When I was far enough from the guard booth, I stopped a man walking toward me and asked him in German, "Please, could you tell me the way to the American consulate?"

Epilogue

I kept my promise to Orlan. I contacted the leadership in exile of the UHVR and related all the information Orlan had given me. I talked to Mykola Lebed and Yuri Lopatynsky. I told them about the underground that still existed in Ukraine and about the difficult conditions under which it operated. I also reported on the leaders in Ukraine—who was still alive and who had died. I also warned them about KGB attempts at infiltrating the UHVR as well as Ukrainian immigrant organizations. After the first shock of disbelief, I think the people who talked with me believed me. I understood their misgivings about my veracity, since my escape following a year-long incarceration in Kyiv was difficult to accept as true.

Lopatynsky, who had been in Ukraine when the Soviets took power, understood the difficulties of operating under that regime. Those who had left Ukraine before the conclusion of the war had a harder time accepting the accuracy of my report. I also spoke to American security agents and accepted the political asylum the United States offered. I was taken to the United States in the spring of 1955 under an assumed name and was further debriefed in Washington, D.C. When I was released, I received residency documents under an assumed name. I also was given help in obtaining a job.

I suspected that the KGB was looking for me and was glad of the precautions that the United States government took on my behalf. Even when time passed and my life normalized, I refused to sink my roots into the new soil and adapt to the new circumstances in which I found myself. I fell into a deep depression, and life stopped having meaning for me.

What saved me was my decision to record what I had lived through and to bear witness to all the brave men and women who had given their lives or their freedom for an idea they believed in. I roused myself. I purchased a typewriter, acquired maps of the places where I had lived and fought, and sat down to write this memoir, in detail, year after year, starting at the beginning and continuing to the end. The events were fresh in my mind. I saw the faces of the people I knew. I heard their voices. I could still recreate the coldness of the underground hideouts, the murmur of trees in the forest, the rustle of leaves underfoot.

As the years passed, I became used to my new country and began to participate in a variety of organizations, but my involvement was not wholehearted. Even when I met former UPA soldiers from the *Zakerzon krai*, I found that I had little in common with them, since they had left before the Soviet terror began.

More lonely years passed. My thoughts were with Orlan and Petro, with my family. I did not know what had happened to them, who was alive and who was not. I tried to learn their fates, and I tried to ascertain what had happened to my son Zenon. I had no success at all in tracing Zenon, since I had no documents to show that I had had a child, and I did not know his exact whereabouts.

During this time, the tuberculosis I had contracted in the bunkers reappeared, and I spent eight months in a sanatorium. This is when I decided that if I got well, I would start living again. I did recover. I obtained a divorce and eventually married again. My second husband is Volodymyr Pyskir, a man who visited me regularly when I was ill. We had two children, a boy Bohdan, and a girl Larysa. I was able to delight in motherhood, which had been denied me with my first two children.

In 1960, I learned that my family had returned from exile to Zadviria, except for my sister Lesia. She married during the exile and did not return to Ukraine until a year later. My family spent ten years in exile in the region of Taishet, Irkutsk *oblast* in Siberia. All had survived.

We reestablished contact through acquaintances. The first letter I received was from my mother. I still have it and remember by heart its opening lines: "Darling [but no name], What a joy it was to learn you're alive. We didn't know where to look for your grave so that at least we could erect a cross on it. And then news came that you're alive and well. I still cannot believe the good fortune and keep thanking God for protecting you."

Unfortunately, I never saw my mother and father again. My father died in 1977 and my mother in 1988. I went back for the first time in 1992, a year after Ukraine's independence. My sisters and my brother and their families met my airplane with flowers in their arms. No one reproached me for what I had done and for the exile my actions had brought upon our family. To the contrary, they told me that even in Siberia they kept worrying about me. Other families that had been exiled complained about those brothers, sisters, and sons whose actions had caused the family to be banished, but my mother never said a word, and the children followed her example. When I wrote to Lesia and asked her if she had forgiven me for bringing so much suffering upon her, she wrote back with a question, "Didn't you suffer, too?" My family was patriotic and politically conscious and realized that we all had been punished for what we believed in.

My family helped me contact my son Petro, whom I also met when I went back after Ukraine's independence.

I continue to maintain contact with my family, and our relations are loving. We not only correspond, but I have also been able to help them financially. They have been able to build a brick house in Zadviria, since the original house had been given to others.

I find it very difficult to write about Orlan. When I went west, Orlan asked me to urge the UHVR to continue the chess game he had set up, and I think that some attempts were made to do so. Perhaps that is why Orlan was not sentenced to death but instead received a prison term.

I saw Orlan and Petro when I went back to Ukraine. Petro, who had been raised by Orlan and Orlan's second wife, brought us together in Kyiv. After so many years we touched hands with great emotion. Yet the burden of our separate lives and responsibilities stood between us like an impenetrable wall. With great sorrow, I realized that time had changed what we once held dear. We talked for a long time and he told me much about the years after we had parted. Slowly, I realized that he was psychically exhausted, not the man with whom I had shared ten turbulent years.

He told me his life was spared when he wrote a "confession." He was later pardoned under the amnesty that Nikita Khrushchev issued following his ascension to power. On his release, he contacted Nastia Suta and took Petro, whom he raised. Orlan and Petro settled in Kyiv where they still live. Until the collapse of the Soviet Union, Orlan was under continuous KGB surveillance, although he was able to return to school, become an engineer, and work in this profession until his retirement.

Yet Orlan's life was not saved because of his confession or the amnesty. I think the KGB decided not to execute him because the regime did not want to create another martyr. His confession as well as the confessions of several other underground leaders who were captured were published, and I heard about them and eventually was able to read them. I remember that when I finished reading Orlan's words, my heart broke. Yet as the years of Ukraine's independence multiplied, Orlan shed his depression and regained the vigor that had made him so charismatic in his youth. In his old age he is dedicating what strength he has to the development of Ukraine's youth. He lectures in schools and before military groups on the history of the struggle for Ukraine's independence.

I have been to Ukraine three times. I saw Nastia Suta and thanked her for raising Petro as her own child. She died in 1997. I also heard about Lemish and Ulian. Ulian was killed sometime in the 1950s. Lemish was captured but not executed, and today he continues his efforts in Ukraine to educate the new generation about what had happened to ours.

I was overjoyed when Ukraine declared independence. A dream of my generation and so many other generations came true. Yet the years of servitude have been hard to shed, and I think it will be the mission of the next generation to create a really independent Ukraine.

Index